D0717964

SEVE

SEVE

THE OFFICIAL AUTOBIOGRAPHY

Severiano Ballesteros

Translated by Peter Bush

YELLOW JERSEY PRESS
LONDON

Published by Yellow Jersey Press 2007

2 4 6 8 10 9 7 5 3 1

Photographs on pages 6 (top), 11, 12, 13, 14, 18, 19, 20 and 21 are reproduced courtesy of Getty Images; the photograph on page 7 (bottom) is reproduced courtesy of Corbis Bettman; all other photographs are courtesy of the author. Every effort has been made to contact copyright holders. The publishers will be pleased to correct any omissions brought to their notice at the earliest opportunity

First published in Great Britain in 2007 by
YELLOW JERSEY PRESS
Random House, 20 Vauxhall Bridge Road,
London SW1V 2SA

www.rbooks.co.uk

Addresses for companies within The Random House Group Limited can be found at:
www.randomhouse.co.uk/offices.htm

The Random House Group Limited Reg. No. 954009

A CIP catalogue record for this book is available from the British Library

ISBN Hardback 9780224082563
ISBN Trade paperback 9780224082556

The Random House Group Limited makes every effort to ensure that the papers used in its books are made from trees that have been legally sourced from well-managed and credibly certified forests. Our paper procurement policy can be found at: www.rbooks.co.uk/environment

Typeset by SX Composing DTP, Rayleigh, Essex
Printed and bound in Great Britain by
CPI Mackays, Chatham, Kent ME5 8TD

I dedicate this book to my children
and to my brothers

From Jack Nicklaus

When historians and the golfing public compare the players who shaped our game and were the building-blocks of the global success our sport enjoys, Severiano Ballesteros ranks up there with the best. Seve has earned his place in golf history, and his career accomplishments deserve significant recognition.

The first time I heard of Seve Ballesteros and saw him play was in 1976 at the Open Championship at Royal Birkdale, where he and I tied for second behind Johnny Miller. After that introduction, I knew he was a gifted young player with untold skills, and I began to follow his career with great interest. For many years, his imagination and his creativity with a golf club and golf ball made him one of the most well-liked and exciting players to watch.

Seve's impact on the golf world, particularly in Europe, is immeasurable. The status enjoyed today by European golfers is due largely to his influence, and his support and passion for the Ryder Cup have fuelled the global fascination for that event.

A great man and great ambassador, Seve has represented his country, his sport and himself with class. I am sure you will enjoy his life story.

Jack Nicklaus

From Arnold Palmer

Perhaps the most significant aspect of golf's tremendous growth in the latter half of the twentieth century was its expansion internationally into many parts of the world where its potential had long been untapped. Continental Europe for one. More than anything else, the exciting exploits of Seve Ballesteros brought this about.

Seve shook up the European golf world when he appeared on the scene in the late 1970s. He and his game certainly impressed me when I first saw him in action at the Open Championships in those years. Clearly, his style and talent that produced his run of major victories in the Open Championship and the Masters during the late 1970s and 1980s caught the eyes of the sporting public throughout the world and brought a great surge in the popularity of the game throughout Europe.

Although Seve is best remembered in America for his victories in the Masters, he also enjoyed considerable success in his limited appearances on our PGA Tour. Unquestionably, he deserves the recognition he has earned as one of the most prominent and popular players in the history of the sport.

Arnold Palmer

From Gary Player

I have always been absolutely crazy about Severiano Ballesteros. Here's a man who came from very humble beginnings, but who worked extremely hard to become the exceptional golfer the world has come to know. One of the many characteristics I have admired most about Seve is that he has not been insular in his quest for success. He has played and won all over the world, and that's what all true superstars do. Seve is one of the most charismatic golfers of all time. He is a very good-looking man with a great smile and he has done a tremendous amount for golf both in his native country, Spain, and throughout Europe, as well as internationally.

I'll never forget the first time I met Seve, which was at the 1976 Open Championship at Birkdale. Here was this exciting young man playing in the British Open, and, wow, what tremendous clubhead speed he had! He reminded me of a swashbuckling pirate or matador. I think everyone remembers the British Open he won at Royal Lytham & St Annes in 1979, when he drove the ball into the car park at number 16, before knocking it on the green, and stroking that long putt across the green and into the hole for birdie. That was some of the best recovery work and finesse I have ever seen.

Seve played with me in the last round of the 1978 Masters, which I won at forty-two years of age, and he could not have been kinder or more complimentary to me. He gave me the most wonderful hug at the end of the round. Now, here's one competitor fighting hard against another, but it was a sign of Seve's true sportsmanship that he could express genuine joy for me at that moment. 'You taught me how to win Masters in future,' he said in halting English there on the 18th green, and, of course, he won his first of two green jackets just two years later in 1980. Seve really loves this game and it means so much in his life. We all look forward to seeing him play wherever he tees it up.

Seve is that rarest of golfers. He combines both great strength and a deft touch around the greens. In fact, Seve taught me a great lesson, because I had always believed you needed soft hands for a soft touch. Seve's hands are actually hard and muscular, so it does not matter how your hands are formed, either you have got that feel or you do not, and he is a true wizard around the greens.

One thing that's not soft about Seve is his fierce competitive nature. People saw him captain the 1997 European Ryder Cup team. I mean, he was buzzing around the course and the matches, getting involved in each one with everything he had. Here is a man who has won five major championships and numerous tournaments all around the world, so his place in the history of golf's all-time greatest players is assured.

I would like to say something about Seve the human being, because that is what matters most in life. You know, we must not mix up a person's competitiveness on the golf course and what they are like off the course.

Seve is extremely considerate of others. He is willing to listen to people's concerns, about golf or otherwise, and offer an understanding suggestion or word of support. The bottom line is that he has a great spirit and an innate warmth about him, and I am proud to say I love him as both a man and a friend.

Hasta pronto mi gran amigo!

Gary Player

Contents

Chapter 1

The Champion who was Born in the Spring

I was born on 9 April 1957 in Pedreña, a small village in the north of Spain across the bay from the city of Santander. My parents, Baldomero Ballesteros Presmanes and Carmen Sota Ocejo, called me Severiano after my paternal grandfather.

With my three older brothers – Baldomero, Manuel and Vicente – we lived in a house that my great-grandparents had built in 1882. Our rooms were above the stables where the livestock was kept, as was then still quite usual in villages. Manolo, as we call Manuel, and his family now live in that beloved place where I was born, a white, two-storey house, which I still cherish.

My parents worked the land, reared cows and fished. I learned a lot from them, above all the importance of work. My father spent many hours on his feet, but I think my mother was up and about even longer. I would see her cleaning, washing, cooking and ironing every hour of the day and late into the night. She brought us up to love, respect and enjoy life and made us feel that we lacked nothing, even in the cramped conditions in which we lived. Mothers are like that – they want the best for their children, and that's all they think about. When I think of my parents I would say my optimistic side comes from my father, who never doubted that I would triumph in life, and my more down-to-earth, realistic side comes from my mother.

When I was born Spain was still ruled by General Franco. Franco had been in power since 1939, the year the rest of Europe embarked on the Second World War, and I reached my eighteenth birthday without having known any other ruler. (When he died in 1975, I was with my brother Manolo in Orlando, Florida, trying to qualify to play on the American circuit. I heard the news on a Mexican radio station.)

My father had believed in Franco: he was sure that he was the man to shape our country's destiny. In fact, he admired the man so much that in 1937, when he was press-ganged into the Republican army during the Spanish Civil War – the Republicans were anti-Franco – he shot himself in the left hand to avoid having to fight. This earned him a twenty-year prison sentence, but he escaped from the hospital where his injury was being treated and joined the Francoist forces, with whom he fought until the war ended.

I grew up in an era when attitudes were extremely strict and harsh. Priests and the military were all-powerful. They were dour, stern and very authoritarian. It was better not to let them see you get up to mischief, and better still if nobody told on you if you had been. I remember several of us kids were once caught scrumping in an orchard. We were taken to the Civil Guard's small barracks on the edge of the village. I was very frightened, because the sergeant – Sea-bream Eye, we called him, as he was half blind in one eye – threatened to smash our faces in. Just imagine, because we little boys had stolen fruit! But the world is a funny place: I bought the two houses where I'd gone scrumping as a boy. I live in one of them now; until she died, my mother lived in the other.

My parents married in 1944. Their first child, Manuel, was born the following year and their second, Baldomero, in 1947. By the time I arrived Baldomero – Merín as we've always called him – was the oldest child. This means, as you must have guessed, that something terrible happened. In the August of the year Merín was born, a lady who helped my mother look after the children took them both to the beach, which was close by. She was walking across the farm when tragedy struck: our horse Blackie put a hoof in a wasps' nest. The wasps immediately swarmed out in their hundreds and attacked Blackie and the lady with my two brothers. Poor little Manolo got the worst of it, as she couldn't protect them both at the same time. She ran off frantically with the baby but that left Manuel to the mercy of the wasps. He was stung from head to toe. My parents rushed Manuel to the doctor but there was nothing he could do for him. My parents returned home distraught and Manuel died within twelve hours, in fact on the very day he should have been celebrating his second birthday. It was a terrible blow. My parents couldn't resign themselves to their loss: they gave the name 'Manuel' to their next child. Then came Vicente, and finally myself. I confess that as I was the youngest in the family my parents rather spoiled me, but, to compensate, my three older brothers gave me all the rotten jobs. Before going to school in the morning, for example, my first job was to clean out the cow dung from the stable. Then I went to school, came home for lunch and went back to school in the afternoon.

I was five years old when I started school. The school was about two kilometres from our house, and sometimes I ran all the way. I became a good runner. As a boy, I even won a 1,500-metre race, beating the second-placed by thirty metres. I still have the trophy: it's the size of a mobile phone. It's worthless in itself, but it's always had priceless sentimental value for me. I keep it in my trophy room because, after all, it was in my cabinet long before anything I won playing golf.

After school, I'd go home to help my father milk the cows. Farmers today have milking machines and modern equipment for this operation, but we had none of that. We did it by hand. I would also help my father take grass from the fields to the stable, and to sow, reap and load the harvest in our horse and cart in order to take it home and store for winter in what we called our barn. In Pedreña smallholders harvested their potatoes, beans and maize and stored them in their barns alongside the hay for the animals, which were treated almost like members of the family.

Clearing out the cow muck certainly wasn't my only task. Every Saturday, for example, I had to clean the whole family's shoes. But looking after the livestock was really my main responsibility, with some help from Vicente, who was the next youngest of us children. Working together wasn't always a happy affair, because we'd fight on the slightest pretext. We hit and swore at each another, but nevertheless we always went around together. He'd often get me into trouble – when I wasn't the one telling lies to land him in it. One of our jobs was to pick the beans and, as I hated doing that, I would just sit there in the field until he shouted at me. Then I'd go home. About fifty metres from the house I would burst into tears and tell my father that Vicente had whacked me. When Vicente got home, my father would hit him, and it was a rare thing for him to lay a hand on us. Then Vicente would get his own back by hitting me, and so on. In fact, whenever any of my brothers hit me, I'd tell my father. My father would always defend me.

Vicente and I were also responsible for taking the cows to pasture and bringing them back at midday. We let them graze freely in a meadow that had an electric fence with a 'shepherd', which was our name for the battery. It was four kilometres from our house, but at least we could play when we got there, without a care in the world, because if a cow tried to escape from the meadow, the fence gave it an electric shock and it would run back into the field. Neither we, nor anyone in our house, had a watch, but we knew when it was time to take the cows back to the stable because at twelve the church bells rang for the angelus.

One day the bells didn't chime. As we were late getting back, my father got worried, and at around half-past two he came looking for us. It turned out that the bell-ringer was ill and the poor man hadn't been able to carry out his duties. So we had had no idea it was time to go back. That's something that wouldn't happen in our age of electronically controlled chimes. The man who rang the bells was called Turín and he was very popular. After his death, a village street was named after him. Turín sang in the church choir and eventually he wrote a song dedicated to my victories.

The story about the bells that never chimed takes me to a bit of family history. My great-grandfather on my father's side was also a Manuel and his trade was founding bells: he spent his time travelling from one place to another to get orders from churches to make new bells. As my grandfather Severiano wasn't very keen on a life spent travelling to the ends of the earth, he decided to switch trades and become a livestock farmer. My parents, who continued in the same line, had a small farm with fourteen milking cows; they also grew maize, sugar beet, beans, potatoes and green vegetables. Before the 1960s, the local economy was based on milking cows and growing maize and vegetables. It was subsistence farming: most people lived on their milk production and crops although they also fished, especially for clams and the shellfish that we called *morgueras*, which you open, squirt with lemon and swallow.

Our village lacked a lot of things. All Pedreña had was a church, a few stone houses, three bars and a pharmacy. At school we didn't even have a cheap football – we had to make do with a ball we made from rags and old shirts. On the other hand, we could easily have a game of marbles. How times have changed!

The only place you could make a telephone call in Pedreña was from a small exchange that was managed by an old lady by the name of Angelita. Naturally, she listened to every single conversation, in particular to the sailors who were away from home for ages and called their families from distant ports once or twice a month. Angelita knew what was happening in every household; to make matters worse, she was the confidante of the village priest. Nobody liked that at all, because he had a habit of telling all in his sermon during Sunday mass.

By the time I was twelve or thirteen things had begun to improve. At the end of the 1960s, only two thousand people lived in the eight villages in the Pedreña district, and we were only three hundred in Pedreña itself; nowadays the village has a population of almost thirteen hundred.

The one thing Pedreña did have was a golf club, the Royal Club of Pedreña. The course was next to the meadow where we grazed our cows, and it was very important to all of us who lived near it. The members sometimes found villagers jobs in Santander; and there was always work going there caddying – which would earn you a few extra pesetas.

From childhood, Vicente and I liked golf a lot and, when we took the cows to graze, we'd take along an 8 iron that one of the club members had given us and practise our short game. We'd almost always play with stones, but occasionally we'd use real balls that we found or stole from the club. Once we slipped over the wall on to the club course and left the cows to graze in the meadow. We played so hard that we didn't hear the church bells. We ran back to where we'd left the cattle, but they'd all disappeared. It turned out that they'd broken the fence and gone back to the village by themselves. They were roaming at will. When we got home, our father was very angry and told us to gather them together and shut them in the stable, which was exhausting and took us more than four hours.

People have often said I was a born golfer, that it was my destiny. They reckon I've been blessed genetically – that my right arm is almost four centimetres longer than my left. (If you're right-handed that gives you a huge advantage when it comes to hitting the ball.) But the fact is my right hand isn't any longer than my left; it's just that I have a slight stoop. It may have helped me to play golf; it has certainly given me back trouble. The truth is the day I was born in Pedreña any idea that I might have a career as an international golfer wasn't even a dream, it was pure fantasy.

Chapter 2

The Lone Ranger

Our family is *montañesa* – after La Montaña, the other name given to Cantabria, because of its mountainous contours. I was brought up in a loving family and I played all the usual childhood games with my brothers. As soon as we had finished with our chores, we would be off outside. We were all sports mad, and we played everything. I liked running and boxing a lot, and I still do both.

Outside the family, I was mainly a solitary, rather taciturn boy. I had a couple of good friends at school, like Corino, *El Zurdi* ('The Southpaw'), who died at the age of nineteen when he fell into the hold of the boat where he'd started to work, but it was only later that I found myself a wide circle of friends, among the boys who worked as caddies like myself. We'd go to the beach and play football.

I say that our family was sports mad, and we were. I even tried my hand at rowing, but I didn't like it, because it was such hard work. Rowing is a traditional sport in the north of Spain, especially in the Basque country, Galicia and Cantabria. Every summer important competitions are held along the coast. My father was Spanish champion in *trainera* racing. *Traineras* are big, open boats with fixed seats where fourteen men sit, thirteen rowers and their cox. Pedreña is renowned in this sport. I remember there was a huge fuss when it was decided that Pedreña's team should only include men from the village itself. As my father and Uncle Andrés were originally from Rubayo – a neighbouring village – they were thrown out of the team. In response, they and other rowers formed a new team in Peñacastillo, a village on the other side of the bay.

I can still remember my father taking the village taxi to go to train in Peñacastillo after finishing work on our smallholding. I really loved accompanying him and I think he liked me to, because he would give me the ham roll and Coca-Cola all the rowers got after their training sessions.

My father was a fighter, and he would never give up. Every year I'd go with him to Solares, a village about eight kilometres away where there was a flour mill. We would bring back enough maize flour to keep us in bread for a whole year. For supper we children would eat a big cup of milk and a bread cake, made from maize flour mixture, as big as a plate, that was baked in the oven. Then we'd go to sleep.

Ours was a family of modest means and we couldn't afford anything that wasn't essential without making lots of sacrifices. In my case, when I was nine, I couldn't even take First Communion like the other children. The First Communion ceremony and party are a big Spanish tradition and the village custom was for children of the same age to take it together in the village church. However, to save the expense of a party, my parents decided I would take my First Communion at the same time as my cousins, Marisol and Maricarmen, got married. There were no photos and the suit I wore was the one my brothers had worn before me.

My mother had inherited the house where we lived from her Uncle Vicente. I think that really upset my maternal aunts and uncles; certainly, relations with my mother's family were strained. Uncle Vicente had left my mother the house because she was the only one of them who had looked after him when he was ill and living by himself. The others only appeared at the hospital when he was dying. When they brought the conversation round to what would happen after his death, they said, 'Well, uncle, we expect you've made your will; as you're a good man, we suppose you've done things fairly?'

'Don't worry, I've treated you all equally,' he said.

They got nothing. Uncle Vicente left my mother the house and several plots of land. The rest of the family, of course, were livid and envious, and as a result some of my mother's siblings badgered my grandfather Marcelino into disinheriting her. Consequently we had almost no contact with my mother's family. But despite everything they did to her, my mother never spoke ill of them. My mother never spoke ill of anyone. She always chose her words very carefully. When she went to the cemetery, she'd take a bouquet of flowers for her parents, for her dead son Manuel, and for Uncle Vicente. When I go to the cemetery to take flowers to my parents and Manuel, I also pray for Uncle Vicente, because my mother loved him dearly.

The family house had a living room and a kitchen with a coal fire where we ate. We all sat at the table, except for my mother who'd stand up to eat because she was always busy serving food or cooking. There was only one washroom, at the back of the house, but for years that didn't have even a bath. Our only source of entertainment was an old radio, but it gave us all a lot of fun, particularly my mother.

As I mentioned, all the rooms were on the top floor; the animals' stables below provided us with heating in winter. Of course, my parents had their own bedroom. So too did Baldomero and Manolo; Vicente and I shared a bed in another.

Our room was tiny. It had just enough space to fit a bed and bedside table. We called it 'the dark room' because it didn't have a window, unlike Manolo and Merín's, which was the best in the house. Sharing a bed with Vicente wasn't easy. He kept pushing me during the night and he would end up shoving me out of bed; every morning I'd wake up shivering to death on the straw mat. What's more, I was always very frightened before I went to sleep, because I could hear large rats prowling in the loft we used as a pantry.

I've always had a very special relationship with Vicente. We were as close as could be, and perhaps because of that we were always trying to get the upper hand. When Vicente came home from doing his military service at the base in Zaragoza, he brought back lots of pairs of trousers with him. It so happened – unusually – that I had some money in my pocket. I bought twelve pairs from him – for fifteen hundred pesetas. I thought I'd got a really good deal, but it turned out that he kept wearing the trousers, even though I'd bought them from him.

'Vicente,' I asked him one day, 'why are you wearing those trousers? They're mine, I bought them from you.'

'Yes,' he replied, 'but our deal didn't say I couldn't wear them.'

Something else I vividly remember are the crème caramels. My mother made excellent crème caramels: a big one for my father and small ones for the four of us. Naughty Vicente would sidle up to me and say as persuasively as he knew how: 'You know, Seve, these puddings are so small, if you only eat one, you won't even notice it; wouldn't it be better if one of us ate both of ours?' Adding immediately, 'I'll give you five pesetas for yours.' And that's how it always ended: he'd have two and I'd eat none. I spent the five pesetas on going to the cinema. But we would always look out for each other. We still do.

Years later, a neighbour rang me at around 11.30 one evening to say that someone was burgling Vicente's house. By the time I got to Vicente's, the burglars had fled, but a neighbour saw their car had a German number plate. I immediately rang my cousin Severiano, who is now mayor, and he put the local police on to the case. They soon caught four Yugoslavs. My brothers gave me a good telling-off. They said I shouldn't have got involved, since the burglars must have been a dangerous crew.

I mentioned that I spent those five pesetas I got from Vicente on going to the cinema. I liked going to the cinema, but money was always tight. El Casino, the village cinema, had an attendant – an excellent person – who'd collect up the tickets; his name was Cuco and to a child he was as tall as Frankenstein. The films were all black and white – some were even silent. They'd première a film every Sunday at 4 p.m., because people went to Mass in the morning. So each Sunday we boys would play at who could roll a coin nearest to a line drawn on the ground. On one occasion I lost and had no money to see the film. I went back home, took a toy boat I had and sold it for the five pesetas I needed to get in. The boat was worth much more, and the boy who bought it from me knew how to make the most of my situation.

Mrs Fidela would park her mobile stall near El Casino and sell knick-knacks, sunflower seeds, chewing gum, hazelnuts and a lot of titbits. As I never had enough money left after I'd paid for my ticket to buy even a sugar-coated biscuit, I had to have all my wits about me. During the intermission, I'd take advantage of a moment when she was selling something to barge a boy in the crush and send a few titbits flying to the ground. While she stooped to pick them up, I would pocket something I fancied, a little bag of hazelnuts, sunflower seeds or whirls, and run back into the cinema. I may have been a shy little boy, but I was also mischievous.

It was in El Casino that I saw *The Lone Ranger* for the first time. The Lone Ranger was special to me: every time I made my plans to watch the adventure series they were showing on television, I felt like him.

Of course, when I was young, we didn't have a television. (We got our first set, like our first clock, very late in the day, when Manolo brought them back after he'd played a golf tournament in Tenerife.) So to watch television, we had to go out. The first set to arrive in Pedreña was set up in one of the bars, El Culebrero ('The Snakecatcher'). It was about two hundred metres from my house and I'd disappear there to see whatever series they were showing.

As a kid I'd often go to sleep in my parents' bed, because my mother was always up late washing up, cleaning the kitchen and getting things ready for the following day. I'd wait for my father to fall asleep and then I'd escape to the bar. As they wouldn't let me in at night, I'd stand in the street spying through the window on Roger Moore playing Simon Templar in *The Saint*, and David Janssen in *The Fugitive*. I couldn't hear a word of what they were saying, but I was fascinated by the images. During the day I had no problems. When school ended I'd run out to catch *Daniel Boone*, which was shown at four o'clock. And we kids never missed an episode of *Bonanza*. As every series was dubbed in Mexico, we found it funny to listen to all the people speaking Mexican Spanish and not our kind.

But golf was what I liked most. Whenever I could, I would slip off to the golf course. From very early on I was a kind of 'lone ranger'. I was seven when I got hold of my first piece of golfing equipment: the head of an old club. It was only that. A head. But when I had that, I searched high and low for a long tree branch that would serve as a shaft; when I found one I slotted it into the hollow in the head and put it in a bucket of water so that the wood would swell and make the shaft fit tighter. No need to say that my rough-and-ready shaft had no grip. I say 'shaft', but I should really say 'shafts', since they lasted no time at all. People get very upset when they lose balls, but imagine what it's like losing a club all the time, for the shafts rarely survived more than a day.

And it wasn't only clubs I had to improvise. I made my first strokes with pebbles. Later my brothers gave me balls to hit, and I'd practise in the meadow and on the beach, with holes I made from a tree branch and a handkerchief. Quite often the holes existed only in my imagination. It's how I started to play golf.

As a young boy I learned by trying to imitate my brother Manolo. I started by concentrating on his swing; and then he spent a lot of time helping me with mine, even to the detriment of his own game. I am sure if he hadn't been so generous, Manuel would have won many more tournaments in addition to the 1968 Biarritz Open, the 1976 Spanish championship and the 1983 Timex Open in Biarritz, when he relegated Nick Faldo to second place.

For my eighth birthday, Manolo gave me a real golf club as a present, a 3 iron. By that time I'd begun to work as a caddie at the golf club although I wasn't allowed to play on the course, because caddies were banned from doing so. Diego Portilla, the caddie master, was responsible for enforcing the ban and did so rigorously, but I never worried about that. My enthusiasm for golf and boyish spirit of opposition made the impulse to do whatever was forbidden quite irresistible. At dusk and at dawn, and on many a warm moonlit night, I'd slip on to the course to play – now equipped with balls rather than stones. Some days I'd even truant. I found it more natural to go and play golf than to stick my nose in a book. After lunch, when I was supposed to go back to school, I'd leave my books and satchel by some big pipes set up to take water from the course, extract the 3 iron I'd hidden there and go on to the golf course. I'd usually make for the second nine holes where there weren't so many people playing. I'd generally manage a couple of holes without any problem, but then I would have to hide so as not to be seen by the members. I'd emerge and play another hole when I saw the coast was clear. Then I'd go back to the pipes, very reluctantly hide my club, pick up my books and go back to school. In the evenings, back home, my parents always asked: 'What did you do at school?'

'Did the best I could,' I'd reply and they were very pleased, convinced I'd been studying hard.

The truth was that I never studied; consequently I didn't pass a single subject. And it gets worse. When I was twelve, I was expelled from school. It wasn't golf's fault, although by then it was my only real school. One day, in class, I discovered a couple of pages were missing from one of my textbooks. I wasn't to blame, but my teacher didn't think twice before punishing me. As was the custom in those days, she made me turn the palms of my hand upwards and hit me hard with a ruler. She badly hurt my hands – and my pride.

When I got home at lunchtime, my parents weren't around, because they were out fishing. Angry and upset, I sat down at the table and found a bottle of wine my father had left ready for supper. I drank a couple of glasses before heading back to school. When I entered the classroom I was so tipsy that I got up on the podium, grabbed my teacher and started to rough her up. They had no choice but to expel me.

In time my parents realised it was futile to force me to go to school, as all I wanted to do was play golf.

'All right,' they said, 'if you want to go to the golf course and play or be a caddie, that's fine, but you must go for private tuition every evening.'

And that was how I both made progress with my golf and improved my attitude to studying. My parents were making a big sacrifice on behalf of my brothers and me by spending money they didn't really have to help us with our schooling. They sent me to the same teacher who taught Vicente – she was the owner of a restaurant called El Puntal. I'd go to her five days a week from half-past seven to nine every night. It was very late for me, but it was worthwhile because I could devote every hour of the day to playing golf. And I did. When my father let me leave school to work on my golf full-time, he gave me a warning I never forgot. Even now I repeat it to my own children: 'Remember, if you want to come first in anything, you have to prove yourself.'

Chapter 3

The Boy who Played by the Light of the Moon

In the nineteenth century the aristocracy and wealthy inhabitants of Madrid wanted to escape the stifling summer heat of the capital. The place they chose as their refuge was the beautiful city of Santander. The city was soon such a popular destination that the royal family came to take a dip in the ocean like the rest. In response, the city built the Magdalena Palace for them. But the palace wasn't the only benefit Santander's royal connection brought to the region.

In the summer of 1928 Santander held several functions to honour the presence of the Spanish king and queen in the city and its environs. One of these took place in Pedreña, on the Contrajón highland. Those present included King Don Alfonso XIII himself, along with many local dignitaries and members of the nobility. That gathering would change the lives of the inhabitants of Pedreña, because it led to the establishment of a golf club, the Royal Club of Pedreña. Everyone there could see the potential of the terrain – its peaceful, sheltered nature and beautiful views – and a subscription was immediately opened, led by the king. The Duke of Alba enthusiastically championed the initiative, as did Her Excellency Mrs María Luisa Pelayo and the Countess of Revilla de Camargo, along with many local dignitaries and members of the nobility like the Duchess of Santoña, Maria Luisa Pelayo, Paloma Falcó, the Duchess of Alba, the Marquis of Villabrámiga, the Count of Revilla de Camargo, Ramon Quiyano, Gonzalo Garcia de los Rios, Walter Meade, the Count of Sclafani and Ramon Lavin del Noval.

Of course, a golf course needs a lot of space. The total area comprised some 68 hectares, and 282 small farms had to give up their land (my maternal grandfather Marcelino was among those affected). For the privilege, the locals were paid less than one peseta per square metre. The prestigious English architect Harry S. Colt was contracted to build the magnificent 18-hole course, while the clubhouse was designed by Don Valentín Lavín del Noval, next to a quay that had disappeared. Gradually, as you can read in books of the time, the character of the region changed: 'Trasmieran cows would no longer graze on the Contrajón meadows, village boys no longer carried fodder for the cattle, but the gentlemen's golf clubs. Customs had changed. The people of Pedreña kept their local expressions, but also got to know golfing slang. In the cattle markets in Solares they could boast they were multilingual.' The village of Pedreña had been shorn of a large part of its most valued possession, its land. But in compensation, I think God had foreseen the gift to the village of other ways of earning a living, because when the golf course opened, it provided jobs for the locals. Later on, because the majority of members were well educated and of good social standing, they were able to find caddies or their relatives jobs in Santander. As the years went by, the villagers were no longer so dependent on agriculture and fishing. The club would bring economic prosperity to Pedreña, providing steady jobs and good wages to caddies and their families. And of course it gave those living in the region the opportunity to become golf professionals.

Nowadays, the Royal Golf Club of Pedreña has a national and international reputation because of such names as Sota, Carriles, Cayarga, Ocejo, Rozadilla, Roqueñi and Ballesteros. In fact, Pedreña is now the number one village in the world in terms of the ratio of golf professionals to inhabitants.

The Royal Club is the course where I had my first experiences of golf. Like lots of other people from Pedreña, my brothers Merín, Manolo and Vicente earned a few pesetas acting as caddies. From the age of six I was eager to follow in their footsteps. At the time, like other kids, I'd search out lost balls on the course to sell back to club members. I also went to see my Uncle Ramón Sota, the club coach, play and train. In 1965, Ramón came sixth in the Masters at Augusta; Jack Nicklaus, Arnold Palmer and Gary Player were the first three. As you can see, he was rubbing shoulders with the best. He bought a car with his prize money – it was one of the first three in Pedreña. He won several Spanish championships, the French, Brazilian and Dutch Opens and a few other tournaments. He became the best golfer in Spain and among the best in Europe.

I loved to watch Uncle Ramón play. He had a good swing and struck the ball consistently. That's how I learned, by watching other people; I can almost say I taught myself. I remember how one night – because Ramón always trained until late – I found a twenty-five-peseta coin on the way home, and he came over and said: 'What a stroke of luck! Don't say anything to your mother and let's go to El Culebrero and have a glass of wine with hot chestnuts.' He's probably forgotten this episode but I remember him taking me to the bar and spending the twenty-five pesetas there.

I may have watched him play in order to teach myself, but there wasn't much communication between us. Ramón was very withdrawn. Once, when I'd just started out as a professional, I played with him, and my brother Manuel, who was just beginning to shine, in the Ramón Quijano Memorial. It was only my third pro tournament and I had a two-metre putt at the last hole. I knew I had to hole the putt to force a playoff with Patricio Garrido. It was a very tense moment for me, because I was so inexperienced. Ramón, with all his experience of international tournaments, came over and said: 'It's now or never.' I played and missed. Perhaps he shouldn't have said anything.

I showed how golf-mad I was from a very early age and followed in my brothers' footsteps by carrying players' clubs and watching them play. I was happy playing, even though it meant truanting or stealing on to the course at dawn or on nights when a full moon was shining. In the autumn or spring, when the days were longer, I'd wait for everyone to leave the club before stepping on to the course. I'd spend hours and hours at the 2nd hole, which is a par 3 that runs alongside the road and can't be seen from the clubhouse. (But you *can* see that hole and a good part of the rest of the course from the house where I now live!) I even made a little course in the field behind our house, with a tomato tin for the hole and a handkerchief on a stick for a flag. I played approach shots for hours and I swear the hole seemed incredibly small. I spent hours and hours practising between the ages of nine and fifteen. If my short game was outstanding it is because during those years I practised approach shots and putts all the time. I even hung up a fishing-net in the stables at home so I could hit balls at it late into the night. My mother would call me in and I'd hear my father telling her: 'Let the boy practise!'

The moment the opportunity presented itself I also started to work on Saturdays and Sundays as a caddie for the club members. I spent the money I earned on going to the pictures and buying titbits I no longer had to steal from poor Fidela. But it was very hard being a caddie, since we weren't allowed to do anything – and certainly not play on the course. They wouldn't even let us practise our swings. I was once punished with a week without work because I disobeyed that rule. Everything was so rigid and class-bound that, when we went to the equipment room, we weren't allowed to walk in front of the clubhouse: we had to go round the back. Members who were eating on the terrace got annoyed if they saw us. They were harsh times and such behaviour was ridiculous!

The caddies were the responsibility of a caddie master, and if we did something he thought was wrong, he'd report it to the club management, which would take appropriate measures, almost always a suspension. Caddies were paid a fixed tariff of twenty-five pesetas per bag, along with a tip of thirty, forty or fifty pesetas, depending on how well your player thought you'd worked for him. Sometimes they claimed you had lost a ball or hadn't been watching the game carefully in order to get out of paying. Given that, we caddies had to be on the alert: I can tell you from experience that the proverb that says hunger sharpens the wit is true. In our case it wasn't 'hunger' so much as authoritarian attitudes and the lack of fairness that sharpened our wits. We were always thinking of ways to rile our charges. As the majority of members were wealthy people who played golf very badly, we'd take advantage of that to steal their balls. We weren't so foolish as to take balls from the bag, for they would have rumbled that straight away, but when they hit a ball into the rough we'd tread on it and bury it. We'd mark the spot and come back later to retrieve it, and then we'd clean it and sell it to the man in charge of the changing room. He'd then re-sell the balls to the members, who could thus buy back their own balls several times. In fact, many members were better players than they thought, because we made sure they lost at least one ball per round.

We caddies couldn't play on the course. Or, to be more accurate, we could play once a year, when the caddies' championship was held.

The caddies' championship had three flights, and which flight one competed in depended more on one's ability than on one's age. The first flight played thirty-six holes over two days; the second, one round in one day, and the third, a mere nine holes. We played with clubs that members lent us, because they were expensive and we didn't own any. We would train with a club a member had given us or even one that we'd stolen. These usually came not from locals but from foreigners. When we were carrying the latters' bags to the car, a club could easily go missing on the way. It was the law of survival.

The same went for the balls we played with. For the championship, it was traditional to play with balls that members had lost but we were supposed to hand them in to Diego, the caddie master, at the end of the 18th hole. So at the 16th or 17th hole we'd start to hide the balls we had left. As Diego would never have believed that we could end up at the final hole without any spare balls at all, we always kept back the well-worn ones to give him. If he got angry he was capable of banning you from the following year's competition.

At the end of each championship the club paid for a celebratory meal, but only those in the first five places of each flight could attend. It was another example of how stingy the club could be. Almost all the club's old guard were followers of Franco, little dictators who mistreated and even insulted us. It wasn't unusual for them to call us idiots. One day, one of them, for whom I was caddying, messed up a shot at the 12th and in a rage picked up his club and hurled it into the distance. He looked at me, pointed in the direction he'd hurled it and said: 'Hey kid, get moving!' And, naturally, I had to fetch it. We caddies had to keep quiet and obey. If you said or did anything they didn't like, the club would suspend you – or even throw you out. This happened to a caddie by the name of Cotera when a member threw his club far away and ordered him to bring it back.

'Hey, for God's sake, get a move on!'

Cotera, who was no doubt already in a bad temper, was very upset by his tone and retorted: 'You know, sir, I've just had an idea. Why don't you go and get it yourself?'

That sort of arrogant attitude was the norm, but not all the people at the club were like that. Men like Valentín Valle or Santiago Ortiz de la Torre, for example, always behaved decently. They acted in a pleasant, respectful and friendly manner towards everybody.

Chapter 4

A Fright on New Year's Eve

One of the players I got to know best as a caddie was an old Englishman I called Mr Michael. He played all over Spain, but he was particularly fond of the Royal Club of Pedreña. Mr Michael was an aristocrat – well, I used to think all Englishmen were aristocrats – who lived in Andalusia. He was a quiet, elegant man who smoked a cherry-wood pipe that I thought he never lit, as it never gave off smoke. I liked working for him – he always treated his caddies very well. Often when he was weighing up a potential shot, he'd ask me for advice, even though he knew full well I wasn't in a position to give him any because of my age and lack of experience. Sometimes, just to say something, I'd suggest a tactic that owed more to my imagination than reality. As he listened, he'd smile good-naturedly and explain why what I'd said wasn't feasible. Over time I realised it was his way of teaching me. One day he said something really strange, and it has stayed etched in my mind: 'The day when you play calmly, enjoy yourself and don't fuss; when you feel what you've achieved is the fruit of what you'd planned, you'll be a great success.' For Mr Michael the best player in the world was the one able to play in a relaxed manner – the one who could have fun. I think he felt that he belonged in this category – even though he wasn't good enough to play in a competitive tournament. One day, he asked me to play with him not as a caddie but as his guest. I played fairly well and I was very happy with the day. 'If you persevere, you'll become the best golfer in the world,' Mr Michael told me as he gave me his putter as a present. It was the last time I saw him.

Another of my favourite players was Dr Santiago Ortiz de la Torre, a paediatrician. Although he was the member who tipped the least money, I never stole a single ball from him. When I carried his small bag for him at weekends, he would let me play with him and his friends. On more than one occasion, the director of the club reproached him for this, but he was a man with a strong personality and replied: 'The boy's good company and I play with him because I'm a member and I'll play with whomever I want to.'

Even though the doctor was a bad player I didn't mind, because when I went out with him I could play on the course and use his clubs. In fact, it was the only way I could since the club's elitist regulations otherwise prevented me. I'm very grateful to Dr Ortiz de la Torre for this and also for his other kindnesses. Occasionally he gave me tickets to see a Racing Santander football match and he always took a genuine interest in my health and my family's. When he saw that I was wilting, he'd make me take a course of vitamins to get my strength back.

When I'd started to play as a professional, I tried to repay him for his kindness. I'd give him new balls as a present, for he always used old ones. I remember once when we were playing the 8th hole at Pedreña – the 8th is a very narrow fairway – he lost two balls. Then he lost two more at the next. When it came to his next turn to play, I said 'Hit away, Don Santiago.' 'Well, unless I cut off a ball of my own, I don't know what I'm going to hit,' he replied.

Long before Mr Michael gave me his putter, Manolo, as I have mentioned, had given me an old 3 iron. The number 3 is a club that's very difficult to control, especially for a young boy like I was, but I couldn't have cared less. Beggars can't be choosers. So, although it was a tricky club, I practised with it all the time. That was how I learned to play different strokes; from a bunker, with a ball in a bad lie, and so on . . . I think the fact I had only a single club to play with and that it was a 3 iron helped me to learn much more in less time. I had to hit high and low shots, short and long shots, on the fairway and from the depths of the rough, all with the same club. If I had had a full set of clubs – or even half a set – each club would have given me different distances and flights of the ball. The 3 iron gave me a huge set of advantages, for thanks to it I developed my ability to improvise and to play the characteristic shots that shaped my career as a professional golfer.

I also have the fondest memories of my first pair of spikes. These were a present from Casimiro Gómez, who was in charge of the male changing room. I took the shoes home the minute I got them – they were leather and were a member's cast-offs – and the first thing I did was to grease them with horse fat so they'd last longer.

Of course, my playing time on the course was always limited. When I did manage to slip surreptitiously on to the course I played with my brother Vicente and two friends, Emilio Cayarga, whose grandfather was my first teacher in Pedreña, and Tasio, who'd give me balls in exchange for use of my 3 iron. They'd come to our house, because you could see the course from there. When the caddie master Diego, whom we nicknamed 'Chin', and the security guard, Quintás, left through the gate we knew it was our cue: 'Come on, quick, off to the course, Chin and Quintás have just gone.' But until I was thirteen I continued to practise my drives, approaches and putts on the beach. At the time, the beach in Pedreña reached to where the practice links are today and the sea almost lapped against the clubhouse. The road that now runs between the club itself and the sea was built, like the practice links, on reclaimed land. At the beginning of September, the sand on the beach at low tide was very smooth and fast. It was a lot like a green. However, as you moved away from the breakwater it got drier and coarser and much like the sand you'd find in a bunker. Playing on the beach was very useful practice but it wasn't enough and, as I couldn't play on the course by day, I started to slip in at daybreak and nightfall, especially on nights when there was a full moon.

It was a very strange experience to walk around a golf course at night, because all the reference points that help estimate distances vanished. The landscape became a grey space where the dark mass of trees made little impact and I found it hard to follow the flight of the ball, especially as I was soon hitting my 3 iron 150 metres. I knew where the shot was heading from the way my hands felt the hit and from the sound the ball made when it hit the ground. I mean that if I didn't hear the ball rebounding off one of the trees that line the fairways to nearly all the holes in Pedreña, I knew that it was a good drive. By practising at night I learned to feel the grass under my feet, to measure distances intuitively and adjust the power of the strokes I wanted to make.

A day came when the security guard discovered the place where I slipped on to the course and told the authorities about me. But I paid no attention and continued my nightly incursions. I was punished several times and was even threatened with expulsion from the club for good. In fact I don't know why I wasn't expelled. I think the first time I legitimately played on the course was when I participated in the caddies' championship. I was nine years old and funnily enough I never won the third flight, though I did win the second the only time I participated, and won the first level a total of four times before I turned professional.

My first attempt was a disaster. I took 51 for the nine holes, including a ten at the par-3 1st – a real record! I improved a lot the following year, and finished second, with a 42 over nine holes from the women's tees. Then I went up to the second flight. At the age of twelve I won with a round of 79, which immediately opened the doors to the top level. I came sixth the first year, but won the next year with a 71 for the first round and a 65 for the second. People were astonished because a 65 was incredible. We were playing from the professional tees and shooting rounds of 65 and 70 caused a sensation. It is still the course record for a caddie. That year, when I was thirteen, was also the first time I beat my brother Manolo over eighteen holes. He was eight years older than me and already playing in international tournaments.

But, as far as I was concerned, the most important prize being champion caddie brought me was that I was now allowed to play on the course officially. I'd be there the whole day, hitting hundreds of balls from dawn until even the cats couldn't see. It was no effort: I was having a great time, doing what I liked, because I wanted to be a champion. While my friends were going to discos and going out with their girlfriends, I played golf or stayed at home. I found this quite natural, because golf was my life.

That same year I went with Manolo to Málaga to caddie for him. It was the first time I had been out of Santander. My brother was playing in the Spanish Under-25s Championship. Unfortunately, he played so badly that at one stage I put the bag on the ground and said: 'Manolo, I could play better than you!' Manolo, adult that he was, bit his lip and said nothing.

In 1972 I repeated my victory in the caddies' championship, beating the runner-up by sixteen strokes. That year, the owner of La Manga, a new course on the coast of Murcia organised a very important Pro-Am to celebrate the club's inauguration. Sean Connery was invited, along with sporting stars like Wimbledon champion Manuel Santana, and important businessmen like Mark McCormack, the founder of IMG (International Management Group), whose team eventually won the tournament. As they had no trained staff or caddies in La Manga they had to recruit from Puerta de Hierro in Madrid, El Prat in Barcelona and Pedreña. I was selected to be one of the caddies and I travelled by bus to La Manga. It was here I saw Gary Player for the first time, and his personality had a huge impact on me.

The first things about Gary that drew my attention were his powers of concentration and strength of will. We called him *Manitas de Plata* ('Little Hands of Silver', after the gypsy guitarist from La Camargue), because he had a magic touch and a fantastic rhythm. He really knew how to get himself out of a bunker! No wonder he was admired throughout the world! He immediately became my hero, simply because he was the first great golfer I had met. I knew of others, like Jack Nicklaus and Arnold Palmer, but I didn't get to meet them until 1975, at the Open Championship in Carnoustie, where, even though I didn't make the cut, both took an interest in me.

But I am getting ahead of myself. Early in 1974, after winning the caddies' championship for a third time, I prepared to make the leap to professional status. However, something happened that came close to setting my future career on a quite different path.

Among the few diversions in the village of Pedreña are the fiestas of St Peter in June, when people go out to have a good time at the fair and dances after eating clams all day, and the fiestas on New Year's Eve. Traditionally the young people of Pedreña see out New Year's Eve by playing practical jokes, like taking a neighbour's cart and leaving it outside somebody else's house, or opening stable doors and letting the cows out, and so on. I will never forget the practical joke we played on 31 December 1973. That night, a group of us village boys invaded the golf course, where drainage work was being carried out. We were singing and telling jokes when we reached the tee of the 6th hole, one of the highest points on the course. A pile of enormous pipes was stacked there and one of us had a bright idea. 'Why don't we roll them down the fairway?' he said. I was the only caddie in our little gang, so I was never going to join in, but before he got an answer he'd given them a push and more than twenty pipes were rolling almost two hundred metres down the 6th fairway. A few days later, one of the boys told the guard about it. The board decided to ban all those involved for one month, but I was the only one affected, because the others didn't play golf.

I had been intending to turn professional in January. Now I had to wait. My future as a golfer hung in the balance. Always worried about my prospects and wanting the best for me, my mother didn't look kindly on the fact that I was idle. She insisted that I should study or find work. The situation became more complicated when my cousin Severiano visited one day and said I could get a job in the shipyards where he worked. My mother was quite taken by the idea. She didn't really think I could earn my living playing golf. It became the only topic of conversation over dinner.

'Look at them,' my mother said. 'They're punishing you for a childish prank. What kind of future will golf ever give you?'

'Let's wait for now; let the boy play his golf. He's still young and it's too soon to be sending him to the shipyards,' my father said. 'In the meantime he can train wherever and we'll see what happens. He's still got plenty of time left to work.'

My father's views prevailed against my mother's wishes and it was decided it would be better for me to wait. Meanwhile I should keep training, caddying and dealing with the red tape involved in turning professional.

For his part, my brother Merín agreed to write a letter in my defence informing the club board that although I'd been with the group I hadn't joined in the tomfoolery, because I was employed as a caddie. My brother argued that the punishment was unfair: I was the only one in the group with something to lose, and, worst of all, I hadn't caused any of the damage. But when this was put to the board, one of the directors said: 'No, he's excluded like everybody else!'

Ironically this director, whose name I'm not going to reveal, was highly regarded by my father. The paradoxes of life!

If it hadn't been for my father's intervention that end-of-year prank could have changed my life. I saw out the one-month ban and in February renewed my membership again while I prepared to take the examinations to become a professional golfer, which took place on 22 March 1974.

Chapter 5

The Flight of the Partridge

When I look back, I'm always amazed by the way everything has turned out. I think my case is exceptional, because I turned professional before I had any competitive experience; I didn't have a career as an amateur like, for example, José María Olazábal ten years later or Sergio García subsequently. I'd hardly been outside my village and never played a course apart from Pedreña. My brother Manolo had taught me everything I knew. The only experience I had came from playing against the other caddies. Moreover, in Spain at that time, there was no golf culture I could draw on, no school or other resource to help my future development. All I had at the start of my professional career were enough clubs and balls to play eighteen holes. Fortunately, things are different now for young people setting out in the sport.

An adolescent is like a partridge: his flight is noisy, but low and short-lived. When I turned professional my situation changed radically. My whole attention was always focused on golf. Although I sometimes think this meant I missed out on many of the typical teenage experiences, the truth is I feel happy about the benefits I've derived from my career, the experiences I have had and their social and economic consequences. But I am also sure that if I could rewind a few sequences, as if my life were a video, I'd do many things differently. For a start I'd have gone to school and studied more, even though it would have meant turning professional at a later stage. I think I'd have benefited, because I'd have been better prepared for playing competitively and I'd have been much stronger physically. But things didn't happen that way and my professional career began at the age of sixteen. All I could bring to the game was talent and a will to win.

I played my first tournament a few days after making my leap in status. It was the Spanish Professional Championship, played in Barcelona on the San Cugat course. As I'd never travelled alone and had to change trains in Bilbao, Merín accompanied me to make sure I didn't get lost *en route*. In my practice round with Pepín Cabo I shot 27 for the first nine holes. I did not use a driver once, because I didn't own such a club. I used a 3 wood on the long holes. I finished twentieth in my first professional outing (Manolo Piñero won the championship). That earned me 2,500 pesetas in prize money – a real fortune for me at the time. Nonetheless, I was very frustrated and when it was over I started crying in the changing rooms. A Catalan golfer nicknamed 'The Tailor' saw me. He came over and told me I had no reason to feel frustrated. I'd done very well given that it was my first game at that level, and I was very young: 'Yes,' I answered, still in tears, 'but I came to win.'

My second professional game was in La Coruña, in a championship on the northern Spanish circuit that also included tournaments in Gijón, Pedreña, Bilbao, San Sebastián and Zarauz. My brother Vicente, who was doing his military service at the American base in Zaragoza, managed to get me a new set of clubs to play with, courtesy of his friend Agustín Cueto. Very pleased with myself, I took them along to my practice round with Merín, who was again accompanying me, but the smile was wiped from my face almost immediately. When I made my first strokes, we both watched in alarm as the heads of my new clubs flew off after the balls. In retrospect, it's a funny story, but it was a crisis for me at the time. The heads weren't properly attached to the shafts, so straight after the round we went to a blacksmith's where I waited several hours while he soldered them. Compared to that, the tournament itself was all plain sailing.

After La Coruña I started to play on the Continental Tour, which was then separate from the British Tour and had its own Order of Merit. The circuit comprised the Opens in Portugal, Spain, Madrid and France. I didn't do very well – I didn't make a single cut. My first professional tournament outside Spain was the Portuguese Open. I had a round of 89 and I came last. It was my seventeenth birthday. Luckily, Manolo was there to support me and hold my hand as you'd take a child across the road. But Portugal wasn't a complete disaster, because in Lisbon I met Dr César Campuzano, one of Spain's leading radiologists and a man Manolo knew from the Royal Club in

Pedreña. He would turn out to be very helpful at the beginning of my career.

Back home from the European circuit, I entered the Spanish Open in La Manga. I didn't play like a world-beater there either, although I did get through the qualifying rounds. I shot a first round of 83, and followed it up with 78. I missed the cut by one stroke. It's not so usual for a cut on the European Tour to be 160 today. But it was at La Manga that I began to turn the corner.

Even so, my financial situation was getting perceptibly darker and darker. My four tournaments in Europe had cost me a lot of money and I'd earned a mere 10,000 pesetas. I had little choice but to return to Pedreña and go back to work on the practice ground. The money I could earn caddying would help pay my travel expenses.

I was very fortunate that in August the Spanish Under-25s Championships were held in Pedreña. I won. It was my first victory as a professional, but it didn't make me jump for joy. The cheque for 80,000 pesetas took a weight off my mind but the victory itself was hardly spectacular. I had turned professional because I wanted to win tournaments; if it had taken me several attempts to win my first one, nothing had yet changed. While my family celebrated at home that night, I was determined that, for me, winning had to become the rule.

After this victory, I came second in the Santander Open. I won the Basque Open in Bilbao (Manolo and Vicente came second). I was runner-up in San Sebastián. I was playing well and gaining in confidence all the time. I was now ready and on my way.

In October I played in the Italian Open in Venice. For the first time I was able to measure myself against some great players. We played only sixty-three holes in this tournament, because fog reduced the first round to nine holes. Peter Oosterhuis won, beating Johnny Miller and Dale Hayes. I came fifth. For me, the most important experience was watching Johnny Miller play for the first time. He was ranked first in the world that year, ahead of Jack Nicklaus, and I was sure I could beat him. And I almost did: at the end of the first round we were joint leaders. The final result notwithstanding, the fact was that neither Miller nor Oosterhuis nor Brian Barnes – some of the best players in the world – impressed me greatly. After watching them I was convinced that not only did I have a chance of beating them; I was better than they were.

In this positive frame of mind I entered the Ibergolf international tournament in November, held on the Las Lomas-El Bosque course in Madrid. I also came fifth here, playing with Gary Player, who beat Peter Townsend. Once more, I had a chance to measure myself against one of the leading players in the world, but even more importantly, in Madrid I received an offer of financial help from Dr César Campuzano. Although we'd already met in Estoril, at the Portuguese Open, Manolo introduced me to him again in the club cafeteria with these words: 'This man is going to be a champion, one of the all-time greats. He has a fantastic future ahead of him. What he needs now is a sponsor and I think you are that person . . . If you don't, I will.'

Dr Campuzano must have liked the look of me. 'He will be the best player in the world,' he said. Dr Campuzano was prepared to back his confidence in my future with financial support. Straight away he gave us 500,000 pesetas so we could both go and play in South Africa.

'Here's some money so you can keep your commitments; if you need more, just ask and we'll do our sums later,' he added. I shall always be grateful for his generosity, although it was the only time I needed his help.

Over time, Dr Campuzano and his wife, Lola, would follow me around the world. I've just remembered a story from when I was eighteen and we went to Valencia in a car Ford gave me.

'Where did you learn to drive like that?' asked Dr Campuzano, once we'd arrived.

'In a neighbour's tractor,' I replied.

'Do you mean you don't have a driving licence?' he asked incredulously.

'That's right,' I said. In effect I had driven for six months without a licence, but that's how things worked then, although I wouldn't recommend it now.

Around the same time, my Uncle Ramón Sota spoke highly of me to Emilio Botín, a banker with whom he used to play. He said I was very promising but needed help. Our family was not unknown to Botín, since my father was his caddie and also looked after his house and garden in Pedreña. Don Emilio, who'd taken a liking to some land near the 8th hole at the club and wanted to refurbish an old house there, had even asked my father to oversee the complicated negotiations with the owners, who didn't seem at all keen on selling the property. My father succeeded in reaching a deal for the complex sale of this land and did so at a very good price for the banker.

Soon, after my Uncle Ramón had spoken about me, I saw Don Emilio on his way out of the Pedreña club. He called me over and said: 'Hey, Seve, I want to talk to you for a couple of minutes. Ramón told me you need some financial help to play in a few tournaments. I propose the following: I'll pay your costs and in exchange you'll give me a percentage of your earnings. That's to say, I'll give you 25,000 pesetas per tournament and you'll pay me 75 per cent of your winnings.'

'Don Emilio,' I replied, 'that's very generous of you, but there's no deal. I've just reached an agreement with Dr Campuzano.'

Dr Campuzano's support was crucial in Manolo and I travelling to South Africa. But my parents also chipped in. They even sold a cow worth 20,000 pesetas to cover some of our expenses, just as they had done for Manolo when he played in the Italian Open.

We flew to South Africa from Madrid via Lisbon. Manolo, who tried to fix things so I only had to worry about playing, was responsible for looking after the money, buying the tickets, making hotel reservations, in a word, everything. And it all went smoothly until we checked in for the flight to Johannesburg.

'Your South African visas, please,' they asked.

'A visa? What's that?!' asked my brother, his face looking stranger than I'd ever seen it.

'It's a permit to be able to enter the country,' they replied.

And we didn't have visas. It was the travel agency's fault: they hadn't told us we needed visas to travel to South Africa. But we simply *had* to get there. Then a guardian angel appeared. Gary Player, who was travelling on the same flight, sent a fax to somebody or other in Johannesburg explaining our little problem. We followed the instructions they gave him and went to the Spanish Consulate in Portugal and they issued us with the wretched visas, although we only arrived the day before the first tournament started.

It was very hard playing in South Africa in the era of apartheid. The discrimination and repression were brutal. I remember how in a Pro-Am one of the amateurs in my team was smoking. He finished his cigarette and threw the fag end on the ground. A caddie rushed to put it out with his foot – his bare foot! Yes, the caddies went barefoot and, when someone hit a ball into the rough, they waded into the prickly undergrowth without batting an eyelid. What I saw horrified me.

Years later, when I played the Million Dollar tournament in South Africa's Sun City, I took clothes and shoes with me and gave them to my caddie:

'Give them to the caddie master,' I told him, 'and make sure he shares them out among all your colleagues.'

The next day I noticed that none of the caddies was wearing the clothes or shoes I'd given them. 'What did you do with the clothes? Why's no one wearing them?' I asked.

'I didn't give them to the caddie master,' he answered, 'I have a big family.'

That was what things were like.

That trip, we played five tournaments in South Africa and I came joint eighth in the Western Province Open in Cape Town. We generally did pretty well – we came back with almost half a million pesetas in American Express traveller's cheques. The return journey was peaceful enough, but our ups and downs weren't quite over. We got the Santander train back home from Madrid and we had just unpacked our suitcases when I saw my brother pick up the telephone and start to sound grumpy.

'What's wrong, Manolo?'

'What do you mean, what's wrong?' he said, looking rather pale. 'Haven't you got our money?'

'But you saw to everything; I never even saw the money.'

'Well, we left the money on the train,' he replied, shaking his head from side to side.

'Hell, after what the trip has cost us, and the expenses we've had . . . that's great news, Manolo.'

I couldn't think of anything else to say, although he was looking at me as if it was my fault. Luckily, the ticket inspector on the train had found the wallet with all the money in it. Manolo had put it down on the train seat and forgotten all about it. Being an honest individual, the ticket inspector gave it back to us. Manolo and I breathed a sigh of relief.

Despite this rather fitful start to my first season, I finished ninth in the Spanish rankings and thirteenth in the European Order of Merit.

As I'd hoped, and it wasn't just my own wishful thinking, the balance sheet for 1975 was pretty positive: I ended the year leading both the Spanish and European rankings. However, my only victory had occurred, for the second year running, in the Spanish Under-25s Championship, in Sotogrande. I finished very well on the main circuit – I finished in the top ten in the Spanish, Portuguese, Swiss and Madrid Opens. My best finish was third place in the Trophée Lancôme in Paris, which was won by Gary Player. My ambition, however, was not just to win Spanish tournaments, but to win on the European Tour. If I signed off a score of 68, I was really annoyed with myself, because I was sure I could have done it in much less. I wanted to play better – I wouldn't accept that was impossible.

I've always been like that: when I face some kind of obstacle I push myself, because if you want to be a champion you have to learn how to overcome setbacks. When spectators were against me, particularly in America, it spurred me on to win and show them what kind of golfer I was. There are players who retreat into themselves when they play a bad shot or hit some hurdle, not realising that a negative attitude will be their downfall. You have to be resilient and spirited enough to keep your temper if you want to win, whether at golf or in life. This is the difference between being a champion and a good player. If you come up against a hurdle it's good to be angry with yourself, but you mustn't confuse positive anger – anger that makes you challenge yourself – with negative anger, that casts you into the shadows. If you're in the dark, you can't see anything – you're simply wasting energy. If you have a bad round or double bogey you have to tell yourself that the next day, the next hole you'll do better; that tomorrow you'll be back among the leaders.

There's nothing worse than feeling sorry for yourself and putting the blame on other people or bad luck. If all you find yourself doing is dwelling on what you did badly, you're on the road to failure. That's why I've always been very demanding of myself and of the people around me. When I became a professional, I imposed an almost spartan discipline upon myself: I would punish myself by not having dinner, for example, when I wasn't playing well or felt unhappy with my game. At such times Manolo would provide the voice of reason. He'd say 'That's a stupid thing to do, Seve. It won't help you at all. I know you've not played as well as you can, but you must eat, relax and sleep properly. Otherwise, you won't be in the right state to play well tomorrow.'

But I wouldn't give in and I punished myself when I thought that I deserved it. I don't know if that works for other people, but it did for me. Nobody becomes a champion without discipline or rigour. To reach your goal you must work hard, persevere and make lots of sacrifices. There's a story about a man who went up to Gary Player, a golfer who sometimes didn't play as well as the final tally on his card would suggest, and said: 'You're very lucky, Mr Player.' 'Yes, you're right,' Gary Player answered, 'and the more I practise, the luckier I get.'

I believe in this maxim completely, because if you are talented, but don't have discipline, perseverance and a spirit of sacrifice, you won't be successful in any sphere of life. There's no other secret to being a champion. That was why I maintained my iron self-discipline. By 1978 winning had become a matter of habit and I was the undisputed best player in Europe.

Getting there took a lot of work. I finished the 1975 season outside Europe, in the United States and Asia. Manolo and I went to play at the American Tour School, where you had to play six rounds and come in the first twenty-five to get a card that would give you access to the tournaments on the PGA Tour. Going into the sixth round, I'd already practically qualified and, at a mere eighteen, it looked as if I was going to become the youngest player on the American Tour. But something happened that was completely unexpected. On the last round, with qualification almost certain – I went round the first nine holes in 33 – I shot 40 on the back nine. I was eliminated by four strokes. Many people thought I'd choked, that I couldn't handle the pressure. But that wasn't the case.

My brother Manolo had just told me he'd agreed with an agent that I'd stay on to play in America for the rest of the year. So I'd be by myself in California for the end-of-year festivities, with no Christmas Eve dinner with my family, no New Year's Eve celebrations with the lads in Pedreña, no going from house to house offering to sing or pray in exchange for tips, which all went towards a special meal. Rather than concentrating on playing as best as I could, I was thinking about how lonely I would be, far from Pedreña, my family and my friends. So I practically threw my card away over the last nine holes. When I'd finished the round, several players came to commiserate, but I wasn't at all miserable. In fact, I was relieved. I'd done it on purpose. I had spared myself the chore of staying in the United States. Before the holidays started I travelled to Japan to play in the Dunlop Phoenix, where I came seventeenth despite a final round of 75.

I returned to Pedreña and spent Christmas and New Year's Eve with my family, though Manolo gave me a good telling-off because of what I'd done in America. I'm not proud of having thrown in the towel on the course, although I think any young man would have done the same in an environment where he felt alien. My flight had been swift and short-lived that year, like a partridge's. Nonetheless, I felt more like a huge bird, like an albatross, preparing to fly very high indeed.

Chapter 6

In the British Kitchen

I always found it a very special experience playing in the British Isles. The first time I did so was in 1975, in Sandwich, at Royal St George's. It was the PGA Penfold tournament; Arnold Palmer won, with Manolo just behind in fifth place. I have to confess that my first impressions weren't very positive. When you enter a clubhouse, you can usually see part of the course, but all you could see here was the putting green.

'Manolo,' I asked my brother, 'where's the course?'

'It's over there, look,' Manuel replied, pointing at a spot I couldn't see.

When we got to the first tee, I realised at once that the club was unlike any other I'd seen up to then. The golf course was in a great hollow, which was why you couldn't see it from the clubhouse.

'They call it "The Kitchen",' explained Manolo.

I was intrigued. Why 'The Kitchen' I wondered, as we continued to explore the course. But before I could tease out the thread of that particular plot we bumped into Jimmy Bates, the Dunlop representative at the tournament and the man responsible for supplying the players with balls.

'Manolo, we must ask him for some balls, because I haven't got a single one.'

I spoke almost no English at the time, so Manuel asked for me. Jimmy gave me two boxes of three balls. That is, a total of six balls.

'Six balls on this course? Have you taken a look at the rough out there?' I asked my brother.

I was quite upset and pointed out to my brother that the grass was so tall you could lose your caddie out there, let alone your balls. I may not have been speaking in English, but from the tone of my voice and the gestures I was making, Jimmy worked out why I was protesting. He turned to Manolo and said: 'Tell your brother I'll give him more balls . . . if he makes the cut.'

So I had no choice but to play with only six balls. I did my best to make them last for two rounds, which is as long as the tournament lasted for me, as I finished in 84 and 78. The rough was horrific and it was very windy, the bunkers were huge and, as if that wasn't enough, I had to play several shots blind. It was very difficult to 'cook' in such a place and it was hard learning to play links golf in the Kitchen. Not long afterwards I went to Carnoustie, on the east coast of Scotland, for the Open Championship. I missed the cut by ten strokes, eight more than Manuel, who also fell by the wayside. Overcoming the problems links courses posed for me was going to be a real challenge. But I came to realise that this style of golf required a player to use his imagination, that it demanded he create shots, and this fitted well with my style of play. It wasn't long before I was winning the Open – three times – and in 1983 I would win the PGA Championship at Royal George's itself.

This was still in my future, but 1975 was a relatively good season. It gave me lots of confidence going into the next. I had come fifth in Portugal, joint sixth in Spain, just behind Manolo, and joint eighth in France. Moreover, when I returned to Royal St George's for the PGA Championship, I managed to complete all four rounds, ending up joint twenty-third. A real achievement. Most importantly of all, my first position in the European rankings meant I qualified automatically for the 1976 British Open.

I worked very hard preparing for my trip to Royal Birkdale that year, but I didn't change my usual routines: I was confident I would play much better than I had at Sandwich and Carnoustie the year before. The week before the Open I helped my father mow the grass in our fields and put it into storage so the cows had fodder for the winter. On the Saturday Manuel and I went to Madrid to watch an exhibition match between Tom Weiskopf, Valentín Barrios, Jack Nicklaus and Sam Snead. From there we flew to England, because my brother had to play in the prequalifying tournament for the Open at Hillside and I was going to caddie for him. Regrettably, Manuel didn't qualify; nor could he say to caddie for me. I was very sorry – I wanted him at my side. As it was, I thought I'd have to use Dave Musgrove, who'd caddied for me in the French Open at Le Touquet that May. But Dave had already committed himself to Roberto de Vicenzo, a great Argentine player and winner of the Open nine years previously. (What a good friend and generous adviser Roberto turned out to be!) That left me in a bind: I didn't have a caddie and I needed to get one as soon as possible. My brother asked Dave if he could find me someone.

'I have a friend,' he said rather defensively, 'who's a policeman. He has never caddied in a big tournament, but I think he's free this week and I know he would like to carry Seve's bag.'

That was why I spent my second Open in the company of a policeman by the name of Dick Draper. As Dave had warned us, Dick had had no professional experience, but he was a polite, pleasant young man. As for Dave, our paths would cross again. He was my caddie three years later, when I won in Lytham. He was also Sandy Lyle's, when the Scotsman won the Open in 1985, held at Royal St George's – my beloved 'Kitchen'.

To get back to the 1976 Open, I remember that it was so hot the week we played in Southport it was like being in the tropics. Everything was bone dry and there were several fires on the course. In these conditions we had to aim to land the ball twenty metres short of the green, as I soon discovered during my practice rounds with the great Roberto y Vicente Fernández, another Argentine. But, despite the adverse conditions, before the tournament I had the feeling I was going to play well, and I did. I still wasn't mature enough to win a prestigious tournament like the Open, but I would become so much sooner than many could imagine.

I began the championship with a round of 69, three under par. It was nothing special but, as the course was so hard and dry, lots of players made a fist of it and at the end of the day I found myself joint leader with Christy O'Connor Jr and Norio Suzuki. It was a really unexpected result, the fallout from which I registered the minute I stepped inside the changing rooms. Doug Sanders was one of the first to come over. Talking to Manuel but pointing at me, he asked a question I didn't really understand, given the precarious state of my English. It sounded like: 'Is this the same boy who caddied for you in the qualifier?'

Nobody knew who I was, but everyone was quick to congratulate Manuel. Soon he was interpreting for me at the press conferences I was to give that evening and the next day, when another 69 put me two ahead of the field.

It was all new to me and I couldn't believe any of it. My brother and I had rented a small house in Southport for the duration of the tournament so we could enjoy some peace and quiet. Before the tournament started we'd go out at night for dinner and a stroll. As it was so hot and the day was so long there was a lively atmosphere in the streets in the evening. But after the tournament got started there was soon such a fuss around me that we had to forget our dinners and quiet strolls. The British newspapers put me on their front and back pages; fans and photographers pursued me the whole time. The constant attention upset, surprised and shocked me but at the same time I found it all very amusing. It stayed that way until I began to suffer from the pressures such high expectations brought with them.

At the end of the second round, it seemed that the confidence I'd always had in my ability to win was being vindicated. I was feeling very happy with myself – it was wonderful to be enjoying my best golf in the most important tournament I'd ever played in. I was too young and innocent to understand the true extent and importance of it all; I couldn't imagine what it meant and, even worse in terms of the competition, I was forgetting I was still only half-way to victory. Manuel, however, had kept his feet on the ground and was unimpressed with my over-confidence. My brother is intelligent and perceptive: he realised that my scant knowledge of English was isolating me from the stir I was causing and reducing the pressure on me. All he needed to do to help me win was to continue to protect me. And he almost succeeded.

For the third round I was playing with Johnny Miller, winner of the 1973 US Open. I began badly – I bogeyed on the first three holes – but I fought back to finish with a 73, which Miller couldn't match. With one round to go I held a two-shot lead. The key thing was to maintain my concentration. Many people thought that was going to be my downfall, but my will to win didn't fail me. My problem was that I was a callow, impetuous youth. I had watched Johnny Miller in the Italian Open in my first year as a professional and he hadn't impressed me. I still reckoned that I was a better stroke-player and could beat him. I was in the lead and was sure I was going to win. But Manuel wasn't so sure when he got into bed that night.

When I arrived at the first tee on Saturday afternoon I was calm and collected. In fact I was probably at my calmest and most collected of all the times I embarked on a final round with victory on the horizon. I didn't feel any pressure on me, simply because I didn't feel I owed anyone anything. All I knew was that this was my big opportunity and I was in the right state of mind to make the most of it. However, suddenly things began to go badly wrong.

I went one ahead at the first hole, to lead by three, but Miller came back at the second with a birdie. I took a bogey and lost control of the game. My problems just accumulated. I made a double bogey at the 6th and a triple at the 11th. Miller was intent on winning, and playing very well, but I didn't give up. I replied with a birdie at the 13th and another at the 14th. I parred both the 15th and 16th. My real problem was not simply that I'd lost the lead; I'd lost the initiative. At the 17th – a par 5 – Miller drew on his experience. 'It's important you finish well, because Mr Nicklaus' – that's what he called him – 'has finished with a good score.'

I was very surprised by what he said. Even more so, because he'd said it in Spanish. Johnny Miller is from California, so I might have guessed he could speak Spanish, but he hadn't spoken a word to me in Spanish over the two days we'd been playing together. It's not something that was highly significant at the time, but when you look back you can identify those little moments that can psychologically upset someone who is already in a mentally fragile state.

When Miller said that 'Mr Nicklaus' had already finished, I glanced at the scoreboard and saw that he was three under par for the tournament, followed by Ray Floyd at two under. I wasn't overawed. I reached the 17th green in two and holed a 7.5 metre putt for an eagle, leaving me two under par. Miller had the tournament in the bag, but I could come joint second if I managed to birdie at the final hole.

It was a tricky situation and it became even more so when my drive went astray at the 18th, another par 5. I'd only hit three fairways all day. I spent a lot of time over my second stroke and managed to drop the ball in the short rough to the left of the green. I needed to hole out in two shots to be level with Nicklaus. I couldn't float the next shot in gently, which would have been the obvious thing to do from where I was, because there was a strong wind that might take the ball into three-putt territory, not exactly what I had in mind. To get what I wanted, I had to risk everything. There are times when you have to choose between giving in and going all out and I was determined to go all out. As two bunkers lay between the ball and the green, separated by only about a metre and a half, I took a 9 iron, positioned myself for a short swing and punched the ball towards the narrow strip facing me. I struck it so confidently that the instant I felt the hit I knew it was good. Better than good, it was exceptional. It stopped just over a metre from the hole. After playing such a shot it would have been terrible to miss my putt, and I didn't. By that time, Miller had finished to confirm his victory, but I got the final ovation from the crowds, and that was very generous of the fans. Minutes later, Johnny declared at the press conference: 'I think it was very good for Seve to come in second; his day will come.'

I was surprised by what he said because I didn't understand what he was really suggesting. I felt just as I had after my professional début at the San Cugat Championship. All I could think was that I should have won the Open. In time I came to see that Johnny Miller was right. I had started cooking a rich dish in the British kitchen.

Chapter 7

The Young Spaniard and Mr Palmer

Like the captain of a boat setting sail, as the 1976 season started I began to see how vast was the horizon that lay before me. By coming second at Birkdale, amongst the world's best golfers, I boosted my presence both on the Tour and in my own eyes. That result had given my self-belief a terrific fillip: I was no longer a young upstart with potential that had yet to be demonstrated. I had shown myself and everyone else that I really had what it takes to win. The truth was that I'd started my professional career with such a bang that the press and general public kept a constant eye on me. As I continued to rise up the rankings, everyone wanted to know who this young Spaniard was.

I was third in Sweden's Scandinavian Enterprise Open, won by Hugo Baiocchi, and third in the Swiss Open in Crans-sur-Sierre, which went to Manuel Piñero. My first victory on the European Tour wasn't far away and, although it took longer than I'd foreseen myself, it came much more quickly than anyone else had imagined. On 8 August 1976 in Kennemer, I won the Dutch Open, beating Howard Clark by eight strokes. I had reached the top, but, as when I won the Spanish Under-25s Championship in Pedreña, I felt it was the most normal thing in the whole world: something that had just been waiting to happen.

I felt unstoppable. One success followed another: I came third in Germany, fifth in Ireland, and joint eighth in the Benson & Hedges International. I won the Donald Swaelens Challenge in Belgium. There were only eight of us in the field and I beat the second by eight strokes. That second-placed player was none other than Mr Gary

Player. Two weeks later I took part in another tournament with a field of eight, the Trophée Lancôme at Saint-Nom-la-Bretèche, near Paris. There I confronted another of golf's three greats: Arnold Palmer.

It was a game I shall always remember. With nine holes to play, Palmer was four strokes ahead of me. He was always a magnificent driver of the ball, but I remember being astonished that day because he was driving so well. When we left the 12th tee, I plucked up my courage to approach him. 'Mr Palmer, you are driving very, very straight today,' I said. I was a nineteen-year-old and he was and still is Mr Palmer. Mr Palmer looked at me hitching my trousers up as I used to do all the time on the course and said very seriously, 'Not as straight as your putts, young man.'

Palmer did the second nine holes in par, but I made five birdies to card a 35 and win by one stroke. After the game, I kept thinking about our brief exchange. I wondered whether he thought my comment about his drive had been made to disrupt his swing or distract him. His reply had been so measured and dry, I thought I'd detected a touch of irony in what he'd said. But that wasn't the case. I hadn't had an ulterior motive in saying what I said; I hadn't even intended to impress him. I had simply expressed my admiration. The way he'd been driving the whole day and flighting the ball in such a masterly fashion was simply wonderful. I was so young and such a novice it never even occurred to me to try to put Arnold Palmer off.

Seven years later I beat Mr Palmer once again in the first round of the World Match Play Championships at Wentworth. Walking out to the 17th, a par 5, he was dormie two, but I birdied the hole to pull one back. At the final hole, also a par 5, Palmer got off to a good start: his beautiful 3 wood went slightly past the green, but as the flag was at the far end, he was on for an almost certain birdie. My second shot fell short, leaving the ball some thirty-five metres from the flag. All I could do was go for an eagle to win the hole and stay alive. I analysed the stroke, took an 8 iron and chipped – and amazingly the ball dropped into the hole. Palmer's didn't and we were all square. I got a birdie at the first hole of the playoff to win the tournament.

'Mr Palmer, don't you think Seve was very lucky to hole out at the 18th?' a journalist asked at the press conference.

'No,' he replied. 'It's part of the game, I've done the same myself to others. That's golf.'

Arnold was a formidable player and polite and courteous as a person. One of the occasions when he impressed me most was the day he won the Spanish Open at La Manga in 1975. A gale was blowing over the course and John Fourie had finished in what looked to be a winning score. I'd also finished and was sitting in the clubhouse with three over par on my card. To force a playoff, Palmer needed to birdie the last hole. The 18th at La Manga, a par 5, is tricky under the best conditions – you have to be wary of the water on the left as you drive – but that day the wind was making it even harder: getting your second shot anywhere near the hole was almost impossible. When his turn came, Palmer struck a very long, magnificent drive. Then he hit a fantastic 4 iron just two metres from the hole. He holed it straight away for an eagle 3. It was wonderful.

As far as I was concerned the way I finished the 1976 season in Europe was also wonderful, since I was perched top of the Order of Merit. I was the youngest player in history to achieve this distinction and, moreover, the first non-British European number one since the Belgian Flory van Donck in 1953. In line with my ranking, at the end of the season I also helped Spain win her first victory in the World Cup, which was held in Palm Springs, California. Manuel Piñero and I beat the local team of Jerry Pate and Dave Stockton, who had recently won the US Open and the USPGA Championships, for the title. It wasn't an easy victory, because the Americans kept putting hurdles in our way. At the 6th hole of the second round I asked Piñero to remove his ball and mark the spot, as the rules allowed: the ball was making it difficult for me to play my stroke. Manuel picked the ball up and gave it to his caddie. Jerry Pate jumped in at this point and accused the caddie of cleaning the ball, which is forbidden in the rules. He immediately called on the umpire to penalise us. Fortunately Piñero stood up to Pate and the umpire wasn't swayed. For the last round we were again matched against Stockton and Pate. We beat them by two strokes, which was precisely the penalty they had called for. Manuel Piñero and I hoisted the trophy as the congratulations rained down – except from the two Americans who were still complaining. I wasn't prepared to let them continue being such spoilsports and I turned to Jerry Pate and said: 'Stop complaining! You lost because we played better than you did!' And that was an end to it. The two Americans simply couldn't stomach losing on home ground.

By the end of 1976 I'd gone from a total unknown to being leader of the European rankings, runner-up in the British Open and joint winner of the Team World Cup. Remarkably I hadn't set myself any particular target for the season, just to play as well as possible and see where it would take me. I think it was ambition alone that took me so far that year. Given the leap I had made in 1976, I decided to set myself a series of objectives for the 1977 season. But life can derail your best-laid plans. Just as my golfing career was taking off I was called up to do military service.

Chapter 8

The General and the Doll

In January 1977 I went to do my military service. Thanks to the fact I'd won the World Championship with Manuel Piñero, I was allowed to join the Air Force as a volunteer. Uppermost in my mind was the Masters, which was just around the corner. I worried how I would find time to practise properly. But nobody was going to let me off the three months of basic training.

I swore my oath of loyalty to the flag in the airbase in Getafe. Needless to say I never saw a single aeroplane and only went to shooting practice once. On that occasion I got through a couple of magazines, shooting with my eyes closed. It wasn't that I didn't know how to shoot – the gun I'd been given was so old and battered I was afraid it would backfire and I'd be hit in the face.

I was obsessed with getting ready for the Masters. Every day I left my base in Cuatro Vientos in Madrid to catch a bus to the city centre. Then I'd take a taxi to the Club de Campo, where I trained. One day, however, I had to go and practise at the golf club in Puerta de Hierro. I asked my cousin Santiago Sota, who was also doing his military service, to drive me there. My cousin had bought an old Citroën that was his pride and joy: 'It only cost me 3,000 pesetas,' he told me. 'Did it come with wheels at that price?' I asked.

The car did have wheels, but no brakes, so you could only stop by using the handbrake; you also had to grip the right-hand door tight to stop it falling off. It really wasn't the most suitable car to turn up in at Puerta de Hierro, one of the most elitist clubs in the whole of Spain. But it was all we had. When we drove up to the club entrance, we were stopped by a guard in a gold-braided uniform and peaked cap, sporting a shiny badge that said: 'Security guard of the Royal Golf Club of Puerta de Hierro.'

'Where do you think you're going?' he asked in an authoritarian tone, looking distinctly frosty.

'This man's Severiano Ballesteros, the world golf champion,' replied Santiago, taking the initiative, but the guard wasn't at all impressed by the title.

'That's right, I'm Severiano Ballesteros – I've come for a spot of training,' I added.

'I can't let you in,' the guard declared, planting himself firmly in front of us and shaking his head.

'Why not? Can you please ask your boss?' I asked.

He gave in reluctantly and went off to telephone. But I could see things weren't going well. 'You watch them send us packing,' I told Santiago.

Sure enough, when the guard got back he accused us of trying to pull a fast one, and told us to get out of it. We had no choice but to return to the barracks.

At a club as exclusive as Puerta de Hierro, no security guard would believe that a raw recruit in a car that barely had doors could possibly be a champion golfer. So when I turned up at Augusta for the Masters in the second week of April, I had not played a single round of eighteen holes in the previous three months.

In the meantime, I was attracting a lot of interest in the American press. *Golf Digest* – the biggest circulation golf magazine in the world – devoted its pre-Masters edition to a preview of the tournament. They had a photo of me on the cover with a headline that ran 'Can this teenager win the Masters?' It was a bold gamble on their part to put an unknown Spanish youth on their cover and I was extremely proud. But their question seemed really silly – more like a publicity stunt – for how could I possibly win the Masters, one of the four most important tournaments of the golfing season, if I hadn't touched a club in competition in almost three months and had spent barely four days on a course in total before reaching Augusta? The result, of course, was a disappointing performance at Augusta, of which more later.

Back in Cuatro Vientos, the Air Force brass-hats, who generally behaved very well towards me, let me practise on the course at the

Barberán Sports Centre where they used to play. I was training there one day when a general's wife arrived. Valentín Hernández, the club pro, was quick to introduce me as a soldier from the base – but also as Severiano Ballesteros, world champion.

'Severiano will be here practising the next few months,' Hernández told the lady.

The woman looked at me and with a smile that didn't conceal her haughtiness, she replied: 'Well, how splendid! We have found ourselves a new caddie!'

The only way I could react was by laughing. But my laughter was wiped away almost immediately, because a sergeant appeared and called me to attention. Sergeant Antonio Bernal, a name I shall never forget.

'Ballesteros, given you've got such support from the top brass, you can paint the tennis, basketball and handball courts for me today,' he rasped. I had to paint them all by myself, but that wasn't the end of it. When I'd finished, the sergeant returned to the attack: 'Ballesteros, as you're such a little favourite, I don't want anyone else' – we were some sixteen soldiers – 'to get jealous. So from now on you'll have to serve everyone their afternoon snack.' And I did just that.

Yes, I remember Sergeant Antonio Bernal very clearly. He's now a retired captain. One day in October 2003, I was watching television and heard that a Spanish soldier called Antonio Bernal had been murdered in Baghdad. He was a son of my old sergeant and had volunteered when the Spanish government decided to send troops to the war in Iraq. I was very moved by the courage and stoicism of the statements Bernal made as a result of his son's death. He said his son had died doing his duty as a soldier.

Almost three years later, in August 2006, I heard a knock at my front door. I could see a very tall man on the security monitor. I couldn't believe it, but it was Sergeant Bernal. I went to welcome him personally and there he stood with his wife.

'Hey, sergeant! How are you?' I exclaimed as I opened the door.

'Seve! Do you remember me?' he asked in an unusually timid voice.

'Of course, how could I ever forget you!'

'You don't know how I grateful I am, because I didn't know what kind of welcome to expect. I thought you might hold a grudge.'

I told him that not only did I not feel resentful, but that I'd tried to track him down to express my regrets at the death of his son and my admiration for his dignity and integrity at such a painful time. We spent several hours drinking wine and remembering our days in uniform.

I must say that Sergeant Bernal was right to think I enjoyed privileges, because the officers turned a blind eye when I left the base at 11 a.m. to go to the golf course and give some general's wife a lesson. Similarly, though I didn't have official leave granted, they let me play in some tournaments on the European Tour. Thanks to my 'special' situation I managed to play in the Italian Open, where I came fifth, and in the French Open, in Le Touquet, which I won by three strokes in front of Antonio Garrido, Manuel Piñero, Ian Stanley and John Bland.

Barracks discipline hadn't got more lax, but I had begun to move in and out fairly freely until, after I came back from playing three weeks in England, I was suddenly stopped in my tracks. One day, I was quietly tying my shoelaces in the changing rooms at the Club de Campo, preparing to play the Madrid Open, when a corporal appeared and told me: 'Ballesteros? You are under arrest!'

'What? How come?' I was really shocked.

'You must come with me immediately. The General has ordered me to take you to him now.'

'Well, I'm not going! I've got to play!'

'That's impossible. This insubordination will cost you dear!'

'I don't care what it costs: I'm not going now. I've got permission from the General and I'm about to go and play!'

The wretched corporal's face was a real picture. He stood there, not knowing whether to drag me off or not, and while he hesitated, I went off to begin my round. As you can imagine, I was nervous and worried. I didn't make the cut. When I went to see the General, he used the intimidating tone the military employ when giving out orders: 'From now on, you must present yourself outside my office every morning at eleven, and knock on my door. I will give you permission to come in. You will come in and say "Awaiting your orders, my General!" You may go now.'

For the moment I couldn't play any more tournaments, but they did let me continue to practise on the Barberán course. The punishment lasted just over a month. My next excursion was to play in the Uniroyal International at the Moor Park Golf Club in north London, where I ended up beating Nick Faldo in the playoff. On my return, I presented myself before the General at eleven, as he'd ordered me to. I took advantage of the opportunity to ask for permission to play in Switzerland, Sweden, Germany, the Open – which that year would be held at Turnberry – and Holland. Then something peculiar happened: 'Very well,' replied the General, nodding, 'I'll give you permission.' He paused as if he still had doubts about what he was about to say. 'But in exchange you must do me a favour . . .'

'Of course, my General,' I agreed enthusiastically, 'whatever you order.'

'I believe that sex shops are all the rage in Germany and, well, I want you to buy me a life-size, dark-haired inflatable doll.'

I was flabbergasted. I couldn't believe my ears: the last thing I expected was for a Spanish general to ask me to bring him an inflatable doll. I put on a poker-face, stood to attention and replied with great discipline: 'At your orders, my General!'

'Just to make sure you don't forget, I'll put this bracelet on your wrist.' And he did just that!

Shortly before I went to play in the German Open, I got a call to say I'd been released from my military service. What a relief! I wouldn't have to go back to the barracks or see the General again. I hope he's not still waiting for his doll from Hamburg!

Now the law has changed and I think it's marvellous that my sons don't have to do military service. It's just as well I did mine when I did, because if I'd had to do it five years earlier – when Franco was still alive – I'm sure I'd have had to endure the whole eighteen months without getting permission to play once. That would have really damaged my career.

When my military service was finished, I got stuck into international tournaments. I played all over Europe, in Japan, in New Zealand and teamed up with Antonio Garrido for the World Cup in the Philippines which I won for the second time.

In the end, the 1977 season finished well despite the difficulties I had training in the months I was doing military service. I managed to become the most powerful driver in Europe. I won eight long drive competitions, beating people like Jim Dent and Evan 'Big Cat' Williams and silenced all the people who talked about my 'tricks' with the driver. You have to hit very straight to win this kind of exhibition competition. I won the European Tour's Order of Merit for the third year running. I had won the Opens in Switzerland, France, Japan, New Zealand, and the Uniroyal International tournament in England, the Dunlop Phoenix in Japan, the Braun International in Germany, and the World Cup. But if 1977 had been a good season, 1978 was going to be much better.

Chapter 9

'The Parking-lot Champion'

The 1978 and 1979 seasons were particularly exciting for me. I had a lot of success and a lot of drama. But what I remember most fondly from that period is a shot I played in the 1978 Hennessy Cup. It was the sort of shot that marks your life and makes history.

In that Hennessy Cup, a tournament in which continental European teams played Great Britain and Ireland (it was the predecessor of the present Seve Trophy), I played Nick Faldo in the singles. Although our team went on to lose the match, I won that particular contest. The shot I'm talking about took place at the famous 10th hole at the Belfry, a 280 metres par 4, where your drive presents you with two options. The first is to take a 6 iron and lay up just short of the stream in front of the green; the second is to go straight for the green. It's a risky shot and before that day no one had attempted it. Nobody had ever dared. When I saw Faldo was laying up short, I decided to take my driver, knowing full well the risk I was running. The entrance to the green was as narrow as it is now and even if you hit the ball dead straight you had to make sure your drive was airborne for 260 metres to avoid dropping into the water in front of the green. It was a real challenge – but I was up for it.

I took up my stance for a fade and dusted and polished the ball, as you might say. The ball landed three metres from the hole. What a strike! What a moment! It was a shame I missed the putt for an eagle, so I made a birdie to win the hole. Later on, when the Belfry staged the Ryder Cup, it wasn't unusual for players to go for the green, but by that time the hole had got shorter. For a while there was a plaque by the hole commemorating this stroke.

That 1978 season turned out to be altogether extraordinary. I won

(*Above*) The crew of the *trainera Castilla*; my father is in the back row, second from the left, and my uncle Andrés is three places to his right

(*Left*) My mother's uncle Vicente (standing on the left)

(*Below left*) My father Baldomero in his cart

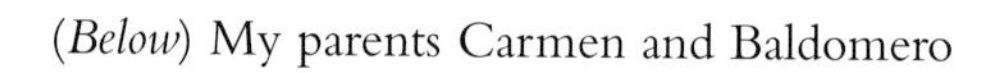

(*Below*) My parents Carmen and Baldomero

(*Left*) Me at school, aged seven

(*Above*) My father and me, 1967

(*Below*) Caddying with my friends at Pedreña, aged fourteen. I'm second from the right

(*Top left*) Practising at Pedreña

(*Below right*) Doing my military service

(*Above*) Practising at the beach

(*Right*) Another putt holed!

(*Above*) With my mother, Carmen.
(Our house is in the background)

(*Right*) On Puntal beach

(*Below*) The Ballesteros brothers:
Baldomero, Seve, Vicente and Manuel

(*Above*) Celebrating my first Open victory, Royal Lytham & St Annes, 1979

(*Below left*) Receiving the Dutch Open trophy from Princess Irene of the Netherlands
(*Below right*) Raising the trophy with Patricio Garrido at the World Cup, 1977

(*Above*) With my brothers and caddie Dave Musgrove (*left*) at the Open, 1979

(*Below*) Putting on the green jacket after my first Masters victory, 1980

Holding the Claret Jug at St Andrews, 1984

six consecutive victories going into November. Maintaining that momentum was always going to be difficult. After the last of the six – at the Japanese Open – I didn't win another until the spring of 1979.

That May the Spanish players on the European Tour would have a very unhappy experience. It made a deep impression on us all. On the eve of the French Open in Lyon, Salvador Balbuena – who had only just celebrated his twenty-ninth birthday – died suddenly. It was a cruel blow. We were all shocked. José María Cañizares, Antonio Garrido and Manuel Piñero, who had dined with him that same night, withdrew from the tournament as a mark of respect. They asked the rest of us Spanish players to follow suit, but I didn't agree. 'Let's play this in his memory and give his family whatever prize money we win,' I suggested.

And that's what we did. We played in homage to our friend. Every day, during the tournament, I would accompany Marcia, Salvador's wife, who had come to Lyon to collect his body. As we'd promised, at the end of the tournament I gave her the cheque I received for coming third.

It had been a terrible shock, and it wasn't easy to forget. After this misfortune, I participated in other tournaments and trained to play the Open, to be held at Royal Lytham & St Annes.

As I had at Birkdale, I received invaluable support in preparing for the Open, from Roberto de Vicenzo and also from Vicente Fernández, my other great friend on the Tour. De Vicenzo knew how to play links courses, and he spent several days teaching me how to approach them. In the light of what happened that week, perhaps his most influential piece of advice was to insist I should hit the ball a long way with the driver: 'When you're teeing off, hit it hard, because the farther you hit the ball, the fewer problems you'll have in the rough – you'll be closer to the green.' On the surface this didn't seem particularly insightful, but its wisdom derived from the fact that Roberto had *seen* what was the best strategy for me. I took note and tried to drive the ball as far as possible on almost all the par 4s and 5s, and then sorted myself out as best I could. A first round of 73, two over par, didn't seem very encouraging and anyone else might have interpreted this result as an indication that the strategy was a failure. This would surely have been the logical conclusion to draw, but I felt I should persist with my game plan, even though it didn't seem at all sensible. With the exception of myself, and perhaps Roberto de Vicenzo, most people were surprised when I made four birdies on the last five holes of my second round to finish with a 65. This result was probably a turning point in the tournament and, very likely, in my life as well.

My playing partner on that occasion was Lee Trevino, who had already won the Open twice. He certainly knew what links golf was about. It was very windy, and what was worse, over the last five holes – which are infamous for their difficulty – we had to contend with it blowing straight in our faces. On the 13th, Trevino came over, adjusting his cap, and said: 'Now that's when we must start playing with our heads.' I did.

I made a fantastic birdie at the 14th. On the next, I holed out from off the green. At the 16th, the easiest of the five, I still can't work out how I missed a two and a half metre putt for a birdie. Nonetheless, I reached the green of the 17th in two, and drained a six-metre putt for a birdie that tasted like an eagle. I managed a bit of everything at the 18th. First, my drive left the ball in a very awkward spot, but then, from 135 metres out, I kept the ball low to end up just under a metre from the hole and well placed for another birdie.

For the third round I was drawn with Hale Irwin, who'd won the US Open just the previous month. Hale was leading the tournament, two strokes ahead of me. Someone told Irwin what I'd just done, namely, to finish the last five holes in 16 against a headwind.

'Are you sure he didn't forget one?' asked Irwin incredulously.

I got the feeling Irwin had little respect for me as a player, perhaps because I hadn't won a major, whereas he'd already won the US Open twice. Even after I'd won, his only comment was that I'd been very lucky and he very much doubted I would win another major. I expect he said this because of the markedly unconventional way I won that Open; I hit some miraculous recovery shots with balls that seemed lost for ever. That's how I read Irwin's gesture on the green of the 18th on the final day when he extracted his handkerchief from his pocket and waved it as if surrendering. I kept to Roberto de Vicenzo's advice, so my apparently haphazard game at Lytham flowed from a perfectly planned strategy. So much so that Roberto, who had missed the cut, turned up for the fourth and final round. I bumped into him at the entrance to the changing rooms: 'Hey, Roberto!' I exclaimed when I saw him. 'I thought you'd gone back to Argentina! What are you doing here?'

'No, *che*, I didn't fly back,' he replied with a big smile. 'I stayed on to watch you win!'

I will always be grateful to him for his wise advice and I took pride and encouragement from the fact that a great master like him should say such a thing. But that is Roberto: at once a great champion, and an excellent human being.

On the 2nd hole of the third round, I drove the ball out of bounds, on to the railway track, and emerged with a jumbo double bogey: it was a terrible start, but my luck was in. Irwin could only manage a 75, like me. This result kept us in the same position for the final round, that is, me trailing him by two strokes. Jack Nicklaus and Mark James were snapping at our heels one stroke behind, with Ben Crenshaw and Roger Davis two behind.

If I hadn't got off to an ideal start for my third round, it was different that decisive final day. I made a birdie 2 at the 1st, and Irwin collected a double bogey, which immediately put me in the lead. As you can imagine, the tension over the next ten holes was dreadful. We all kept frantically conceding and winning back strokes from each other. Even Davis and Isao Aoki managed to take the lead at one point. The afternoon was shaping up for a frenzied finish. But it was all over at the 13th, when, to everyone's amazement, I made a birdie. I say amazement because I put my second shot in a fairway bunker sixty-five metres from the green, only to leave myself with a nine-metre putt from the fringe of the green with my third shot. I'd recovered the lead, and I wouldn't lose it again, although that didn't become clear to me until I'd teed off at the 16th. Baldomero and Vicente came over and told me: 'Seve, you've gone two up. All you have to do now is to play your game.'

Before my first shot at the 16th, I was under the impression I was leading Irwin and either level with Nicklaus and Crenshaw or one stroke behind. When my brothers told me I had the outright lead, I saw the way was clear and told myself: 'The time has come. I'm going to win the Open.'

I concentrated even harder. From eighty metres out I put my second shot on the green and holed the six-metre birdie putt to increase my lead to three shots. The Open was mine for the taking. However, the next hole turned into an incredible adventure. In normal conditions, I'd have taken an iron off the tee, but as I was playing so well, I was feeling quite fearless. I followed Roberto de Vicenzo's advice, and pulled out my driver. I hit the drive so hard that the ball ended up in a nearby parking lot. Obviously, I'd intended to get the ball on the fairway but this wasn't quite the disaster it appeared to be. As I stood on the tee, rehearsing the drive, I told myself 'Seve, don't go left'. When you're thinking along such lines, it's easy to steer the ball to the right, but I knew it wasn't a bad direction to go in. The wind direction, the fact the 16th had a slight dogleg right and the spot where they'd placed the flag all went in my favour. In fact, I reckoned that a mistake to the right might even help me: I would be able to hold up my approach shot in the wind. To many people, when I ended up in the parking lot, it looked as if I'd played myself out of the championship. I hadn't at all: the ball was less than ninety metres from the flag. The birdie I scored practically secured the championship for me.

It seems impossible after that 16th, but the last two holes were equally exciting and tense. At the 17th I saved par by getting down in two from a bunker by the green, but I had to hole a good three-metre putt for my four. That week I had been in the greenside bunkers fifteen times; on fourteen of those occasions, I had saved par. At the 18th I used my driver again, but this time I went to the left, where there were no great obstacles. I told Dave Musgrove, my caddie at the time: 'I think I can get away with a bogey here and still win by two strokes.'

'You can, Seve,' he replied, looking me in the eyes, 'but I want you to finish in four, because I've made a bet that you'll win the Open under par.'

And that's what I did: I put my second stroke just on the green, avoided taking any risks and two-putted from thirty metres out. I finished the tournament one under par and ensured Dave won his bet. I was three ahead of Nicklaus and Crenshaw, who came in joint second.

Irwin, who'd ended with a 78, six behind me, commented that I was 'the parking-lot champion'. I wasn't hurt by his remark or by the fact that my style of play was getting a lot of people's backs up.

There is no rule in golf that says you have to win in a specific way, only that the winner is the one who cards the fewest strokes. I take the rule literally. Say a player drives down the fairway, goes for the green and holes his putt; his opponent goes for the fairway, ends up in a bunker and finds the hole from there. Both will have played the hole in three. If I may say this, my short game was such that I could achieve things that few others could contemplate. This was my strong suit. But I enjoyed watching my opponents trying to second-guess my next move. 'You're never sure what Seve's going to do', people said, and that can be very demoralising for an opponent. I've often wondered if this was why I had so much success at matchplay. I've always thought the key to matchplay is to impose your game on your opponent. In a one-on-one match, the best thing that can happen is to have your adversary concentrating on your game, not his own. Before he took out his white handkerchief to signal surrender, Irwin must have been thinking, 'How the hell can I beat this guy?' When he couldn't find an answer he talked about me being 'the parking-lot champion'. Later in our careers, when I came up against Irwin in a matchplay tournament, he suggested we should split the money for third and fourth position. Naturally, I refused, and went on to beat him.

That week I won in Lytham because after seventy-two holes I had the lowest score. At the end of the day that's what people will read in the history books. And those books will also say that at the age of twenty years, three months and three days, I was the youngest Open champion in the twentieth century. I also became the first non-British European to have won the tournament since the Frenchman Arnaud Massy in 1907.

Winning the Open was one of those moments a champion must toast with champagne. A television interviewer asked me how I would mark the victory and I replied: 'I don't drink, but I think tonight will be different.' I celebrated with my three brothers, who had provided me with moral support at every stage.

Winning my first Open was undoubtedly one of my greatest triumphs. Nonetheless, for me, it was like winning the 1974 Under-25s in Pedreña or my first tournament on the Tour in 1976: it didn't thrill me as much as you might have expected. I won't say it left me cold, because you don't win a major every day of your professional career, but in my innermost self it was something I had been sure I would achieve sooner or later.

As in 1976, I knew my victory would be important but I could never have imagined how much winning the Open was going to change my life. It changed everything: from work commitments to the amount of travelling, to media interest. There were even greater demands on my time, and I suddenly had a huge responsibility thrust on my shoulders. The worst aspect of all was the intrusion into my private life. The situation got even worse when I won the Masters, the very next major I played, and I felt under pressure to keep winning major tournaments. When you go out to play to enjoy yourself and aren't worried about the result, but simply let things happen, it feels so much better than going out programmed to win and trying to force the outcome. Believe me, I've been there: it is totally different; the results are never the same.

But back in 1976, now I'd won the Open, I knew one major wasn't going to be enough: I wanted to win everything; I wanted to be a great champion. So I set out on a quest. Once again Roberto de Vicenzo's advice was a revelation. I'd always admired Roberto's enormous hands – they reminded me of my father's, who also had enormous hands from working the land and rowing. One day when we were chatting, Roberto started drumming his fingers on the table. I looked at his hands and stared at the beautiful gold ring set with a diamond he was wearing.

'I won it at the Houston Open,' he said proudly when he noticed I was looking at his ring.

'Roberto, what does a player need to become a great champion?' I asked. Roberto was definitely a great champion, even though he never won a major.

'Look, Seve, to be a champion you need to do the following: first, you have to be able to eat every kind of food under the sun; second, you have to be able to get your head down in any kind of bed; third, you need to know how to love women, but not so much that it distracts you from your game,' Roberto replied.

Roberto taught me that generosity and a spirit of sacrifice are the virtues that transform a player into a great champion. In his own way, he was telling me he knew why I had won the Open. The 'parking-lot' champion was simply a champion.

Chapter 10

Hard Knocks in the Garden of Eden

My first experience of the Masters was in 1977. The Masters is unique among the four major tournaments; entry is only by invitation, not based on a player's position in the rankings. I probably received mine thanks to a letter Johnny Miller sent to Clifford Roberts, at the time the president of the Augusta National Golf Club. Miller wrote to Roberts telling him I was a young Spaniard who was playing very well, who'd just come second to him in the Open at Royal Birkdale, and that I had a very promising future. He suggested Mr Roberts should invite me to play in the Masters. Mr Roberts obviously agreed.

Augusta was love at first sight. I was smitten. I felt at ease right from the start and even in my first interviews I was telling reporters that the course was just right for my style of play. I also said I was sure I would win the Masters some day, which was a reflection of how much I liked the course and how confident I was it would bring out the best in my game.

My entry into the tournament couldn't have been more dazzling; my exit was less so. For the first round I was paired with none other than Jack Nicklaus. I suppose they thought it was a good idea to put the Spanish youth – the number one player in Europe – alongside the best player in the world. As you can imagine, the fact that I was playing with Jack Nicklaus was a great source of motivation. I hit a good drive at the 1st. The 2nd wasn't so good: the flag was at the back of the green – I went for it and over-hit. It seemed almost impossible to get my recovery chip anywhere near the flag, but I somehow managed to hole it for a birdie.

Over the course of the round I chatted to Jack in my shaky English. He behaved in a very pleasant, courteous manner towards me right from the start. His attitude was very important for someone so young, playing so far from home and with a such a superstar. I remember remarking that it was a very tricky course. 'Yes, it's the kind of course you have to play several times to get the hang of,' he replied.

Nicklaus's observation had both a positive and a negative side. The good side was that with time you got to know the slope of the greens and discovered the problems the course posed. The bad side was that the more you played and discovered how incredibly demanding the course is, the more you ended up playing defensively.

On the Friday I took a seven at the 18th and made the cut only by a whisker. However, my good fortune was short-lived. Only the top twenty-four finishers were guaranteed an invitation for the following year. At the end of Sunday's play I wasn't one of them. I'd done reasonably well for someone playing one of the world's most prestigious courses for the first time, but I was left feeling very despondent. When one of the lady organisers saw the look on my face, she came over and said: 'Don't worry, we usually give players we've invited for the first time a second chance.'

And that's what happened. I was invited back the following year. I made the cut easily, but at the end of the third round I was seven strokes behind Hubert Green, the leader. I thought I was completely out of the running, even though I was three under par, like Gary Player, who I was paired with on the final day. I finished with a 74; Gary won with a 64. After the first nine we were level at two under par. But Gary played the back nine wonderfully. He came back in only 30, one better than the runner-up.

Playing with someone like Gary Player is a great learning opportunity, and what I learned from him the day he won the Masters is that you can't lower your guard for a single moment, you always have to play with maximum concentration, because you never know what may happen.

That day, on the fairway of the 13th, after he'd hit his second stroke, Gary came over to me and said: 'Seve, I want to tell you something . . .' He looked around and waved his club gently at the group of fans following our game. 'These people think I can't win any more, but I'm going to show them they're wrong.'

I was very impressed by what he said. He had iron self-control and, although he didn't have to prove anything, he was determined to prove himself to himself and everyone else; to show the doubters yet again that he was still capable of winning a major. This is why I consider his 1978 victory so wonderful. It was his third Masters and ninth victory in a Grand Slam tournament.

In the meantime, the Masters was still a struggle for me, though it began to get better. In 1979 I came in the first twenty-four again, joint twelfth to be exact, and that gave me the right to participate in the tournament the following year. This time things were going to be different.

By 1980 things had changed a lot at Augusta and my position on the Tour was more secure. I knew the course – I'd played it three years running – and came as Open champion. And for the first three days or, to be more precise, the first sixty-three holes, I played like a champion. But the confidence I derived from having played Augusta before and having won the Open weren't the only factors that helped me get the famous green jacket awarded to all Augusta's champions.

The previous summer when I won at Lytham St Annes I'd been finishing my follow-through Arnold Palmer style, lifting high and bending to the left. My back began to hurt a lot, so over the winter I shortened my swing. That helped me win the Masters. But the difference in my game wasn't just physical. There was something even more vital: the attitude and mentality I brought to my game.

It so happened that in 1979 when I played the Prat Open near Barcelona, I got to know a woman called Gloria, who is still a very good friend. Gloria's mother worked with Dr Alfonso Caycedo, a Colombian teacher who'd spent a long time in India researching transcendental meditation. Dr Caycedo taught sophrology, a discipline that helps fight stress and brings harmony to the mind through a variety of exercises. These exercises include not only a mental side – visualising what you are trying to achieve – but also various physical contractions, so that when you face moments of great tension your body can cope. Gloria suggested it would be a good idea if I visited Dr Caycedo and I followed her advice.

By taking this step I think I became one of the first Spanish sportsmen to prepare himself mentally to confront critical moments in his sporting life. During my consultation with Caycedo, I explained what I did, and although he confessed he knew very little about golf, he said he thought he could help me to develop my mental attitude and to have greater self-control. This was one of the areas I most wanted to improve after being astounded by Gary Player's mental discipline.

I told Dr Caycedo how I prepared to play my strokes and how I often imagined them before actually playing them, how I could see and feel them.

'In a way, you practise sophrology intuitively, but what do you really hope to achieve?'

'To win the Masters!' came my answer immediately.

The next time I visited him he'd prepared a tape of exercises for me. The treatment consisted of learning to relax myself physically and mentally to play a particular tournament. Following his instructions, I visualised every single aspect of the Masters, the atmosphere, the tension, my on-course attitude. I really could see myself there. This was how I won my first Masters so astonishingly easily. I should say that I won my second without practising any sophrological exercises, but nonetheless I must recognise that in their day these exercises were a great help. I am a person who believes firmly in the power of the mind. We do everything through the mind: we see, we think, we feel and we act. It may seem arrogant, but when I reached Augusta that year I was already expecting to win the Masters. For the very same reason, when the moment of victory arrived I didn't feel very emotional. I asked Dr Caycedo about this and he said:

'Do you know why? Because you'd already seen yourself as the winner, and already experienced that emotion within yourself. You can't emotionally experience the same victory twice.'

A month after playing the tournament, the exercise tape broke. But I continued to play well. I won the Madrid Open, that year held at Puerta de Hierro, with a 63 for the second round, a new course record.

In 1997 I tried to do the exercises again, thanks to a copy of the tape that Gloria got me, but it no longer had the same effect. This showed me that the exercises could help, but in the end everything is down to you, to your attitude, your will and effort, and also to your ability to confront the hard knocks that come your way, especially in Augusta, golf's Garden of Eden.

Chapter 11

The Fruits of Paradise

You have to be physically and mentally ready to enjoy the fruits of Paradise. After the 1980 Masters I was in a wonderful state of mind and playing magnificently. Winning the Open the previous year had put me in the best possible frame of mind to tackle the big tournaments. I think I played the best golf of my life from tee to green that week at Augusta. My game had terrific rhythm and I led the field by four strokes after the second round. Manolo congratulated me:

'Great, Seve, you've played really well, try to hold on to the lead tomorrow.'

'No,' I replied, without even thinking about it. 'Tomorrow I'm going to play them all out of the tournament.'

And that's what happened. When I teed off on the final day, I led by seven strokes. I began with a sequence of birdie, par, birdie, par, birdie, playing with Jack Newton. When we came to the 10th I was already ten strokes ahead. I over-relaxed, thinking I'd already won the tournament. It was this that eroded the quality of my game over the final nine holes. It suddenly seemed as if I had lost all motivation, as if I was unable to concentrate at all.

I only needed to shoot two under par for the back nine to beat the tournament record of 271 – shared at the time by Jack Nicklaus and Raymond Floyd – but I wasn't even aware of that fact. Perhaps if somebody had mentioned it to me before the 10th, I might have maintained my concentration and won without breaking sweat. I should say that it doesn't always work that way. They say, for example, that Arnold Palmer lost the 1966 US Open Western to Billy Casper because over the last nine holes he stopped concentrating on winning and became obsessed with the idea of beating Ben Hogan's tournament record. This distraction led to him scoring bogeys rather than the birdies he needed and he threw away a seven-stroke lead. As a result Casper caught up with him and won the playoff. But in my case I think I would have played the last nine holes better if I'd had the extra motivation of going for a record.

When a young player prepares himself to play the last nine holes of a major tournament holding a ten-stroke lead, he finds it easy to think winning is a foregone conclusion. And so I made a silly mistake at the 10th, took three putts from just over seven metres to finish with a bogey. I made par at the next hole, but at the 12th I took a double bogey, because I used a 6 iron and the ball was caught by a breeze that blew up just as I made contact and deposited it in the water. Newton made a birdie at the 11th and again at the 12th. My lead was down to five strokes. Things got no better at the 13th, where I mis-hit the ball into the stream just in front of the green and finished with a bogey. Again Jack got a birdie. All of a sudden my lead had been cut to a meagre three strokes.

It was astonishing, because from being ten up and only needing to go through the motions in order to maintain my game, I was now at a critical moment. The worst that can happen in such situations is for one to panic. Fortunately, that didn't happen. I told myself to wake up. The 14th was completely different – I'd changed my attitude. I went back to being the player I'd been at the beginning of the round. Though I didn't have the best start, driving into the trees on the left, I hit my second shot perfectly, dropping the ball four and a half metres from the flag. The resulting par was enough to calm me down and silence some of the spectators. I particularly remember how, as I walked over to hit my second stroke, I heard a man shouting in the crowd 'Go for it, Jack!' I recognised the person cheering Jack on as someone who had said he was a friend of mine, and felt something surge within me. 'What's this guy saying?' I thought and responded with that magnificent second stroke. It was a vital shot, because I put an end to my bad run and preserved my three-stroke lead.

At the 15th Jack reached the green with his second, but I now had other problems. Gibby Gilbert, who was playing in front of us, made his fourth consecutive birdie at the 16th to go ten under par. Gilbert was only two strokes behind me. I realised I had no more margin for error. I needed to hit my second straight and true. I did just that. I put all my heart into it and hit a terrific 4 iron which left the ball only six metres from the hole – a certain birdie on this par 5. I didn't miss and my lead over Jack Newton increased to four strokes. In the subsequent press conference, Jack Newton declared : 'Gentlemen . . . it's time to give Seve the star treatment.'

This victory made me only the second non-American to win the Masters. (Gary Player had been the first.) Perhaps that's why the following year the club changed the classic Bermuda turf used by golf courses all over the southern United States to Penn turf.

I felt very happy. I thought that the victory of a Spaniard in one of the most important golf tournaments in the world would receive blanket coverage back home. All it got was a mention on the three o'clock news the following day.

Despite all the mishaps I had tasted Paradise, as success in the Masters might be described. I felt complete bliss when the previous year's champion, Fuzzy Zoeller, put the winner's green jacket on me, following the tradition that began over thirty years previously.

I tasted the ambrosia of success at Augusta once more, in 1983. The tournament was played in the same week as my birthday and victory was like giving myself a fantastic present. On this occasion Craig Stadler helped me into the green jacket.

I must admit that I didn't play particularly well on this occasion – certainly not as well as I would have liked. I put lots of fight and feeling into my game and the Americans liked that a lot. They compared my charisma to Arnold Palmer's and said I could go far if I decided to play on the American Tour.

The weather wasn't good that Masters week. On the first day it rained heavily enough to suspend play for almost an hour. It also rained on the second day, but despite all that I managed to take the lead. Forty-nine players made the cut, and at the end of the third round Raymond Floyd and Craig Stadler were joint leaders. I was one stroke behind, even though I had three-putted three times. Tom Watson was in top form and was also well positioned. People thought Stadler was the favourite to win for a second year running, thus equalling the record of Nicklaus, who had won in 1965 and 1966. But this final day was to be a very close fight: of those of us in the mix, several had already won the tournament and were hoping to wear the green jacket again.

At the start of the round I told myself: 'Seve, you're not at the top of your game, but if you put your heart and mental strength into it, you can show the Americans your true spirit.'

Although I wasn't on my best form, I was feeling good and the adrenalin was flowing. I attacked the first hole like a lion pouncing on its prey. I preferred it that way. My start was explosive. My card for the first four holes showed birdie–eagle–par–birdie. This wore my rivals down, so much so that Tom Kite later said: 'While we were in our Chevrolets, Seve was driving a Ferrari.' I kept the aggression up as far as the 9th and then decided to play more calmly in order not to spoil the final stages.

I was playing with Tom Watson, the reigning US and Open champion. People usually say that the Masters really begins with the final round. Nonetheless, at no stage did I feel harassed by Watson's game, even though, as many of you will be aware, he has a degree in psychology from Stanford University in California. He not only applied that knowledge to his own game, but also tried to use it to influence mine. At the 15th both our second strokes had left us a short distance from the green. It was his turn to play first, but he waved to me to go before him. The third stroke was a tricky affair: the 15th hole is usually protected by a whirling wind, and if you do manage to reach the green you have to be very careful not to let your ball roll back into the water at the front. I realised that Watson wanted me to play first to see what my ball did. His idea was no doubt that that would give him an advantage and a chance of clawing back my lead. But I was experienced enough not to fall for such a ruse.

At the last hole, when I already had the tournament in my pocket, Watson renewed his attack. I was about to play my second stroke, when he came over and said: 'You've played really well today, Seve!'

'Thanks a lot,' I replied pleasantly but curtly.

Then I promptly leapfrogged the green with my third stroke. Fortunately, I holed the return chip for par. Watson must have made some comment about this afterwards, because a journalist said to me at the press conference: 'You were lucky to hole that chip, because if the ball hadn't hit the flag and gone in, it would have rolled way past; with that slope it wouldn't have stopped until it hit the edge of the green.'

'That's true,' I replied, 'it was a possibility. And if I'd taken five putts I'd also have lost the Masters.'

Cesar and Lola Campuzano, Manuel Martínez, Adolfo Morales, Jorge Ceballos and my father were among the few Spaniards who witnessed my second Masters in Augusta. I was pleased for them and for Nick de Paul, my caddie, who had dressed in blue, my lucky colour. I had broken with Augusta's obligatory custom of using the local black caddies in favour of Nick, so having him at my side for my victory made me especially happy. But your relationship with an important tournament like the Masters certainly doesn't stop when you walk off the last green. One way or another it's always linked to your life as a champion. And in my case, my memories of a later Masters, in 1986, will stay with me for ever.

Chapter 12

Travels with my Father

For me, the 1986 Masters will for ever be linked to the loss of my father. In the autumn of 1985 the doctors found my father had lung cancer. As soon as we were given the terrible news, my brothers and I decided to take him to Houston, Texas, a place that is recognised for its advances in the field of cancer research. He was operated on there and stayed for more than a month of post-operative care looked after by my brother Manuel. We were all aware of the seriousness of his condition, but I didn't think the end would come so quickly – or perhaps I didn't want to accept that it would.

I always had a very special relationship with my father, because he, unlike my mother, understood how my family's fortunes had changed and knew how to make the most of it. He was sixty-seven and enjoying the fruits of my sporting triumphs when the illness attacked him. I went to fetch him when he was allowed to leave hospital. We returned to Spain on the last day of 1985, New Year's Eve.

It was a very hard journey for him and he was feeling quite poorly when we got to Madrid. He wanted to get home as soon as possible, but the only flight to Santander had been cancelled because of bad weather. I couldn't take him to a hotel in the state he was in. He was in enormous pain.

'Is there no way we can get home?' he kept asking, the pain reflected in his face. 'I so want to be home, Seve,' he'd say.

'Don't worry, father, I'll find a way to get you home.'

Which is what I did. I moved heaven and earth to get my father back to Santander that New Year's Eve. The only possible way was by air, because the train journey would be too long and uncomfortable for him. So I went to Gest Air, a company that hires out aeroplanes.

Although we'd been told it would be impossible to land at Parayos airport, we managed it and arrived home in the evening. It was the last time I travelled with my father.

Obviously, I cherish very precious memories from the many trips I took with my father. On one occasion we flew from Akron, Ohio, and my father had a window seat. I could see him looking down, silent and deep in concentration. Finally I couldn't restrain myself any longer and asked him: 'Why are you looking out of the window so thoughtfully?'

He turned his head towards me, still staring at the landscape below and said: 'It's just that since we left, I've seen nothing but houses and more houses, buildings and more buildings. Are there people living in all those houses and buildings?' he asked totally seriously.

'Yes, of course,' I replied.

'Damn me! What a lot of people! And what a lot of potatoes and beans you'd have to sow to feed that lot!'

My father came from peasant stock – he was thinking of how hard he'd have to work to feed so many people. With our horse he sowed enough crops for the three hundred inhabitants in our village of Pedreña. Given the backward state of Spanish agriculture under General Franco, my father knew nothing of the machinery used by North American farmers. We lived in two different worlds.

Even though he was happy accompanying me, enjoying luxuries that would have been previously unthinkable, I suspect my father sometimes harboured a nostalgia for the old days. He had gone from spending hour after hour sowing, reaping, ploughing, and looking after the livestock, to not doing anything at all, apart from tidying the garden and planting a few potatoes, tomatoes and other bits and pieces in his little plot. I sometimes think it had been a mistake to take him away from the life he was accustomed to, because work is such an important part of a man's life. As the saying goes, 'A man retired is a man done with life.'

He started to play golf to amuse himself and overcome boredom. Although he'd worked as a caddie at the club in Pedreña, like almost everybody else in the village, he'd never played. And so he had no idea about the difficulties the sport involved.

'Did you win easily?' he would ask when I got back from a tournament, convinced it was all very simple for me.

'No, not at all, do you think I just arrive, play and win?'

'Bah, golf is really easy!' he'd respond.

When he started to play, he began to see that golf wasn't 'really easy'. Golf requires skill and lots of practice. But on the whole, my father was well equipped to adapt to change and enjoy the good things that life can offer. He liked to live well.

My mother was completely different. Her 'thing', as they say nowadays, was quite the opposite. When I was a child we didn't have a fridge, let alone a washing machine. My mother would put our dirty washing in a tub, lift it on her head and walk down to the village wash-house. (It still exists; it's about 150 metres from our house.) She'd do her washing there. My mother ironed, cooked, did the housework and also helped in the fields and went fishing. She worked eighteen hours a day. She'd look at me and say with resignation: 'Son, you should have been a girl, then you could have given me a hand.' You have to remember that we were five brothers and not a single sister.

My mother was set in that way of life. I never got her to go to the cinema, although we did once go to a football match between Racing Santander and Real Madrid. She had been very marked by Spain's past, by the sufferings of the Civil War and Franco era. The privations she had experienced had made her extremely conservative. Whenever I brought her a present the only thing she could think to say by way of a thank you was: 'Ay, my son, that must have cost you the earth!' Rather than enjoying her present she worried that I should have been saving 'for the future, because you never know'.

After she died, my brothers and I went to her house, the house I'd had built for her on the plot of land next to mine, with rooms all on the same level, as she had wanted. We sorted out her clothes and it was very sad to see the huge number of dresses and pairs of shoes in her wardrobes that she'd never worn. My mother was a woman who would thank you for any present you gave her, but she would rarely put it on. 'I'll wear it some time, when there's something special,' she'd always say. But that special day would never come.

She was a very simple woman, not at all vain or arrogant. When I asked her: 'Mother, why not wear one of those pretty dresses you've got in the wardrobe?' she'd reply, 'No, the people in the village know who I am.' She was also a very considerate person, who wouldn't dream of speaking ill of anyone or interfering in the lives of others, particularly those of her daughters-in-law. She occasionally went to

Mass, but she wasn't very religious. For whatever reason, she was fairly sceptical. She was a great non-believer in things; she didn't even believe the Americans had reached the moon. She'd say, half-jokingly, 'Go on with you, Seve, I bet they've landed on a beach and are just pretending that what we can see is the moon.'

Television and telephones were a mystery to her. Though she wasn't illiterate, for she wrote very well and read with great facility, she always acted very ingenuously. Intrigued by the constant march of technology, she'd ask me: 'How is it possible for them to be playing a game of football in Valencia and for us to watch it at home, on a screen? How is that possible? It's very strange. And when you are so far away, how can we talk on the phone? Where does the voice travel? Through a cable, down a tube . . .?'

My mother was really only worried about the well-being of her children, particularly anyone she thought was in difficulties.

'Ay, my son! Imagine the state Manolo must be in with the expense of having four children! What he must spend clothing and feeding them and sending them to school. Do you think you're paying him enough money?' she'd ask me. (Manuel was employed by one of my companies.)

'Yes, mother, don't worry! Manuel's well paid. And if not,' I added jokingly, 'he's got a father-in-law who's pretty well off and I bet he'll help him out.'

'Ay, don't be silly, my son! What do you think his father-in-law is ever going to give him? He'll never give him anything! If you don't give him what he needs . . .'

What she didn't know was that Manuel had and has his life and the lives of his family completely provided for. But my mother was driven by a desire to protect her children. She would always speak up for anyone she reckoned was weak or in need. I was very sad she passed away without properly taking advantage of our new situation in life. But I also think she was very happy in her way, especially when she could watch me triumph in what was my passion, golf. She was so excited at keeping press-cuttings in which I figured: 'I want you to come home, son, so I can show you the cuttings . . . you wait until you see the lovely things they say about you.'

I travelled with my mother quite a lot, although not as much as I would have liked, because she preferred to stay at home, protecting her world and looking after her garden. Although we were now adults, she still saw us as children who needed to be under her wing and, as you all know, the place where a mother really feels in control is in her own home.

The first time my mother travelled with me outside Spain was to London. She watched me win two World Match Play Championships and the 1984 Open, which I consider the most brilliant moment in my career. I remember how the tournament organisers welcomed her with a huge bouquet of flowers. So many people were hanging on her every wish that she spent the whole time on cloud nine. But it was hard going to get her away from her usual surroundings – 'No, let me stay at home, *that's* a long way to go,' she'd say – and she found flying a traumatic experience: 'Ay, my son! How awful! Are you sure *it* won't fall?'

'No, mother, *it* never falls,' I answered, not thinking anything of it.

'And what about the accidents you see on television? How can this scrap metal fly?' she'd say in the aeroplane, incredulous, swaying her head from side to side.

When we got off the plane in London and she heard everyone speaking English, she was taken aback: 'They all seem very nice but I can't understand a word they're saying! What strange words they use,' she looked at me in surprise. 'Can you make yourself understood with them?'

'Yes, of course, mother.'

'It's incredible. How did you ever learn all this? It will always be beyond me.'

My mother came to watch me in Madrid, Málaga and some other cities in the south of the country, but what she really enjoyed was going out to lunch or supper with my brothers and me on a Sunday.

My father, of course, was completely different. When he was young, he had always enjoyed himself with the *traineras*, on trips with his fellow rowers or to livestock fairs, where he went to sell the odd cow. He liked eating with his friends, playing cards, going to football matches and, sometimes, to the cinema. But, as he gave all the money he earned to my mother, who ran the household affairs, he was often short of cash for his personal needs. Every so often, I'd slip him an envelope with some pocket money.

My father liked to try his luck, because he said you had to go in search of luck. My mother didn't, though she always complained she never won anything on the lottery:

'But, mother,' Baldomero would say, 'how will you ever win if you never buy a ticket?'

Luck – bad or good or whatever – plays a part in all our lives. It's true we forge our own destinies, that we make our own lives, but there are always independent forces that affect us. I remember how after playing a tournament in Sun City, Vicente and I thought we'd stay on in South Africa for a couple of days to rest and sunbathe. We were going to fly back to Santander via Lisbon and Madrid. However, we weren't used to being on holiday and we got bored straight away, so we decided to bring our departure forward. Back in Santander, I was watching television at home with my father when they showed images of a terrible accident in Barajas airport. Two aeroplanes had collided in fog; six crew members and eighty-seven passengers in the two planes died. Vicente and I would have been in the crash if we'd kept to our idea of having a couple of days' holiday in South Africa. One radio report even included our names in the passenger list. When he heard them being read out, my father started to cry. I gave him a hug.

'Father, don't grieve. Lady Luck is still on my side.'

In 1983 my father came to watch me when I won the Masters. We flew from Atlanta to New York and from there to Madrid in an Iberia plane. As we had to wait seven hours in Kennedy airport, I asked him whether he fancied going for a drive around the city. He liked the idea, as I thought he would. Then I thought, 'As my father came to Augusta and saw me win, I'll give him a present. I'll hire a chauffeur-driven limousine.' (He used to see them on television sometimes, and he always found them fascinating.) After I'd made the necessary phone call, I said: 'All right, father, when you see the biggest, most spectacular car that you have ever seen arrive, that'll be the car we will ride in to see the city.'

After a while, a limousine stopped in front of us. It was eight metres long, with a bar and television and it could seat eight to ten people. A driver emerged from this enormous luxury piece of junk and addressed me in English, naturally enough.

'What a big bloody car!' exclaimed my father after a few seconds. 'It's like the ones you see in films! Is it for us?'

'Yes, father, it's for us.'

Then the driver opened the door for him. I watched him get in totally astounded.

'What a fucking big car!' he exclaimed. 'You could live in it! And who's paying for the bar, all those drinks and whisky?' he asked nodding his head towards the bar.

'Don't worry about that, father, you enjoy yourself. We're going for a ride round the city.'

'All right then, mine's a whisky,' he said making himself comfortable.

I poured him one and then watched him sitting there so happily, downing a whisky in New York at eleven in the morning.

'I'd give anything for people in Pedreña to see me drinking a whisky in this car . . . And with a chauffeur . . .'

'Where would you like to go now?'

'I've always thought I'd like to visit that really famous bit. You know, the one that's in all the films.'

'I know! You want to go to Harlem!'

I told our chauffeur and, after a long spin round Manhattan, we reached Harlem. But of course it wasn't usual for a car like that to be driving through Harlem in those days, and we began to attract a lot of attention from the locals. Some, no doubt surprised, even stood up when the car went past. My father wanted to have a better view of the streets and the people, and asked for the smoked-glass window to be lowered. He took one look at the landscape, turned to me and said: 'Fuck, Seve, this place is scary, I think we'd better clear off before something nasty happens!'

As we'd already had a big tour, we drove straight back to the airport. I think it was one of the high points of my father's life, because when we got back home, he never stopped telling all his friends in the village about it.

On another trip to the United States – also to New York – we stayed in a hotel with twenty-seven floors. We were on the twenty-third. The lift on one side of the hotel only went to the fifteenth floor; the one on the other went right to the top. My father was jetlagged because of the time difference, so he got up very early for a look around. He noticed that there was building work going on right under our hotel.

'I'm not surprised the Americans are so advanced,' he commented admiringly. 'Look, it's 3 a.m. and they're still working.'

'Yes, father, they work around the clock.'

'It's incredible!' he exclaimed. 'I'm going downstairs to see how they do it and what kind of tools they're using.'

He went downstairs and I went back to sleep. When I woke up two hours later, my father still wasn't back. I was worried and straight away went down to look for him. Much to my relief, I found him sitting in the foyer.

'About time you showed up!' he reproached me. 'I've been sat here more than an hour and a half. I didn't know what to do.'

'Why didn't you come back up?'

'I tried several times, but this lift doesn't have a number twenty-three. How the fuck do you get to the twenty-third floor?'

'Father, this lift only goes up to the fifteenth; you have to take the lift on the other side to get to the twenty-third.'

'Bugger, Seve! If you hadn't come down I'd never have known.'

My father acted like a simple man; a man who could appreciate the work and success of others. On one occasion in South Africa, where I had gone to play in an exhibition match with Lee Trevino, Jack Nicklaus and Gary Player, my father came with me to have dinner at Gary's ranch. It was a very pleasant meal and the atmosphere was very relaxed. However, when we got back to the hotel, I noticed that my father was very quiet.

'What's the matter, father? Are you feeling ill? Didn't you like the dinner? Didn't you enjoy yourself?'

'No, it's not that. I ate well and I had a very good time, but,' he paused rather too long I thought before continuing, 'do you know what I'm thinking, son . . . ?' He paused again and I looked at him, waiting for him to continue. 'I thought our house was the best in the world, but, after seeing this gentleman's, I realise it's nothing special . . .'

My parents had just moved into a simple but very nice house that I'd given them as a present. They were very proud of it. So I was surprised by his comment.

'Well, it's better than the one we had before,' I said surprised.

'Yes, but I thought we had the best house ever . . .'

Gary Player's ranch had made a huge impression on him: there were lots of horses, a house that was a real mansion and an army of servants. He was very sensitive to this kind of thing. He was also very struck by the beds supplied on our flight from London to Tokyo. After my father got into bed, he couldn't stop saying: 'Bugger! This is the life, Seve, this is the life! I wish people in the village could see us now, because if I tell them they won't believe me. Two lovely ladies wait upon me, give me everything I ask for . . . I've had something like four whiskies, I'm half addled, I'm sleeping in a bed way up high in the sky . . . It's incredible! This is the life, son, this is the life!'

But it was a life that would soon slip away from him, although I didn't want to accept that. One night, when he was convalescing at home from his operation, I told him:

'Father, I see you're well on the way to recovery, so I'm going to America to play a few tournaments to prepare myself for Augusta. Then I'll come back for you and you can come with me for the Masters – I think I'll dedicate it to you this year.'

At the time I could only play small tournaments in the United States – I'd lost my card (i.e. my entitlement) to play on the main PGA Tour because I'd not played the required minimum of fifteen tournaments the previous year. For this reason, I entered the Florida Cup Classic – part of the Tournament Players' Association Tour. I finished joint second. My prize money was just $1,375. I'm almost certain there were never more than three hundred spectators there on any of the days.

Although I kept my momentum going on the course, I found it very difficult to concentrate on my game. I was constantly thinking about my father. I knew from my brothers that things were not going well and, finally, towards the end of February I received the news I feared most. Baldomero rang me the Wednesday before the next tournament I was due to play.

'Seve, I think you'd better come home.'

I returned immediately. My father died a week later, on 4 March.

Chapter 13

Times of Grief

My father's illness had drastically curtailed my preparations for the 1986 Augusta Masters. Caring for him became my and my brothers' priority. But that meant I couldn't train properly. In the first three months of that year I hardly played at all: three rounds in Florida, four in the Spanish PGA Championship and two in New Orleans, where I was defending my USF&G Classic title, though I didn't make the cut.

Despite my lack of preparation and the fact that I was still deeply affected by my father's death, in April I travelled to Augusta with my brother Vicente, who was caddying for me. I played the whole tournament on emotion rather than technique or strategy. Nonetheless, when I reached the 15th hole of the last round I was in the lead. But life and golf had another unpleasant surprise in store for me. With only four holes to play I lost what would have been my third Masters title.

For me, the saddest part of the whole tournament was that my father couldn't be there to watch me. And as I didn't win, there was no victory to dedicate to his memory.

Surprisingly, despite my lack of preparation, my father's recent death and my dispute with Deane Beman, the head of the PGA Tour, who'd suspended my card, before the tournament I was rated one of the favourites to win. When journalists questioned me about the Beman conflict, I nipped it in the bud by answering: 'Forget Beman, this tournament is much more important than Deane Beman!'

Given what an important figure Beman was in American golf, I'm not sure how that went down in the media, but I do know the impact it made on the bookmakers. Half-way through the tournament I was on 139, 5 under par, my rounds of 71 and 68 giving me a one-stroke lead over Bill Kratzert in second place.

As I said, my game was highly charged, because I wanted to win the title for my father. On the Saturday, I went round in par (72) – not exactly what I wanted, but it left me only one behind the current tournament leader, Greg Norman. I was level with Nick Price, who'd just set a new course record with a 63, Bernhard Langer and Donnie Hammond. Tom Kite, Tom Watson and Tommy Nakajima were behind us, and Sandy Lyle and Jack Nicklaus were even further adrift.

In the final round I was paired with Tom Kite and, as I'd anticipated, he was out for revenge. Tom and I had played each other in the Ryder Cup singles seven months previously at the Belfry, where I halved our match by making three birdies in the last five holes. Right from the first green Kite started niggling about Vicente, who was caddying for me, because he claimed my brother had moved when he was trying to putt. It is possible Vicente moved, but it was completely irrelevant: the putt was less than twenty centimetres, and Vicente had certainly not intended anything unsporting. However, Kite started gesticulating as if my brother had tried to impede him intentionally. At the tee box at the 2nd, Vicente came over and asked me: 'What's wrong with this guy? He's out of order!' I shrugged my shoulders and continued to play. I was determined not to lose my concentration.

When we reached the 8th, I was already one under par and Kite was one over, but he holed from seventy-five metres for an eagle. Right then I caught sight of Tom Watson walking down the slope of the 9th gesturing to Kite as if to say 'Come on, Tom, you can beat him!' Despite the difficult pitch shot I was facing I hit the ball confidently and found the hole. Then I turned round to see the look on Watson's face, but he'd already walked off down the fairway. The shouts from the spectators must surely have let him know, much to his disappointment, that my ball had rolled in on top of Kite's. A real piece of theatre.

This shot gave me a one-stroke lead over Greg, although that was to be short-lived. I pushed my drive at the next hole to the left, the ball fell among the trees and ended up in a very bad lie. I found it hard to accept the ball could have landed there – I was forced to conclude that a spectator must have kicked it, for there was a big crowd round my ball. I took a bogey. My eagle at the 13th brought me back to nine, under par overall and put me two strokes ahead of the field. So far, so good. I played all my strokes to perfection, particularly the 6 iron second. Vicente was delighted by how things were going. He shook my hand in congratulations.

There was such a tense atmosphere on the course that some people thought my brother had made this spontaneous gesture to congratulate me in advance on certain victory and accused him of a lack of sportsmanship. But neither he nor I thought it was over and done with – far from it. I couldn't allow myself the luxury of losing my concentration. All I was thinking about was holing my putt and carding an eagle.

The 14th was the point where it all began to go haywire. I started off with a perfect 3 wood. The strike flew through the air from left to right as if on its way to a certain birdie. However, a television cameraman had carelessly wandered into the middle of the fairway and the ball rebounded off him some twenty-five metres. Now I was faced with a considerably longer second shot to the green. I had lost my chance of getting a birdie; now I had to work hard to save my par. Whenever I think of that moment, I'm more and more convinced that that unexpected obstacle signalled the beginning of the end, because from then on it all began to go catastrophically wrong.

The disaster happened at the 15th. My tee shot couldn't have been better: it went long and straight down the middle of the fairway. But both Kite and I had to wait ages for our next shots, because Nakajima and Watson were still to putt on the 15th green. The delay had come about because Watson had suggested to the Japanese player that they should wait until Nicklaus putted at the 16th. Nicklaus was on a tear, and the crowd was going wild. He now faced a putt for birdie, and Watson didn't want to risk being disturbed if he made it. The whoops of delight indicated that Jack had holed his ball.

My problem now wasn't just that Jack was only one behind me. The long wait before hitting our second stroke meant Vicente and I had time to worry about which club to choose. Before such a vital shot, those eight minutes seemed an eternity. In the event, rather than using the 5 iron I had already intuitively picked out, we selected a 4 iron: 'Come on, Vicente,' I told my brother, 'I'll play a nice, gentle 4 iron.' At the 16th at Augusta it's always better to over-hit rather than play within yourself, because it's essential to clear the water in front of the green. To put it plainly, you're better off long than short. I now know I made a mistake: although the 4 iron wasn't an intrinsically bad choice, it would have been more sensible to hit a 5 iron, which is what you would normally do when pressure is mounting in a game. In these circumstances, you must hit the ball hard, not pull your punches. Unfortunately, that's just what I did. I tried to play the shot delicately. As a result I hit the ground before I hit the ball. It was such a bad stroke there was no way I could make up for my error. The ball went into the water and, as it turned out, with it went any chance I had of winning. Vicente panicked and shouted: 'Shit, we're going to lose!' But I didn't accept defeat. 'Calm down! It will be all right in the end! We can still win!' I tried to raise his spirits. The fact was that when I walked on to the sixteenth tee, I was eight under par and tied level with Nicklaus. I still felt I could control the situation.

There has been a lot of speculation as to why I hit that stroke so badly. Some say that I was so incensed by my exclusion from the American Tour that I was obsessed with rubbing my victory in Deane Beman's face, others that I'd been intimidated by Jack Nicklaus because he had the whole crowd behind him, others still that I was too caught up by the idea of winning in order to render a posthumous tribute to my father. In principle, I knew that if I won the Masters it would be a good response to those who were applauding the fact that I wasn't allowed to compete in the top American tournaments, but the pleasure of 'revenge' could wait until we'd finished on the course. As for Jack Nicklaus, I have to say that, even respecting him as all golfers do, he didn't intimidate on the course then as he might have done ten years earlier. Moreover, if a player tries to intimidate me, the only thing he succeeds in doing is to make me feel even more determined. And I didn't feel the pressure of the crowds, because all of us players have fans out there. I was twenty-nine and had played at the highest level for ten years; none of this could disrupt my game. It is true that I wanted to win at all costs for my father, but, while I was playing, I kept that very much to myself. If that shot cost me the tournament, it was mainly down to the long wait, and poor choice of club. But my father's memory may have had something to do with it.

Everything came together in the final holes to enable Jack Nicklaus to win. My fate was definitively sealed at the 17th, when I three-putted from the edge of the green after my first putt went some four metres past the pin. In the end, Jack was the champion. Greg Norman beat me by two and Tom Kite by one.

The crowds at Augusta behaved very well towards me. When I was coming up the fairway on the 18th, people applauded me loudly. I responded, waved my peak cap at them and threw kisses, although I kept a tight rein on my emotions. That afternoon, God was on the side of Jack Nicklaus. The harshest blow for me wasn't so much losing, as not being able to dedicate a victory to my father, as I had pledged. Perhaps it had been destined to be so.

Chapter 14

The *Forza* of Destiny

Sometimes when I think back to the 1986 Masters I can't stop myself from crying silent tears. Over time I have accepted what happened, but it still hurts. There's a lot of truth in the saying 'The worst thing about knowing how to lose is to have lost in the first place'. Perhaps it was destiny.

Destiny in golf is a strange thing. Take the last hole of the 2000 USPGA Trophy, which gave Tiger Woods a remarkable third consecutive title. What happened at that 18th hole was incredible. Woods had to hole a three-metre putt to tie with Bob May and he did just that. When you attempt a three-metre putt, you can have perfect sight of the break, hit the ball with the exact amount of oomph required and do everything under your control to perfection but a single blade of grass may send the ball off course. And there's nothing you can do. At other times, you can get it wrong, and that same blade of grass or gust of wind will hole the ball for you. Such is the *forza* of destiny. The putt that Tiger Woods sank at that final hole, when he most needed to do so, must have been the work of destiny. As I've said already, you forge your own fate. But there's no denying that things sometimes happen that make you suspect our script is written in advance.

I often have the impression in spite of myself, that the defeat I suffered at Augusta in 1986 helped write a very special chapter in golfing history. My downfall had seemed unthinkable; but Nicklaus's victory was equally remarkable. At forty-six he had become the oldest winner ever. Apart from the mishaps and factors I've mentioned, I also paid the price for my lack of training. Nicklaus himself even said that the stroke I played at the 15th was the typical stroke of a player who's short of match practice. Nevertheless, I have no excuses. If I could play the shot again I would use a 5 iron . . .

The following year I was on the point of winning but then lost in the playoff. When you suffer a series of setbacks like the ones I suffered in Augusta over those years, it hurts deep inside. After I beat Tom Watson at St Andrews in 1984, he never won another major tournament. But at St Andrews Watson was beaten by me. At Augusta in 1986 I beat myself.

However, I'm not the only one to suffer this sort of setback. There are other cases in point: Doug Sanders missed the shortest of putts at the 18th at St Andrews and it cost him the Open in 1970; Tony Jacklin lost the Open, at Muirfield in 1972, when Lee Trevino holed a fantastic series of chips and snatched a title Jacklin thought was his; Ed Sneed lost the 1979 Masters because he took three bogeys at the last three holes.

It's extremely hard to come back from these misfortunes, but it's not impossible. Tennis player Goran Ivanisevic did so when he won Wimbledon in 2001 after losing the final three times. I did so at Lytham St Annes in 1988 when I won the Open. That's why I understood Ivanisevic's tears. These victories are really important because they put you back on track to the goal you've given yourself.

Of course you can feel sorry for yourself. Doug Sanders says not a day goes by when he doesn't remember that putt he missed, but these regrets are pointless. If you stop and think about it for a moment, we've all had our missed opportunities. What you have to do is to concentrate on not slipping up again and not let your grief overwhelm you.

If I keep referring to the 1986 Masters it's because of the way I lost and, above all, because of my father. I may have been on the point of victory in 1986, but one must also recall that I was in the same situation in 1982 when I finished one stroke adrift of making the playoff; in 1985 when Bernard Langer won; and in 1987 when I lost in the playoff with Larry Mize and Greg Norman. That tournament was also a big setback, but what really makes defeat or victory special is the emotional burden it leaves you with, and that's determined by the way you win or lose.

The 1987 playoff was, as I said, a setback, but it didn't impact on me more than any other defeat. It's true that Greg and I were favourites, but when you are playing sudden death you always think that anything is possible, because golf isn't a game of certainties.

I reached the tee box of the 10th, the first playoff hole, in a confident state of mind and hit a good drive. So did Greg and Larry, who hit the longest drive of all. My second stroke – a 5 iron – was also very good, rather to the right of a pin that was set quite deep. Unfortunately, the green was dry and hard, and the ball rolled to the back, some nine metres from the pin. Norman landed more than four metres away and Mize three, which was a good distance to be from the hole. I hit the putt very fast. Some people say I was rash – that I was trying to rattle the putt in. In fact I wasn't trying to hole it, just to get as near as possible. I reckoned that neither Mize, who was near to winning a major tournament for the first time, nor Norman, who was desperate to win the Masters, would hole their putts. And I was right.

My problem wasn't that my putt overran by almost a metre, but that I missed my next shot. Generally, when you miss a short putt you feel your hand slipped or you've over-hit. But the video of the tournament shows clearly that I was astonished the ball didn't go in. The pictures also show I didn't do anything out of the ordinary with my hands or with the club face. I missed the shot because I aimed badly. I should have aimed at the centre, because it was a straight putt, but I hit it to the left. I got it wrong because the shadow projected by the beautiful trees around the green in the twilight interfered with my sight of the line and I misjudged the roll of the ball. So my Masters ended there.

Finally, destiny decided in favour of Larry Mize at the next hole and he won the tournament. He pulled off an astonishing stroke, one of those when the ball goes in every once in a thousand times. Naturally I was extremely disappointed and when my brother Vicente and I walked back up the fairway to the 10th, we didn't speak; we were distraught and cried tears of rage. How could I have missed that putt, after I'd practised that stroke and told myself 'I have to win, after what happened last year'? But if I analyse my game in the cold light of reason, I recognise that although I'd holed three putts from four and six metres during the last round, I hadn't managed to hole anything from two and a half metres the whole week. Besides, although I'd made only eight bogeys over the four rounds, which is unusual for Augusta, the eleven birdies I'd made weren't enough. That's where I really lost the tournament. As we can see, the *forza* of destiny, to evoke

Verdi's famous opera, sometimes manifests itself in the shape of things or acts that are quite inexplicable, which we call miracles if they're helpful and catastrophes if they're disastrous. Sometimes they seem to depend on tiny things, as silly as changes in the weather or quirks of behaviour.

Chapter 15

My Moment of Glory

Tee-off times and the weather can be crucially important in the game of golf. Throughout my sporting career, as you can imagine, I've had good and bad starting times in major tournaments. Take links golf. When you are playing by the sea conditions can be completely different at 7.30 in the morning from how they are at 3.30 in the afternoon. Given that links golf – via the Open – has been so connected to the high points of my career, this has always been of great importance to me.

Because I was born by the seaside, I know that tides greatly influence the climate and winds. Sometimes, if you play in the afternoon – often the case in one of the first two rounds – you can see the changes in the weather influencing the game of the competitors on the course. The worst that can happen in the Open is to have to play your first round late and in bad weather. The golfers who have preceded you have signed cards in the 60s; now the rain is starting to fall and the wind is sweeping across the course and you know you've lost any chance of winning the Open before you've played a single shot.

Obviously no golf tournament is won on the first day, but it can be lost. And it happens more frequently in the Open than in any other. I don't think the Royal & Ancient Golf Club of St Andrews, the tournament organisers, can be blamed, although you have to recognise it is often unbending in its attitudes. (Perhaps it cannot be otherwise.)

Here's an example: I believe that Royal Birkdale and Muirfield are two courses in the rotation system for the Open where they could send players out from two different starting tees at the same time. However, this isn't possible if more than a hundred and fifty players are competing. In that scenario there would be games that would finish the first nine holes before the tees at the 1st and 10th were clear, which would lead to huge hold-ups in play. But, despite that and although I expect it will never happen, it would be interesting for the R&A to some day test a system of simultaneous two-tee starts, as the United States Golf Association did for the 2002 US Open.

Although it isn't perfect, the Open remains the most important tournament in the world. I had my deepest emotional experience in my golfing life when I played the 1984 Open at the cradle of golf, the Old Course at St Andrews. In the last round, I went out with Bernhard Langer, with Tom Watson and Ian Baker-Finch the pair behind us. They were both eleven under par and Bernhard and I were nine under. I wasn't at all anxious. I had been feeling so confident throughout the tournament that I'd brought the press conference to an end the previous evening by telling the journalists: 'I'll see you all here tomorrow.'

It was obvious I didn't mean I was going to be there as runner-up. I'd already beaten Watson in the Masters the year before; and, though I thought Langer was very good, I didn't think he was ready to win a major yet. (Perhaps I was wrong. The following April he beat me to don the green jacket of Augusta.) I felt Baker-Finch was simply too inexperienced to stay in contention, unlike seven years later when he won the tournament.

Contrary to the way I had played at Lytham five years before, I spent the afternoon looking at the scoreboards to find out how things were going. I made a birdie at the 5th to tie with Watson; another birdie at the 8th made me outright leader.

I was playing confidently, but Watson seemed to be having problems with his putts. He three-putted three times in the first five holes. I took a bogey at the 11th but although it might have appeared that way, I wasn't at all interested in aiding Watson in his attempt to equal Harry Vardon's record of six Open titles. Over the subsequent holes, anything seemed possible; Watson made a birdie at the 13th, but I retaliated with one at the next hole. We both felt that victory was within our grasp.

When Bernhard and I reached the tee at the 15th, it had got considerably colder. I proceeded to dress for the kill – just like a bullfighter. I took the navy-blue sweater that I'd worn at Lytham five years before out of my bag and pulled it over my white polo shirt. But, as we say in Spain, don't sell the bearskin before you've caught the bear. The first rule of golf is that you must control your emotions. You should never imagine yourself holding the trophy aloft before the game is over: golf is too unpredictable. Though I was well aware of this, after my birdie at the 14th I told myself: 'you can win now'. But as soon as you've said something like that, you get an attack of anxiety just thinking how far there's left to go; we still had to play the renowned and much-feared Road Hole.

Watson and I maintained the status quo through the 15th and 16th and we were tied when we came to the 17th, the Road Hole. It was the most demanding par 4 – and in my view the trickiest hole outright – in the world. I'd only made five bogeys in seventy holes over the tournament; three had been at the 17th.

I knew I had to get a par.

So I prepared myself and as on previous days, I aimed left – a lot to the left. And, as on previous days, the ball found the rough. The lie wasn't too bad. But the flag was just under 190 metres away and I didn't really have any choice but to steer the ball to the right. It was a difficult stroke and, if I missed, I was finished. If I veered to the left I might find myself in the road bunker or be left with an impossible chip; if I over-hit, I'd have to play my third stroke from the road.

I gripped my 6 iron firmly and hit the ball as hard as I could. The ball took off from the rough slightly out of control, as I'd anticipated it would. My eyes followed the ball but all my fears were groundless. It ended up in the middle of the green, to the right, just where I wanted it for a two-putt over some fifteen metres. I relished the par as if it were a birdie.

That wasn't the end of it. On my way to the last hole, I looked back to watch Watson preparing to play his second stroke at the 17th, from an ideal position on the right-hand side of the fairway. I told my caddie, Nick de Paul, that we needed a birdie at the 18th to guarantee victory.

I hit a pretty good 3 wood off the tee. I followed up with another good sand wedge that left my ball about five metres below the hole. The putt had a clear borrow to the left, but as I struck the ball, I felt I had overdone it. I hadn't. It rolled sweetly towards the hole, then seemed to hover on the edge of the cup, before finally going in as if in slow motion, perhaps impelled by my powers of mental suggestion, so strong was my desire that it should drop in.

This was the happiest moment of my whole sporting life. My moment of glory. My most fantastic shot. So much so that the picture of me gesturing in triumph is now the logo for my companies. My brother Baldomero is right when he says: 'There are two kinds of players in the world of golf. Some turn themselves into a commercial product and try to achieve great success in the marketplace, and others devote their youth to achieving sporting and social success, generously dedicating themselves to this task and to the public. Seve belongs to this last category, and that's why he's not a product but a symbol.'

When the ball dropped in, I knew I was the champion. I was no longer worried by what Watson might do at the 17th. But despite the fact I knew I had won with my final putt, after signing and giving in my scorecard, I went off to watch him. I didn't know that he'd made a bogey before I putted, which meant he needed an eagle at the 18th to force a playoff. It was beyond him.

Later on, when I watched a video of Watson's second shot at the 17th, I discovered where he'd made his mistake. While I'd been able to cover almost 190 metres with a 6 iron, he'd used a 2 iron – wasting the perfect position his drive had given him. I really don't know why, because Watson never offered an explanation. Perhaps he misjudged the distance from the flag; perhaps the adrenalin made him believe he was stronger than he really was. Whatever the explanation, he made the wrong choice of club. Even so, he played a splendid third shot and almost managed to save par.

Watson is one of the greatest players in the history of golf. Between 1975 and 1983, he won the Open, the Masters and the US Open – as well as many other victories we've mentioned. His sporting record speaks for itself. For me, he's a great individual, a good person whom I have always admired and respected deeply. I think it's mutual because he once said this about me: 'Seve isn't just a great golfer. He works miracles communicating with the public. I could never have imagined a Spanish golfer making such an impact on the general public in the United States and Great Britain.'

Even so, Watson was rather despondent when congratulating me later. I quite understood. I knew what he must have been feeling, since that Open was very important for him. If he'd won he'd have equalled Vardon's record. But that was my moment of glory. The wind – which is always changing by the seashore – was blowing in my favour.

Chapter 16

The Round of My Life

To win the Open at St Andrews is the dream of every professional golfer. The Old Course is the birthplace of our sport; it is the world's most famous course, the one with the most tradition. And the Open is the oldest championship of them all. This is history and there is none richer. What's more, in my opinion, the Open is the trickiest tournament to win: it always attracts the world's best players, and links golf is always subject to changeable weather conditions. But my best round in the Open – perhaps even the best of my entire career – wasn't at St Andrews in 1984. It was that fantastic round of 65 with which I finished to win once again at Royal Lytham four years later.

That 1988 Open will always stay fresh in my memory, both because of the birdies I hit and the emotions I went through.

Right from the start, as storm clouds gathered on the Thursday morning, I was in the thick of the action. I began strongly, with five birdies in the first seven holes, but on the back nine things began to get more difficult, as often happens at Lytham. I made bogeys at the 14th and 18th, after having to drop two balls that were unplayable. Nonetheless, my score of 67 gave me the lead after the first round.

The game proceeded hotly contested, with the lead changing all the time: at the end of the third day, Price was in front, on a total of seven under par. Faldo and I were trailing by two and Sandy Lyle by three. The rest of the field was far behind. After the awful weather on the Saturday, our final round had to wait until the Monday and, most unusually for a major tournament, we teed off in threesomes. Nick Price, Nick Faldo and I set off together for the final game.

Usually people prefer to play in twos, because playing in threes is slower and makes it more difficult to concentrate. But that afternoon neither Price nor I were affected. I admit I was quite surprised to find myself so in control of my nerves and emotions. I don't remember ever being in a position to win a major tournament and being as relaxed as I was during that round.

Coming off the 6th hole, Faldo and I had hit a very good rhythm. We were both within a stroke of the lead, hot on Price's heels. However, at the 7th Faldo began to fall away. He three-putted, whereas both Price and I made eagles. At the 8th, the game became even tenser: I holed a six-metre putt for another birdie which brought me level with Price, and we matched each other stroke for stroke over the next two holes. On the 11th, the emotional pitch rose even higher when I holed another six-metre putt for yet another birdie. It was incredible. I was six under par for the last six holes but held the lead by only one stroke. Nick Price was obviously at the top of his form too. To crown it all, I mis-hit the ball at the next hole for my first bogey of the day and Price was back level.

We were both playing spectacularly well. At the 13th, Price hit a magnificent second shot that miraculously failed to go in, though it got him another birdie. It was a very tense situation: I couldn't let him get away from me. I made a very good second shot, leaving me with a five and a half metre putt for a birdie, down a gentle slope from right to left. It is the kind of putt you always think you can hole but you often miss under pressure. And I was under tremendous pressure now. But I didn't falter, my touch was sound and the ball went in.

When we reached the 16th, the scene nine years earlier of my famous 'parking-lot birdie', the game was still equally tight. Price and I were level and in the lead. I told myself I had to do something special. I had to take a risk and attempt something extraordinary. So I decided to split the fairway down the middle with a good drive and follow up with a 9 iron. I very nearly holed in two, but the resulting birdie restored my lead to one stroke. And that was how we reached the tee on the last hole.

As you can imagine, the expectation couldn't have been higher; but the outcome didn't simply hang on one decisive shot. Many factors come into play at such a moment and not all, wind included, are necessarily in your favour. I thought the best option in those conditions was to take a 3 wood off the tee, but I'd not used that club the entire week and it wasn't the best idea to start experimenting now. So

I chose my driver, aimed for the left of the fairway and hit it with fade, to bring the ball back into the middle. But the wind played a bad trick on me and took the ball much further to the right than I'd wanted. There was a bunker on that side and I was afraid that was where the ball was heading. Luckily I was safe for the moment, but the danger from the bunkers remained. I'd only been in a bunker four times over the whole week – I didn't want to repeat the experience.

The 18th pin was positioned in the right half of the green and I told myself: 'Seve, you need a par to win. Don't worry if you miss the green to the left – you will have plenty of room to play to the pin.' I plumped for a 6 iron for my second stroke. The ball was in the semi-rough, but in a decent lie. I aimed left of the green in the hope that the wind would carry the ball on to the putting surface. However, the flight was so true that the wind didn't affect it. The ball ended up left of the green. My first thought was that I'd been left an easy chip, but when I got to the ball I saw it was badly positioned, on an incline. It was a complicated, challenging shot. I reached for my 9 iron first, but then realised that could be dangerous. Finally, I decided on the sand wedge – to loft the ball two or three metres before it would land on the green and roll towards the pin. When I struck the ball I knew I'd caught it just right. The ball was heading for the hole. Even today I wonder why it didn't go in – it was going at the right speed when it skimmed the rim. Anyone who has watched footage of that stroke no doubt wonders the same thing.

I'd made the par I'd been looking for to win the tournament, but things were still in the balance. Nick Price had a long putt for a birdie to draw level. My caddie, Ian Wright, started celebrating as if I had won.

'Wait a minute, Ian,' I said trying to calm him down. 'Nick's still got to putt.'

'He won't hole it! I'm sure he won't!' Ian replied euphorically

'If you'd seen the things I've seen!' I replied, biting my lip. I was remembering how Greg Norman had lost the USPGA Championship in 1986 to Bob Tway and the 1987 Masters to Larry Mize.

Price putted. He over-hit it, it went wide and he missed the return. Even so, Nick Price had played brilliantly that day – it made it an unforgettable final, and the 65 on my card made it the finest round of my career. In fact, that round for me easily rivals the wonderful 'Duel in the Sun' in the 1977 Open at Turnberry between Tom Watson and Jack Nicklaus. It's why I went over to Nick Price at the end and said: 'Nick, you played as well as I did; the only difference is that I was luckier. All I can say is that if you carry on like this, you'll win the Open sooner or later.'

And it was so, because he won it three years later. Nick is a great champion, a friend and a gentleman.

This Open was the fifth Grand Slam tournament I had won, but it meant much more to me than just another major title. I had been going through a bad patch after the 1986 Masters. In 1987, I'd missed the opportunity to win when I three-putted in the playoff and I'd also lost out in the US Open and USPGA Championship. Other people had scaled the peaks of world golf since I'd won my last major, at the Open four years before. Sandy Lyle, winner of the Open at Royal St George's and the Masters; Bernhard Langer, who'd taken the Masters; and Nick Faldo who'd won the Open. I wasn't exactly forgotten on the European golfing scene, because there'd been glorious Ryder Cup victories in 1985 and 1987, but I was aware of the fact that I needed to do something to recover lost ground and regain the place I deserved among the great players. I needed individual success at the highest level.

The 1988 Open was equally wonderful for me in another way. It was the first time since we'd started dating that the woman who would become my wife had accompanied me.

I'd first got to know Carmen Botín many years before, when my brother Vicente went to do his military service in Zaragoza and I replaced him as the golf coach to her family. I used to give them classes on Mondays, Wednesdays and Fridays in Santander, which I'd reach by crossing the bay in a flat-boat, and on Saturdays and Sundays in Pedreña. I spoke to them all very deferentially, even to Carmen, who was then only eight. Time went by, and I met the young girl again when she was sixteen. She surprised me because, as I was travelling, I hadn't had the opportunity to watch her grow up; she came to watch me in the World Match Play Championship in England in 1981. At the time she was studying at St Mary's School Ascot, not far from London, the school our daughter would attend years later. As I won, my brother Vicente and I organised a party, and invited her. That was all it was, to begin with.

The following summer, her parents were holidaying in Pedreña in a house near ours and she came over one day to borrow some pepper. Obviously my mother gave it to her, but as she was leaving I took the opportunity to ask her out to the cinema. I thought she'd say no, but she agreed. After that we met gradually over the years, though nobody knew: they thought we were only good friends. Then we got closer, but our courtship never led to any formal engagement since we saw each other only sporadically. I was travelling all the time and Carmen was studying abroad, first in England and then in the United States.

Our relationship was now eight years old, and the fact she was present at that crucial moment in my sporting career made me very happy. New horizons were opening up in my personal life. I had seen the family my brother Baldomero had created. He had two lovely children; I wanted to have a family like him. I took the plunge and told Carmen that we should either get married or split up. To me she was just a normal girl. The fact that I was thirty and she was twenty-three, and that she could be quite insecure, didn't enter my head. I just thought she was the ideal person to start a family with.

In the back of my mind, I worried about the impact marriage and family might have on my career, which was in the critical phase that had been ushered in by my father's death and the loss of the 1986 Masters. Until I won the Open again, I had begun to wonder whether my position at the top was under threat. But the manner of my victory ended such fears. The memory of how I'd lost the Masters began to fade. I married that November. Now that time has passed, I know my fears about the impact marriage would have on my career were well founded. The 1988 Open was my last victory in a major.

Chapter 17

The Princess and the Pauper

On 27 November 1988, nearly five months after winning the Open and three after returning from Japan, where I'd won the Taiheiyo Club Masters, my seventh tournament of the year, Carmen Botín and I were married. At twenty-three, she was still very young, but I was sure we would overcome that, understand each other and be happy together.

It wasn't only Merín's obvious happiness that prompted me to tie the knot. I have always been obsessed by the idea of having a family: it's something I believe in, because I owe what I am to my family. In this I'm like any other Spaniard. Our lives are centred on our families, much more than inhabitants of other countries. In Spain children usually live with their parents until they get married. It's the opposite of what happens in the United States, where children leave home as soon as they come of age and families only see each other a couple of times a year. In Spain, children with and without jobs alike stay in the parental home, because they have a guaranteed level of comfort they couldn't afford if they lived by themselves. I'm a case in point; I lived with my parents until I was thirty-one.

I owe my family a lot. My parents and brothers looked after me right from the beginning. Even now I need my brothers' love and support to feel happy and secure. When I won my first cheque for playing golf it wasn't for myself. I mean I didn't do it thinking as an individual, but as a member of my family, which was supporting me to help me win. For this reason, almost the first thing I did when I had made some money was to build a house for my parents. I lived there until I got married; now Manuel and his family have it. So when I got married I was really looking forward to creating a family with Carmen.

I've always thought a relationship is a very private matter. It shouldn't be exposed to the public gaze. However, the Spanish press, particularly the more popular magazines, had been speculating for ages about the marriage. Carmen comes from a wealthy, important family so for them the banker's daughter and the golfing champion made a great story. Given my background, they were calling it a fairy tale – 'the princess and the pauper'. One day they would say we'd got married and the next that we'd broken up. Even so, we weren't prepared to turn our private lives into a circus for the media.

Our wedding was a family affair. It was so discreet that only our closest relatives were invited. (There would have been hundreds if we'd invited all the family on both sides.) To avoid unpleasant intruders we told some people in confidence that the ceremony would be held in Carmen's parents' house; in fact, we'd planned to hold it in her grandparents' house in Santander right from the start. I didn't tell anybody; I only let my mother know the week before. It upset the media, but it was the one way to maintain our privacy. The only mistake we made was that, on our honeymoon, we sent some photos a relative of Carmen's had taken to be developed. Somebody in the laboratory worked out what the film was, made a copy and, much to our fury, sold it to a news agency.

The paparazzi pursued Carmen and myself for a long time until they realised we weren't prepared to share our lives with the public at large. As part of this strategy and to avoid ambiguous situations with the mass media, I took the decision right at the start not to ask for money for the interviews I gave, which is what usually happens with anyone the press is interested in. If they wanted to publish something about me, it had to be about me as a golfer, because that was why I was famous. Though many will find this hard to believe, it meant journalists respected and appreciated me. On more than one occasion, when Carmen and I were courting and she came to watch me play in a tournament, I'd ask the photographers not to take photos of her and they listened.

For instance, in 1985, when Carmen came back from Brown University in America to watch me in the Ryder Cup at the Belfry, I asked the photographers to leave her alone because I was afraid it might cause problems for her with her university. Brown knew she was travelling, but not that she'd come to England to watch me play. There was no problem and they all readily agreed to my request. I owe them my gratitude.

The nastier element of the press wrote that I'd done good business by marrying the daughter of the richest banker in Spain. (They still do from time to time.) Nothing could be further from the truth. It's true Carmen belongs to one of the most powerful families in the country: her father ran the Banco Santander, the current Santander Central Hispano that recently took over the Abbey National in the UK. However, this had nothing to do with my marrying her; we had been together for eight years, known each other for over twenty, and it was time to start a family. As I like everything to be clear and above board, and to avoid giving any ammunition to the scandal-mongers, I made it one of the conditions of our marriage that we should do so with a legal division of property, which Carmen agreed to.

The house where Carmen and I went to live was and is mine. I think it's the best place on earth. As I've already said, I'm a big family man and I don't like going off on holiday, because I travel enough the rest of the year and everything at home is just as I want it. It's a large house, with airy, open spaces and no pretensions. It stands at a spot in Pedreña from where I can see all the way from the Bay of Santander to the Cantabrian Sea, and from the golf course to the Cantabrian mountains. There's a big garden with hundreds of trees. I had the house built myself and it is my paradise. It's where I brought Carmen to live.

Soon we began our family. Javier, the eldest, was born in August 1990, Miguel two years later and Carmen in 1994. I am very proud of them all. One of the things Carmen and I agreed on was that they should grow up like normal children. We tried to stop their photos appearing in the press; we didn't want them being recognised in the street.

From the moment the children were born I began to find travelling and being away from home for long periods of time a real bind, because I missed them. I had no choice but to accept the situation, and I understood there was no way around that. The life of a professional golfer has given me great sporting pleasure and fulfilment, but it came with a price: I missed out on many of my children's experiences of growing up, and they suffered too as a result of my absences.

Marriage and children radically change a sportsman's way of life. In my case, it meant I was unable to be single-minded about what I was doing. When I married, I had to stop thinking only about myself – my time was no longer simply my own. And after my children were born that was even more the case. But, although I never won another major the happiness children bring was and is more than reward enough, for no sporting victory can mean more than your children.

Despite the rewards of family life, it was very hard at the beginning. I had to learn to be more generous, to share with my wife and then with my children. When you decide to have a family you have to understand that you must devote your time to them; they are now your main source of happiness.

Chapter 18

The Thorn of the US Open

In 1991, the year after Javier's birth, the Open Championship returned to Birkdale, the course which had almost seen my first victory. From whim or by pure chance, I was paired with Johnny Miller – who had beaten me all those years before. I responded with a very good round, including an eagle and a 370-metre drive (albeit downwind). I felt I was regaining my best form. I carded a 66 for the first round, four under par. (Over the past fifteen years par had been reduced from 72 to 70.) However, I was two strokes behind Ian Baker-Finch and Mark O'Meara.

At first glance, in that position I held a reasonable psychological advantage, given that I was the only one in the top eleven on the scoreboard who had won a major before. I was in with a chance of winning the Open again, although I still wasn't at my best. I've always had confidence in my potential and now I imagined that the others would be intimidated by the prospect of getting their hands on the claret jug. I was wrong. However self-confident you may be, there's nothing you can do when on the last day the guy in front of you goes round the first nine holes in twenty-nine strokes. Baker-Finch had an incredible tournament. He finished with a round of 66, which gave him a two-stroke margin and the 1991 Open. The Open has been a big disappointment to me ever since.

In 1993, at Royal St George's, when Greg Norman won with a brilliant round of 64, my game was nowhere good enough to threaten him. In 1999 I didn't even make the cut. That year the Open was played in Carnoustie. Paul Lawrie won, after a playoff with Jean Van de Velde and Justin Leonard. It was a really surprising fourth day, and Van de Velde had his infamous catastrophe at the final hole.

Fortunately I've never had a blow from fate like the one Van de Velde suffered there. That doesn't mean I don't have my own bad memories of competing in the majors. Of course, I had my disappointments at Augusta, but one of the biggest thorns in my side is that I never won the US Open. It's true that winning three Open Championships and two Masters is no small feat, but if I'd been able to add a US Open to that it would have been the icing on the cake.

For me, the US Open has completely negative vibrations. Think of this: when I made my début in 1978 at Cherry Hills, Andy North won with a bogey at the last hole. It's a tournament where I never felt at ease, because it never rewarded the talent or imagination of those playing. I don't say this because I never won it, although I came near a couple of times, but because no one, not even the spectators, goes there to enjoy themselves. The US Open is a cold tournament: it lacks passion, not only in comparison with the Open Championship or the Masters, but with any tournament in the world. Perhaps the only time it got to be exciting was in 1982, at Pebble Beach, when Tom Watson found the hole with a chip from off the green to snatch victory from Jack Nicklaus.

When I think of my personal history with the US Open I always come back to the 1980 championship. On the plane journey there I'd had a presentiment that an unpleasant surprise was in store for me. So when I arrived at Baltusrol, New Jersey, where the tournament was being held, I had a strange feeling. It disappeared as soon as I stepped on the course, but not for long. I played the first round but that was it. I was disqualified when an unforgivable error caused me to arrive late for my second round. I was foolish enough to get confused and think that tee-off was at 10.45 when in fact it was at 9.45. Clearly my presentiment had been spot on, although it wasn't directly related to my game as such.

Everything seemed to conspire against me that day. Despite our confusion over starting times, Baldomero – who was caddying for me – and I had left our hotel with plenty of time so we could hit a few warm-up balls on the driving range. But the morning started to look very black when we got stuck in a monumental traffic jam. When we finally arrived, I was upset because I wasn't going to have much time for my warm-up. Then, the moment I got out of the courtesy car, somebody shouted: 'Seve, where'd you get to? They've been calling for you at the first tee!'

I went to look at the tee-off times. They were right: I was late. I ran to the tee but when I got there my partners had already hit their respective second shots. The rules were clear, and I had to be disqualified.

I felt very upset and Baldomero felt even worse, for he thought that he'd been at fault. But there was no point feeling sorry for ourselves. All we could do was go home. The following year we almost had a repeat performance.

In 1981 I played the USPGA Championship for the first time. I went over to Atlanta with Baldomero, who was caddying for me again. On the Friday a big storm meant lots of games – though not mine – had to be suspended and finished on Saturday morning. For this reason, the organising body decided to reschedule the third round games and play in threesomes and off two tees. Nobody informed me of the change, but luckily, as I wanted to be on the course early, I had asked the hotel to give me a wake-up call at 8.30. I had just put the phone down when I got a call from the club, saying I started at the 10th hole at 9.10. The course was half an hour away by car, so Baldomero and I leapt out of bed, dressed hurriedly and shot off to the club without eating breakfast. 'What the hell will they think in Spain if we turn up late again?' mumbled Baldomero. 'They'll say we're a couple of idiots.'

Luckily we arrived in time. But just in case, I was already thinking of excuses, because I wasn't prepared to appear in golf history with a unique entry to my name: winner of two majors in two consecutive years, then disqualified from two others because I'd arrived late. Besides, I suppose gaffes of this type are always happening. Just remember Pedro Delgado's in the 1989 Tour de France: he missed his start time in the time trial, and that cost him victory in the end.

To return to the US Open. In 1983 we went to Oakmont, on the outskirts of Pittsburgh, Pennsylvania. I started well, using my 1 iron because I decided I didn't need the driver. I finished the first round two under par and joint leader. At the end of the third round, although I had lost my head slightly to leave myself two off the lead, I was still, interestingly enough, five strokes ahead of the eventual winner, Larry Nelson. He shot a 65 and a 67 for the last two rounds. Strangely, I took a 69 and a 74 over the same eighteen holes. But on the last day, when play was suspended by a tremendous storm, I realised that the US Golf Association had placed the tees a long way back and had broadened the fairways by extending them almost two metres into the first rough on either side. That undoubtedly helped those who were using drivers and made it more difficult for someone like me who was using a 1 iron.

The US Open and I were never *simpatico*. Despite my record, the organisers refused to give me invitations. Whenever I participated in the US Open it was because I qualified. The only year I was invited was during the controversy over Arnold Palmer. When I saw I wasn't invited, and Palmer had been, I made a statement to the effect that the USGA should manage the invitations it had at its discretion more sensibly so as to invite the best golfers of the day. This comment created a big stir because many people thought I was referring to Palmer. That wasn't the case at all. I'd never for one moment thought that Arnold Palmer shouldn't be at the tournament. Quite the contrary. Palmer is a living legend, a fantastic golfer whom I've always admired. The only point of my comment was to get the attention of the USGA so they would invite me. I reckoned it was unfair of them to exclude me. I really believe I deserved better from them.

In 1985 the tournament was at Oakland Hill, Michigan. At the last hole I needed a birdie to force a playoff. But it wasn't to be, because I only made a par. Once again Andy North took advantage of the situation, even though he made a bogey at the last, just as he'd done in 1978. It was incredible!

I came third in 1987 at the Olympic Club in San Francisco, which was the best finish I ever managed in the tournament, five strokes behind the champion, Scott Simpson. Two months later I lost once more in the USPGA Championship, held in Palm Beach, when again I was five strokes behind the winner, Larry Nelson.

It was very disheartening. The US Open and I just didn't hit it off. We were truly incompatible. And it didn't get any better. In the 1990 US Open at Medinah, on the outskirts of Chicago, I did something completely out of character. On the last round I was three under par, trailing the joint leaders, Mike Donald and Billy Ray Brown, by four, and tied with Hale Irwin, who would eventually go on to win the tournament for the third time. At the 2nd hole, a par 3, I put the ball in the water. It was a tricky situation, but not that serious; but rather than putting my character and will into winning the tournament, I crumbled. That was the only time in my entire professional career I didn't fight as I ought to have done to secure victory.

Subsequently, in 1992 and 1993 I decided against participating in the USPGA Championship. My back was torturing me more and more and I wasn't prepared just to turn up and miss the cut. I preferred to rest and prepare myself for the Ryder Cup. I never again played in the USPGA. And the thorn of not winning the US Open continues to wound my professional pride.

Chapter 19

Tribal Warriors

The sport of golf is everywhere, but it is a relatively small world at the top. A large tribe with a few, highly trained warriors, who go into the field accompanied by their shield-bearers, the caddies, to join battle armed with only clubs and balls. There aren't many who manage to enter the cohort of the very best and only exceptional warriors manage to play more than ten seasons at the highest level of their game.

Golf is incredibly demanding and it is extremely hard to stay at the very top. People say the most brilliant period of a top-notch golfer's career is marked by his first and last victory in a major tournament. In my case, my golden age was between 1979 and 1988. My brother Baldomero takes a different view. He extends my state of grace back to long before I won my first Open: 'Very likely nobody will believe me, but I can assure you that Seve played his best golf between the ages of thirteen and seventeen. He was truly wonderful in this period. He never missed a single shot, and had an almost supernatural vision of the game. He always knew which club to select for the stroke he had to make. The shots Seve's magic hands played out of bunkers were unparalleled. He was the best at approach shots, because he used so much backspin to make the most of the second bounce. What's more, his putting was lethal. He had a perfect touch and an excellent grasp of the break and borrow. His golden age began long before his first Grand Slam. Over the years he gained in character, experience and determination but he was in full control of his technique from childhood.'

Bobby Jones, Ben Hogan, Tom Watson and Nick Faldo, among others, played some ten seasons at the highest level. In the whole history of the sport, you can say that only Jack Nicklaus, Arnold

Palmer, Gary Player and perhaps Lee Trevino have been at the top for more than ten years.

It is hard for people to imagine the sacrifices that players must make to reach the top and stay there. You often hear people say, 'These young men just appear, hit balls, play, collect their cheques, then go back to their many homes across the globe and act like celebrities.' Described like that, a golfer's life seems a bed of roses, but the truth is something else.

When you know the demands and the efforts you have to make to be at the very top you can really appreciate the unique qualities of the best. In this sense, I think Jack Nicklaus is particularly impressive. What I most admire about Jack is not only the way he was able to play at the highest level for so long but how he took so much satisfaction from his game. His professionalism, his judgement and self-control on the course were admirable, as were his relaxed, friendly attitude towards his opponents and the way he always managed his time to attend to his golf, his many business interests and his family. He is simply extraordinary.

Nicklaus's understanding of the sport and, as journalists like to say, his ability to 'read' each game is unrivalled, as far as I'm concerned. I'm not at all surprised he is a touchstone for all the players who have come after him. I'm sure that if a survey were carried out today to find out who is the best golfer of all time Jack would come out top by a long way. Of course, many might opt for Sam Snead. Snead was active for fifty years and died at the age of ninety in 2002. He was a terrific athlete, with undoubtedly the best swing ever to have been seen on a golf course. But however great Sam Snead and Jack Nicklaus are, Gary Player must also come extremely high in my list of terrific players.

If you consider the difficulties he always had to confront, I feel Gary performed even greater feats than Jack. As a South African, Gary had to travel very long distances to pursue his career, and air travel in the period when Gary was at his best was much more problematic than it is now. Nicklaus, on the other hand, crossed the oceans at most twice a year. Once for the Open Championship and again, if he felt like it, for the Australian Open. Although there were Match Play Championships and Ryder Cups too, the fact is he almost always played in his own country. So in this light, Gary Player's successes were as amazing as Jack Nicklaus's. It's true the latter won double the number of major tournaments, exactly eighteen against nine, but in Gary's case you must bear in mind that he had to work much harder to achieve greatness and then maintain his position at the top.

Non-American players, including Player, Nick Faldo and myself, have always been forced to spend a lot of time away from home. This required an extra effort that is easy to forget. As Baldomero says, for me 'America meant far away, words that carry negative rather than positive connotations'. I have always felt very rooted in my land and attached to my family.

Equally, and I know I'm not alone in this, I deeply admire and respect Arnold Palmer. He played a very important role in making golf a popular sport. He not only increased interest in the professional game, where he was a key figure in establishing the prestige of the Open Championship during the sixties, but he also had a huge influence on amateur golf. Arnold, with whom I unfortunately played less than with Jack or Gary, is a very charismatic, thrilling player who could excite spectators even when he wasn't playing well. And he had a terrific marketing campaign behind him: I don't think there's ever been – even now with Greg Norman and Tiger Woods – a player who had better commercial backing for his career.

After Jack Nicklaus, the best player on the modern Tour is Tiger Woods. His game is very accomplished and he knows how to play every stroke in the book. When he won four majors in a row, between the US Open in 2000 and the Masters in 2001, he was possibly the best golfer in the world in every facet of the game. What most impressed me about his game during that period was the way he putted: he didn't miss a single putt. He is as thrilling to watch as Nicklaus, although Woods drives the ball very long, achieving distances that outstrip any other player.

However, Tiger lacks one virtue that Nicklaus had. Jack was a player who never defeated himself. In this respect, Jack is Tiger's superior. Take the 2001 Dubai Open when Tiger had problems with his drive, hit the ball into the water and lost to Thomas Björn. I never saw Jack do anything like that in twenty-five years. It's an aspect of his game that Woods must improve, though I do think that Tiger will better Nicklaus's record.

'Tiger plays very aggressively because he always goes for the flag,' José María Olazábal commented to me one day.

'Yes,' I replied. 'When I bought my BMW I was also very sure of myself. Until I had an accident . . .'

Another great tribal warrior is Nick Faldo – the only European player who has won more major tournaments than me. Some people say the mistakes others made helped him win some of those crucial tournaments. For example, in the 1987 Open, played at Muirfield, Paul Azinger finished with two bogeys; in the 1989 Augusta Masters, Scott Hoch missed the simplest of putts at the playoff hole; the next year, also in the playoff, Raymond Floyd hit the ball into the water, and in the 1996 Masters Greg Norman's play went to pieces. But obviously you have to go in search of good luck and you have to be there to take advantage of the opportunities, and Nick Faldo was there. Even so, I can't help but envy him. How I wish someone had given me a similar present at a crucial moment in a Grand Slam tournament!

Nick and I have been more colleagues than rivals, as we were once members of the same Ryder Cup team. The victory we won for Europe at Oak Hill in 1995 made us very close. A few weeks after this magnificent triumph, Nick wrote me a very affectionate, warm letter, in which he stated I'd been a great inspiration to him and to European golf. Nick is a friend whom I respect highly, both as a player and a person.

Now that I've mentioned friendship I must say that I've come to know the tribe very well over the years: caddies, players and organisers. I cannot say I've made many very close friends. Although there's a lot of camaraderie on the European Tour, much more than on the American Tour, it's difficult to befriend someone with whom you share the ambition of being the best in the world. This doesn't mean you can't have a polite, pleasant relationship with all your opponents, because, as the saying goes, politeness isn't a source of weakness. I include my main rivals in this category, including Tom Watson, Greg Norman and Bernhard Langer, for example.

In my contests with Watson, he always showed himself to be a tenacious competitor, with enormous self-confidence; his main virtue was his ability to repeat his wonderful swing and, at his peak, to be the best putter around. A powerful combination, that gave him very good results. Greg, for his part, is a player who, despite being hugely talented, has won just two major tournaments when he might have won several more. He has lost playoffs in the four major tournaments, which has led more than one person to comment that he's better at the business of golf than at the game itself. He's a great character. As for Bernhard, I suppose everybody will agree he is a true gentleman on and off the course. He's always known how to get the best out of his game. He's demonstrated his mental strength by overcoming the yips that prevented him from putting well. He is very religious and a good person.

As you can imagine, the experience I have accrued also means I can observe and express an opinion on the qualities of other warriors in the tribe who are playing now. I think that José María Olazábal is a great competitor. Apart from being an exceptional person and an excellent colleague in the Ryder Cup team, Olazábal works fantastically hard and is among the best players in the world with long and medium distance irons. He has more than enough talent to add more Grand Slam tournaments to the two Masters he has already won.

Another interesting player, Ernie Els, has one of the most fluent swings in the world and an excellent rhythm, although he lacks aggression and mental stamina. For his part, Sergio García possesses huge natural talent, enormous skill and has an innate instinct when it comes to playing golf. He and Tiger are the most interesting players to watch, alongside Adam Scott and Henrik Stenson.

There's another player who deserves a special mention and people often ask me about him, especially after he won his seventh European Order of Merit in 1999, thus beating the record I'd held until then. I'm obviously referring to Colin Montgomerie who is, in my opinion, one of the finest players currently in action despite the fact that he has yet to win a major tournament. As number one in Europe for seven consecutive years Monty has demonstrated that his play is far superior to that of other players who are judged to be great. His problem is that if he doesn't win one of the Grand Slam tournaments he will never be seen as belonging to the league of great champions, which is where I would place him.

I rate Monty's career much more highly than Paul Lawrie's, for example. After winning the 1999 Open, played at Carnoustie, Lawrie has won just one tournament, the Dunhill Links in 2001. He appeared happier with this victory than any other player participating would have been. When a player wins one major tournament and doesn't go on to more, people usually think that his most outstanding victory is a stroke of luck. They said this of Orville Moody, who won the US Open just once, and even of Andy North – although his three Tour victories included two US Opens. Perhaps, when Lawrie won the Dunhill Links he thought he'd killed off the accusation that he'd won just one major out of pure luck. But his career is neither as attractive nor as distinguished as Montgomerie's. Nonetheless, Lawrie deserves all my respect as a player and person.

As regards Lee Westwood, Darren Clarke, Thomas Björn and Luke Donald, among others, let's just say that they are players with considerable talent. They could all win a Grand Slam tournament. Jeff Sluman, for example, won one and he doesn't play any better than they do. But as we know, in golf luck often wins out over logic. The best warriors in the tribe don't always win.

Chapter 20

Comanche Territory

Journalists, usually war correspondents, dub areas of conflict on the planet 'Comanche territory'. For a long time, the 'Comanche territory' in my particular world was the Royal Golf Club of Pedreña. As a child, it was the forbidden land where I could play only at night. Later on, it continued to be out of bounds, for the same basic reasons, although the conflicts took a different form. The truth is some of the people who have run the club may not have been able to stomach the fact a caddie became a world figure in the sport.

When I began to win major tournaments, few of the club directors bothered to congratulate me and, as far as I know, they never came to watch me play anywhere. I'm not suggesting they should have crossed the world to follow me, but not to make it to Madrid! A notable exception is José Ramón de la Sierra, who was Club President for years, and to be fair most ordinary members have always acted in a friendly, courteous manner to me.

In marked contrast, the people of Pedreña have always been behind me; we have always shared strong emotional bonds. When my brother Baldomero is asked what I'm like – because he is the oldest, he has always been very close to me; he knows me better than anybody else – he'll tell you: 'Seve's roots are his hallmark. He is one of those people who feels close to his place of birth and very attached to his family. This rootedness – to his land and to his family – has marked his character and career, they're what have helped him forge his legendary status in golfing history.'

Baldomero is quite right. At the beginning of my career my neighbours formed a supporters' club that followed me wherever it could. It was always there to welcome me when I returned from a great victory.

But while the people of my village always made me feel one of them that was never true where the club was concerned. When the Spanish Golf Federation organised a national tribute, even Princess Elena attended. Was anyone from the Pedreña club there? Of course not. Perhaps for them I will always be a caddie, moreover, a caddie with the *cheek* to build a nice house opposite the club. I suspect that these people couldn't accept that a kid who didn't have the money to go to the cinema, who'd started from nothing, was now triumphing on five continents.

My brother Baldomero used to have a regular foursome at Pedreña. When the game was over, they'd sit down for a while for a drink and a chat. One afternoon the conversation got round to Eduardo de la Riva, who had played Pedreña for years as an amateur. At the time I was thirteen or fourteen; Eduardo was quite a bit older. He was an excellent golfer; he would go on to win the Spanish championship outright, a victory he repeated no fewer than seven times.

'Eduardo could easily beat anyone the way he's playing,' Jaime Botín, Carmen's uncle said.

'Except for my little brother putting out there,' replied Baldomero, pointing at me.

'What do you mean?' he asked. 'You can't be serious.'

'Don't you worry, Don Jaime,' interjected Ramón Rozadilla Senior, 'this can soon be settled with a wager . . . Thirty thousand pesetas will decide who is the best!'

My brother accepted without a moment's hesitation.

Then a famous director of the Club who'd been listening in on the conversation and didn't want to be left out butted in. 'I bet on Eduardo,' he said. Later Eduardo's father joined in too. Logically enough, his money went on his son.

Once the bets had been laid, Baldomero came over and spoke to me: 'Seve, would you be prepared to play Eduardo?' I agreed, but he added, 'Yes, but you must beat him.'

'Of course I can beat him!' I replied totally confident. 'My only problem is I don't have any clubs.'

'Don't worry, you can use mine.'

I rushed off to get his clubs and put on the old spikes Casimiro had given me. Just as I was putting them on Rozadilla came in, looked at me very sternly and said by way of putting the pressure on me: 'A lot of money has been bet on this game.'

Although I had no idea of the amount of money at stake, it seemed a matter of life or death. Perhaps just as well, I only found out what I was playing for later. Thirty thousand pesetas was a lot of money in the seventies. As far as I was concerned, being allowed to play the Pedreña course in the afternoon was a big deal in itself. Normally I was only allowed to play before 11 a.m.

Eduardo and I set off at around 4 p.m. accompanied by our respective contingent of supporters. Eduardo's comprised his father, Jaime and others; mine my brother, Rozadilla and several caddies. I don't think I was in the least bothered by the money my people might lose, because I always went out to win. I played so decisively I was already five ahead after the 9th, having taken only 32 to Eduardo's 37. At the 10th – a 180 metre par 3 – I took a 3 iron and knocked the ball to two metres from the hole. Eduardo missed the green. As I had a practically unchallengeable lead, Jaime said, 'It's all over! We can go now. We've seen all we wanted to see. We have to accept the kid is better.'

That was the end of the game. They slapped me on the back, hugged me, and shouted gleefully as they led me the 400 metres from the tee at the 10th back to the clubhouse.

'Well, Don Jaime, you'll be inviting us to the Masters now,' quipped Baldomero.

'When your brother's playing the tournament,' he replied. Baldomero and Jaime got on very well together and they've played lots of golf together over the years. But my victory didn't go down too well with everyone. I think they were annoyed less by the fact that Eduardo lost than by the fact I had beaten him. Maybe they thought that as he was one of their kind he must be naturally superior to an uneducated boy who carried their clubs to earn some pocket money. Later, some resented the fact that I went on to win titles, trophies and renown. When I married the daughter of the most powerful banker in Spain, it was the last straw.

Today the old Comanche guard still dominates the club through its descendants, and in my opinion it is no better run today than it was then. My view is that the course badly needs improving, given that the club celebrated its seventy-fifth anniversary in 2005. I would say that over the past few years the course has been in the worst state that I have ever seen it. In fact it is so dreadful that by the end of my career I would go to Maeztegi, Bilbao, and Golf Santa Marina, Cantabria – both courses I had the pleasure of designing – for my practice sessions.

The basic point of conflict is that for me the people who run the club behave like a bunch of second-raters. My only hope for the future is that things will change over time. Because of financial problems the club experienced a few years ago, the old guard was forced to let new people in, liberal professionals and young entrepreneurs. These new members conduct themselves in what I believe is a much healthier, more transparent way.

I personally don't feel any spirit of revenge towards the people who run the club, even though I feel they have always acted resentfully towards me. I am being frank here, and it upsets me to say so, but in my view some of the people in charge are trying to preserve the club as it was forty years ago. The way we professionals were treated speaks for itself. We could not even practise with our own balls (an essential aspect of major competitive golf): we were forced to use the ones made available to members through the machine in the clubhouse. Eventually, I was forced to make it plain to them that I would never accept the discourtesy that had been shown to us in the past. Like the vast majority of the world, I live in the twenty-first century. It's time for a change and I can't understand how these people can be so out of touch with the contemporary world.

Nobody should think I say all this out of prejudice against the rich. This is not a case of 'haves' versus the 'have-nots'. I have always thought that wealth is a blessing and poverty a misfortune. Poverty brings sadness, hunger, sickness and ignorance. But many people think being rich is only about money. In fact someone who is well-educated, cultured, who has an aim in life and, above all, who respects other people and everything that surrounds him, is rich. There are material riches and spiritual riches. I believe spiritual riches are more important than the material kind. The latter aren't to be scorned, because they can further our well-being and happiness, but having money won't necessarily make you a better person.

I never played to make money. I played to enjoy myself, to be the best I could in a sport I feel passionately about. However, this passion for golf doesn't make me forget I am a human being. I live in a world where there are many people in need; I must help as far as I can. Life has been good to me; I want to be generous and supportive in return. I am very proud I have such a good relationship with the people of my village. Pedreña is much more than a golf club. Since the 1980s I have organised an annual tournament for children and I also help in many charitable activities, although I don't make a fuss about it. Success can soon be forgotten – it comes with a sell-by date – but not for people who are conscious of their roots. They will always leave a trace.

I'll give one example. A young man from Pedreña was paralysed in a motorbike accident. I felt for him – for his suffering and his family's – but so often you are powerless when things like this occur, because there's nothing you can do. As it happened this time was different. I saw a newspaper article about a special car for the handicapped. I asked my secretary Rosario to find out about these cars and how much they cost. Rosario is very efficient and we soon tracked them down. I ordered one and when it arrived I took it over to the young man's house. Neither he nor his mother could believe their eyes. They were so moved – I will never forget their faces. I thought that was an end to it, but after a while I discovered that the mother was bringing my mother milk every day. I went to see her and told her she didn't need to do this.

'I don't know how to thank you for what you did,' she said.

'Madam, neither you nor your son have any reason to thank me. I'm just happy that I was able to help you, though I wish it had been for some other reason.'

On another occasion, a lady asked me to visit her twelve-year-old son who had contracted apparently terminal leukaemia. Let's call him Martín, as we both want to safeguard his privacy. His dream was to meet his sporting hero, who happened to be me. Any illness must provoke compassion, but when it is a child it goes even deeper. Whenever I can help, I give whatever is necessary in each individual case to find a cure, but unfortunately it would be arrogant to think that you can always restore a person to good health.

We agreed on a time for our meeting and I prepared myself over the days beforehand as if I were going to play a tournament. I wondered why I was so stirred up by this case; it wasn't the first time I'd had to carry out a humanitarian mission and it won't be the last. Why did this one seem so special?

I was accustomed to using my intuition to help my game, so I tried to use the same approach as I prepared to meet the boy. I imagined myself talking to him and taking him a present. But I couldn't imagine his face. I think that deep within myself I didn't want to form a well-defined image of him, because it would make me grieve in advance.

Our meeting went well beyond anything I was expecting. Martín was small and his hair had fallen out because of his treatments. He was waiting for me in a big hospital bed, looking at me with huge blue eyes that seemed to come straight out of a poem. I remember feeling that Martín seemed so full of life. His gaze held a determination to see much more than he'd ever seen up to then. I felt that at any moment he might get out of bed and walk out of the hospital, but in fact, his illness was at an advanced stage and there was very little hope.

I immediately got on well with the young boy. He was very excited to have me next to him – he only knew me from television – and I felt somehow that our meeting had been preordained. This mutual sense of recognition, of having been waiting for each other, struck an immediate chord of sympathy between us. On that first visit we told each other about our lives. He told me about his family and city, and I told him some of my memories of childhood. When we met subsequently – I visited him several times – we talked about all kinds of things: golf, games, but never about his illness. The cancer seemed to be developing in a body that was refusing to pay it any attention, as if it was allowing the disease to progress until one day one or the other would become exhausted.

One morning when he was too tired to speak Martín asked me to talk him through one of my tournaments. I tried to describe every second for him, from the moment I stepped on the golf course to the prize-giving ceremony. It was no easy task. I took a long time over the task, exercising my memory and my storytelling ability to make the memories come alive so that Martín felt he was really experiencing them. I'm not sure why, but I chose to start with the Masters. My gifts as a storyteller are limited, because by nature and as a result of my profession I'm a silent person, but I was able to meet Martín's expectations. He smiled at me with those incredible eyes of his, while I described every move, the dialogue I had with myself as I was selecting a club, the restrained celebration at each hole and, of course, the great final victory. My story was so extensive and detailed I still tend to think someone was telling the story through me, that it wasn't my memory or imagination. After a couple of hours, Martín shut his eyes for a moment, but when I fell silent, thinking he was asleep, he pressed my hand and urged me to go on. When I finished, the boy opened his eyes and hugged and thanked me for taking him to that great tournament in Augusta.

In my life I have enjoyed many hugs from people I love, but Martín's hug was quite different and was re-energising for us both.

That was the first in a series of tournaments I visualised and narrated shot by shot so Martín could watch them mentally. I would come in, sit down next to him and he'd ask: 'Where are we going to play today, Seve?' After a time, the boy became an expert. Sometimes he would interrupted me to debate why I'd chosen a particular club or stroke; he almost seemed to be seeing what I could see, and his comments were always pertinent.

Finally one day I had to travel to play in a major Japanese tournament. I was afraid it might be the last time I would see him. Our goodbyes were brief and casual, like those of two friends who will see each other the next day. He assured me he would accompany me by watching me play – I had described a previous tournament I had played there to him. He even gave me advice on how to play various holes that I always found very demanding.

When I got back, much later than I'd hoped because of a second tournament and other commitments, I hesitated about going straight to the hospital. I spoke to his mother, who encouraged me to go and see Martín. From the tone of her voice, I thought there might be good news, and I found that very heartening. When I got there I discovered that Martín had been moved to another room, his fair hair had grown and become unruly, and he'd got a better colour in his cheeks. He reproached me for being away for so long but he was very pleased with the gifts I had brought: some caps with tournament logos and a miniature game of golf he could play in his bedroom. His mother told me happily that Martín had made a quick recovery; apparently it was for good. The boy had exhausted his enemy, and imagining himself walking along fairways in the near future had been one of the stimuli that had swung the contest in his favour.

Martín is now completely recovered. He is a young man who plays golf and has completed his studies to become a lawyer. He comes to watch me whenever I play in England and occasionally we have dinner together and talk of other times.

I don't think I can heal anyone. That wouldn't be the right conclusion to draw. But I'd like to underline the importance of visual imagination when you have to meet a challenge, even in the uphill struggle we sometimes have to sustain against illness. Seeing ourselves win and wanting passionately to win are, I believe, the first steps to victory.

In the same way that I feel secure with my brothers, I also feel loved and protected by the people of Pedreña. I have an everyday relationship with them. We say hello when we go into a bar and they invite me to have a coffee, or I invite them and, whenever I can, to play cards or billiards. But unfortunately the same cannot always be said of my relationships with the rest of my fellow country men.

The year 1985 was a very successful one in my sporting life – I won the Spanish Professional Championship, the World Match Play Championship and, as a team member, the Ryder Cup – but it proved dramatic in my personal life: we had to take my father to Houston to be operated on for cancer. One day that year I happened to bump into the then president of Pedreña in the club lavatories and, while he was washing his hands, he said to me:

'Congratulations, Severiano! I've just learned that the President [of Cantabria, Díez de Entresotos] is going to confer on you the Silver Medal of the Cantabrian government.'

'Look . . .' I paused, measuring my words carefully, 'tell the President from me he shouldn't plan to give me the Silver Medal . . .'

'Why not, Severiano?'

'It's quite simple . . . I've been given gold in several countries in the world and I won't accept silver in my own.'

'But Seve! How can you say that?'

'Just tell him I won't accept it. I'm sick of being politically correct.'

And in fact they didn't give me that or any other medal. Nor have I ever been given the Santander Trophy for the Local Sportsman of the Year. They didn't lack the opportunity: I was nominated several times, but always sharing the honour with other sportsmen. What's more, one of the jury members voting for Local Sportsman of the Year belonged to the Pedreña club.

I have the feeling that golf simply isn't highly rated in Cantabria. It hurts me and I don't understand why. One of the things I learned from my father is to rebel against unfair decisions, and, of course, this kind of rebuff or total lack of recognition happens everywhere. The grass isn't necessarily greener elsewhere. I remember that in the mid-eighties, when Barcelona was campaigning to stage the Olympic Games, Pascual Margall, the mayor at the time, asked me if I would promote Barcelona by wearing the 'Barcelona 92' cap. I was delighted to accept and wore it throughout the world for two years without being paid a cent. Then, when Barcelona won and held the best-organised Games of the twentieth century, as people said at the time, nobody gave me a word of thanks.

Barcelona got the Olympic Games because it presented an excellent case but it would not have done so without the political weight of the influential José Antonio Samaranch, who was then President of the International Olympic Committee and the much smaller, though disinterested support of others, among whom I modestly include myself. I don't know if anyone else ever received a note of thanks but as far as I was concerned I was Olympically ignored. I reckon that my contribution to supporting the candidacy of Barcelona 92 throughout the world merited an invitation at least to the inaugural ceremony. I was upset they didn't bother; they didn't even send me a note to say 'thank you very much, Seve'. My support for the Olympic ideal and my efforts to make golf an Olympic sport were no doubt why I was awarded with the Olympic Order in 1998.

The same situation obtains with the Spanish Federation of Golf, though this deserves another chapter. Here I simply wanted to mention some of the Comanches you always come across in life, particularly those who clearly believe the saying, 'A prophet is not without honour, save in his own country'. A saying that is not true in my case, because I certainly am among my own people. In the end, they are the only ones that matter to me.

Chapter 21

The European Arnold Palmer

In 1976, four weeks after playing the Open at Royal Birkdale, I won my first tournament on the European Tour, the Dutch Open. Only two years after that I had my first victory on the American Tour, at the Greater Greensboro Open. My winning sequence continued with my first Open in 1979 and first Masters in 1980. Yes, these were milestones in my own career but they were also important for golf in Spain and Europe.

I played golf because I liked doing so; because it was my ambition to win tournaments and become the best player in the world. When you begin in this spirit and don't know the bitter experience of defeat, you don't even think about the possibility of losing. You only think positively. Spelled out like this, and starting out from where I did, my ambitions must have come across as pure fantasy – especially to my fellow professionals. My Uncle Ramón Sota, Valentín Barrios and Ángel Gallardo, among others, always told me it was impossible to beat the Americans. Their technique was far superior to ours, they said; that's why they were so much better than us. For my part I felt I could beat anyone. When I won in America for the first time, I wasn't surprised. 'Well, it isn't so difficult, after all,' I said to myself.

Eithout wishing to seem arrogant, I think that victory was crucial for European golf, because my fellow players saw that the door to America had opened up for them. I'm sure players who had beaten me on the European Tour told themselves: 'Well, if Seve can do it, so can I.' And Europeans began to parade through the United States – first Bernhard Langer, Sandy Lyle, Nick Faldo and Ian Woosnam and, later on, José María Olazábal and Paul Lawrie.

I had become an inspiration to many golfers and perhaps that was what led the press to call me 'the European Arnold Palmer'. Of course, such a comparison is highly flattering to me. I could understand why I was being compared to Arnold: we both gave the impression that we could defeat our opponents and the course itself by subjecting it to our will; the passionate nature of our play attracted enthusiastic fans who enjoyed our unpredictable style. It goes without saying that this is also why we attracted sponsors and television cameras to our respective tours in the United States and Europe.

Nevertheless, given the international spread of my victories – more than seventy in sixteen different countries, something that very few have achieved – I identify much more closely with Gary Player. As I've already mentioned, I met Player in a Pro-Am at La Manga in 1972, where I was caddying. Sean Connery was playing there as an amateur, but it was Gary Player who really impressed me. *Manitas de Plata's* game was really striking, and then there was his attitude and the way he would fly out from South Africa to challenge Europeans and Americans in any part of the world. Gary Player was afraid of no one and that's why I identified with him 100 per cent.

But I am getting ahead of myself. Although I had tasted victory early in my career, I was desperate to win a Tour event in my home country. Two weeks after winning the Masters I fulfilled that personal ambition when I won the Madrid Open. It was really wonderful: my family – which had come to the capital to celebrate my victory at Augusta – and King Juan Carlos himself were there to watch me beat Manolo Piñero by three strokes. That season, when Sandy Lyle headed the Order of Merit for the second year running, I also won the Martini International and Dutch Open. The following season was very good from a sporting point of view too, although, like James Bond in the Cold War, I found myself embroiled in a conflict over appearance money which would see me excluded from the 1981 Ryder Cup. I was really upset by this at the time because I felt much more at ease playing in Europe than in the United States. Now that so many things have changed in my life I feel happier there.

My preference for playing in Europe was understandable from a cultural perspective. Moreover, my fans over here, particularly in the United Kingdom, were and still are very affectionate towards me. They've always been behind me. My brothers saw that straight away. Baldomero puts it this way:

'Seve could have done extremely well in America, but then perhaps Europe would have missed out on his leadership. Seve's style of play, the way he is, fitted Europe better than the United States. He was in his element in Europe – muddy courses, rain, cold and wind are what he's used to and they are the mark of high quality play. Most players can do reasonably well in good weather. The ability to play well when everything is against you is what distinguishes the great from the merely good. Seve always responded to a challenge: he was at his best facing great rivals in adverse conditions. He stayed in Europe and forged a reputation that will be difficult to rival – above all in the British Isles, where he managed to win people over through his game, character and passion. Seve was devoted to the general public and they were grateful. He gave the Tour a boost at a time when it was stagnating. He opened up frontiers, and players grew by his side, as did the game itself. Even the Ryder Cup became a major event and that's why European golf is now as powerful as American golf. But would it have been the same without Seve? However you answer this question, the fact is he opened up new perspectives in Europe. Fortunately, after Seve, European golf produced players as powerful as Faldo, Woosnam, Lyle, Langer, Olazábal, Montgomerie and others who, like Sergio García, will join the band of the chosen few.'

Although my game soon attracted many admirers among the European Tour's sponsors – like Joe Flanagan in Ireland, Len Owen in England, Lionel Prevost in France and Sven Tumba in Sweden, all of whom would become great allies – my attachment to playing in Europe didn't always guarantee plain sailing. 'Political conflicts', for want of a better description, significantly reduced my sporting commitments in 1981. By September I had played only three tournaments in Europe, of which I won the Scandinavian Enterprises Open.

After overcoming my dispute with the Tour's organisers, I played the European Open at Royal Liverpool. I paid for my lack of training when I let slip a four-stroke lead to lose to Graham Marsh on the last day. A week later I played well in the last round at Dalmahoy to end up one stroke off the playoff at the Players Championship. I returned to Spain to fulfil another personal objective, winning the Spanish Open for the first time, at El Prat near Barcelona.

Encouraged by this, I decided to tackle a few more hurdles. So, armed with Gary Player's fighting spirit, I went to Wentworth in England for the World Match Play. I was the last participant to be invited – Jack Nicklaus and Tom Watson had not accepted their invitations – which left a sour taste. Given that I was the only European player on active service who had won a Grand Slam and that the tournament was being played in Europe, I felt that, with all due respect to Tony Jacklin, I deserved better.

At that time I was of the opinion that the behaviour of IMG (International Management Group) – the organising body, which could invite whomever it wanted to – was strongly influenced by its close connections with the European Tour managers I had dared to challenge and by the fact that I had refused to join their portfolio of players. I was also fully aware that even after Nicklaus and Watson had decided not to play, IMG's prime candidate was Sandy Lyle who had just signed with them. Nonetheless, thanks to the persuasive gifts of my manager, Jorge Ceballos, IMG finally invited me and not Sandy Lyle. Their decision may have been influenced by the fact that if they'd decided to do without me, the general public might have seen my absence as an extension of my exclusion from the Ryder Cup team.

Naturally, these weren't the best possible conditions in which to play a difficult tournament. I wasn't surprised when I received a low seeding and I prepared myself to play all four days of the competition. It made the final outcome all the sweeter.

I began by beating my old rival Hale Irwin 6 and 4, and then went on to defeat the defending champion Greg Norman 8 and 6. After winning my semi-final against Bernhard Langer, who was number one in Europe that season, by 5 and 4, I defeated Ben Crenshaw in the final with a birdie on the last green. Carmen was there to see me play in this tournament, and that rounded off a terrific week.

And so autumn of 1981 arrived, although I still had a lot to play for that season. After playing two tournaments in Spain, in which I finished second and third, I travelled to the Australian PGA championship, which I won by three strokes. Then I flew to Japan for the Dunlop Phoenix, which I also won by three strokes, and on 31 December I landed in Sun City, South Africa, for the Million Dollar Challenge. Only five golfers were playing apart from myself: Jack Nicklaus, Lee Trevino, Johnny Miller and Gary Player, the organiser and our host. In the final I lost to Miller in an exciting playoff, but the company of Baldomero, who caddied for me on this occasion, and Gary Player's hospitality were priceless, unforgettable prizes.

Chapter 22

Trouble on and off the Course

After 1981, the 1982 season was a little disappointing. I managed just three victories in Europe – the Madrid and French Opens and the San Remo Masters – although I did retain the World Match Play title. The following season was to be much more fruitful. In 1983 I won the Masters and Westchester Classic in the United States, the Million Dollar Challenge in South Africa, and three titles in Europe.

That year I made a late but triumphant return to the links of Royal St George's, Sandwich, where I'd played so poorly in 1975. This time, the PGA Championship would treat me differently. I won the tournament, two strokes ahead of Ken Brown and three ahead of Ian Woosnam. This was quite an irony, as it turned out. For the first round I was drawn with Woosnam and Brian Waites. We were all on the green of the 6th, a par 3. I had left my ball about seven metres from the hole, and Brian was quite a lot nearer. Ian had managed a fantastic shot to leave himself only a metre away. When it was my turn to putt, I bent down to gauge the break. Off to the side of the hole I saw a glove marker. A Pro-Am had been played there the day before and I told myself, 'These blasted amateurs never pick up their markers!' As many of you know, amateurs usually mark their balls with a marker that comes with their gloves. I thought one of them must have left this one. I picked it up and threw it into the bunker. When I walked round to check my putt from the other side of the hole, I saw Woosnam looking at me rather taken aback.

'What's the matter, Ian?' I asked.

'You've just thrown my marker into the bunker,' he replied.

'Sorry, it was a mistake, I thought it must have been left by an amateur. You know they use these glove markers.'

'I know, but you threw my marker . . .'

We went to the bunker to look for his marker but we couldn't find it, so we put another one down where we thought his had been and carried on playing.

It seems incredible, but this kind of thing often happens in golf. A year earlier, for example, when I was playing the Pro-Am before the Spanish Open at the Club de Campo in Madrid, my team and I were seven under par after the 11th. At the 12th my amateur colleagues had a few problems and took their time playing – to such an extent that I forgot to hit my last putt. I suppose I must have played it in my head. I went straight to the tee at the 13th and drove off! It was only then that my partners told me I hadn't finished the 12th. Reasonably enough, I couldn't count that hole. This shows how hard it is to keep your concentration in golf and how much you can lose over a silly mistake. It wasn't the only time I was disqualified because of errors you would have to call stupid.

It happened to Padraig Harrington at the 2000 Benson & Hedges International – he was disqualified because he forgot to sign his card and it cost him the tournament. Something similar happened to me in 1983, at the Dunlop Masters. Although I didn't forget to sign my card I added up my score wrongly and, giving myself one fewer stroke than I'd really played. I was subsequently and rightly disqualified, but the judges didn't inform me of the fact until I'd finished playing the tournament on the Sunday. What's more, they waited until I handed in my fourth-round card in order to tell me.

Tony Gray, the umpire, came over and said: 'I've got bad news for you. You've been disqualified.'

'Why?' I asked taken aback.

'It happened on Thursday,' he replied, showing me the card with the mistake.

'So why didn't you tell me then?' I asked, even more taken aback.

'Because we've only just realised,' he said by way of an answer.

I can only wonder whether they didn't inform me of my disqualification when they checked the cards that same day because it suited them to have me playing the whole tournament. Of course, mistakes do happen. But regrettably there have been many such points of friction throughout my career and I ended up on the sidelines on more than one occasion.

Sooner or later these tensions were going to have an impact on my career, but for the moment all was going well. In 1984 I won the Open, the World Match Play title and the Sun City Million Dollar Challenge. The following year I won my fourth World Match Play title in five years, four stroke-play tournaments in Europe and the USF&G Classic in New Orleans.

Despite my conflicts with the Tour, I continued to strive all out to remain right at the top. During my period of grace I was in the top five of the European rankings every year except 1981 and 1982. In 1986 I regained the top spot, but my failure in the Masters that year undermined my confidence and damaged my game considerably. It's true I won six tournaments on the Tour that year, but I could and should have won several more.

My first victory was in the Dunhill British Masters, which was held in Woburn. But in between Augusta and Woburn I squandered a two-stroke lead over the last eighteen holes of the Cannes Open. I 'gifted' victory to John Bland, who beat me by four strokes. Nothing like this had ever happened to me before, and then I did it again in the Italian Open, to David Feherty, and in the Madrid and Spanish Opens, in both cases to Howard Clark. Clark is one of those players who are always very punctilious towards their opponents. I've played with him in the Ryder Cup team, and of the four occasions we were together, Europe won three times and on the other managed a draw to retain the Cup. Howard was a very good team-mate but as an adversary he was something else. For example, in the last round of the 1986 Madrid Open we teed off together, and at one of the early holes Howard's ball ended up in some surface water. He asked me if he could drop his ball without being penalised because in his view the water was there 'by accident'. As I wasn't of the same mind, I told him he couldn't take a drop. When he heard me say no, he got angry and started to stamp the ground so that the water appeared on the surface. Seeing the way he reacted and wanting to avoid a nasty scene, I suggested he called the umpire.

'I don't understand why you reckon I can't drop my ball,' he said angrily.

'My problem is that I can see you're getting very worked up,' I replied calmly.

The umpire found against him. I held a two-stroke lead, but this episode damaged my concentration so that, from the 12th onwards, Howard met my errors with his own successes and won the tournament. Three years later I won the same trophy by one stroke. The result was different, but not so Howard's character. At the end of the game he complained I'd been annoying him the whole day. According to him, I was looking at my putts when it was his turn to play. In fact, all I was doing was studying the break for my ball while he did the same. I hardly need to add that I stopped doing that as he positioned his ball. But Howard may be the kind of person who needs to blame someone else to excuse his own mistakes. He's the kind of player that can get under your skin and put you out of the game. At any rate, one must say he was a very competitive player.

After Woburn I won four of the next five tournaments I played, the Irish, French, Dutch and Monte Carlo Opens. A funny thing happened in Monte Carlo. I was in the hotel with Adolfo Morales, my lawyer at the time, and my brother Vicente, and I was messing around with my clubs in my bedroom. One of the two suggested I should hit a ball through the window into the garden in the Casino rotunda. The ball flew out of the window – and broke a window in the Casino. When my brother went down to retrieve the ball, not knowing what had happened, he faced five policemen. Vicente pacified them, explaining it had been an accident, and promising that it wouldn't ever happen again.

The tournament I didn't win – and of course it was the one I most wanted to win – was the Open, held in Turnberry that year. But I was never in contention. I had to shoot a final round of 64 just to finish joint sixth. Greg Norman won after playing incredibly well in a week of horrifically bad weather.

Some of the victories I did record that season were a source of additional personal satisfaction. For example, my victory at the Dutch Open, held in Noordwijk, coincided with the tenth anniversary of my first victory on the European Tour – in that same tournament. Just as I had the first time, I won by eight strokes, this time against Pepín Rivero. Apart from the sentimental value, this victory made me the first player to win a million pounds in career prize money on the

European Tour. I was also the first to go above a million dollars on the PGA Tour. It's worth remembering I needed ten seasons and thirty-six victories in Europe to earn that amount, and now it's common for a winner to carry off a cheque for a million dollars. But winning back first position in the European rankings was much more important for me that season than all the money I had won.

The next season was again a poor one. I won only the Suisse Open in Cannes – in a playoff against Ian Woosnam one week after I'd lost another against Larry Mize and Greg Norman in Augusta – and the Larios APG and the Spanish Professional Championship. The high point for me was being part of the European victory in the Ryder Cup.

I began to lose ground after that 1987 failure in Augusta. It put me off my game for the whole of that season. I couldn't get the reason I'd missed that putt in the playoff out of my mind. It took me a long time to recover my confidence. Despite my victory the week after in Cannes, I'd begun to miss my short putts, particularly the vital ones. Golf is a very psychological game, and when you do something really bad and it gets inside your head it's a struggle to get rid of it.

The mishit in the Masters cost me very dear, not so much in my overall game but because I lost that final punch, the sure touch that brings victory. It meant I didn't win every time I could have. But in the twenty-three tournaments in which I competed in 1987 I finished in the top ten six times – eleven times second or third – and I never once failed to make the cut. Moreover, I brought Europe four out of a possible five points when we won our historic victory in the Ryder Cup at Muirfield Village. All this showed me and everyone else that I wasn't ready to be played off the course. I would continue playing my best golf.

Chapter 23

The ETPD

Some people have claimed that I opted to play in Europe more than in the United States because I received appearance fees from the European Tour. This is not true. The basic reason was that I felt more at ease in Europe – it is the environment I am familiar with. My family and friends live here, and the general public, particularly in Britain, have always acted warmly towards me.

Tournament organisers pay appearance fees to guarantee the participation of players who attract spectators and mass media attention because of their talent and charisma. Obviously, in my case, the fees represented an extra financial incentive for me to stay in Europe, but if it had been about money, as my brother Baldomero always says, the American Tour 'offered me more sporting opportunities and rich pickings'. However, I've always put golf before money. Business acumen and marketing strategies could certainly have made me a multi-millionaire, but I never wanted that kind of double act. Those who argue I didn't know how to market myself have just got it wrong. I've always preferred to be a player who wins on the course. I'm sure that if I'd tried to combine sport with business it would have been bad for my career. In the end I've earned much more than I could ever have imagined and I am grateful for that, but this income is the result of work, sacrifice and my family's unwavering support.

I played for thirty years in Europe, and I always felt a sense of responsibility towards the fans, sponsors and promoters that was independent of any appearance fees. In those years I was what Tiger Woods is today. As the statistics show, I missed very few cuts in Europe, a mere handful in the 190 tournaments in which I participated in the fifteen years from 1976. It's a disaster for a sponsor if a player he's endorsed packs his bags after two rounds. That rarely happened in my case: in this period, I won forty-one tournaments and generally finished in the first five or ten places. If I say this now it is to make it quite clear that I was very aware of my contribution to the development of the European Tour when I had my differences with those who ran it.

The root of the controversy was the attempt by Kenneth Schofield, the Tour's executive director, to get rid of appearance fees. I reacted by refusing to play – and that cost me half a season and my place in the 1981 Ryder Cup team. My argument was that I had a right to money because I was number one and because I felt they should take into consideration the fact that I'd chosen to play in tournaments in Europe even though prizes were much smaller there than in America. Besides, it wasn't as if I had invented appearance money.

The first British professionals were paid to play from the moment the Open started in Scotland in 1860. And in modern times Tony Jacklin began to be paid after he won the Open in 1969. By the mid-1970s the PGA European Tournament Players' Division – born out of the amalgamation of the British Professional Golfers' Association and the original Continental Tour, and predecessor of the present European Tour – had already established two categories for European players in relation to the payment of appearance fees. One stipulated that members of the Tour had a right to payment if they'd won at least one of the three major tournaments at that time – the Open, the Masters and the US Open – or if they'd won the Order of Merit in the previous year. The other category comprised non-members, who could always receive appearance money.

When it dropped these categories, the new Tour management agreed its members could receive a maximum of $10,000 for expenses, while players from the USA or anywhere else could negotiate their own fees. By this time I was earning $25,000 per tournament and, as Tony Jacklin was on his way out, you could say I was the only European golfer who'd won a major tournament. I interpreted those decisions more as a personal attack on me than as a change of strategy by the Tour directors.

I felt that they had established a system that served Jacklin well while he played in Europe, and then kept altering it to give me exactly the opposite treatment. So before the new rules could fully come into effect I resigned as a member of the Tour, anticipating that, during the weeks when the Madrid and Italian Opens were being played, I wouldn't be given permission to play in Japan. I was very upset about not going to Madrid – because I'm Spanish and would have been defending my title – but the problem that had arisen was more important than that tournament. While the Tour tried to reduce everything to a question of money, I saw it as an issue of principle. In retrospect, I think both sides could have handled their differences more imaginatively and thus avoided a lot of unpleasantness.

To make my position crystal clear I sent a letter to friends and associates on 25 May,[1] which I copied to Ken Schofield and Deane Beman of the PGA Tour in the USA. I wrote this letter in order to

[1] This is the text of the letter:

Recent months have been difficult and turbulent. Lots of things have been said about me and I have yet to make any statement in my defence. I sincerely hope this letter serves to answer all your doubts and questions, and stop the need for any further speculation.

In almost six years of participation in the ETPD Tour, I have only once asked permission to play in one tournament that conflicted with the official calendar. Three years ago I was invited to play the Chunichi Crowns Tournament in Japan, that celebrates the Emperor's birthday. As twice winner of the Japanese Open and the only non-Asian winner of the Japanese Open I believe I cannot defer acceptance of their invitation any longer. I received 10,000 dollars to cover expenses as did other participants. I anticipated a fortnight's stay and communicated as much to the ETPD at the beginning of the year. The forthcoming response was that I needed their permission, although I wasn't a formal member of the ETPD, and my notification was purely a matter of politeness. Nevertheless, to avoid any possible wrangling, I sent in my request for permission to play. I have also been in contact with the Madrid and Italian Opens who have stated they won't oppose my trip to Japan.

After reading in the press that I was going to be fined and/or suspended if I decided to play in the Japanese tournaments, to avoid further problems, I made a third contact with the ETPD to explain my plans and respectfully ask them to grant my request for permission. As I received no reply, I sent a further statement saying '... I tender my temporary resignation as a member of the ETPD'. If the ETPD had opted to approve my request on my return to Europe, I would have signed my ETPD membership form and the whole matter would have been over and done with. But the ETPD not only did not answer my request, but additionally issued a communiqué that was frankly damaging to my profile as a sportsman and which the press re-printed under the following headline: 'Ballesteros, expelled from the membership of the ETPD and from the Ryder Cup list'. This was totally false. I wasn't even a member of the ETPD; and yet I had made every effort to abide by confused rules that they were changing by the day, in order not to upset the ETPD or tarnish its prestige. These efforts of mine came up against a series of new norms that were clearly directed against me. I was very disappointed.

express my frustration and annoyance at a situation that threatened to create a division that would be lasting and damaging for both sides. But nothing was done. Subsequent events aggravated the situation.

Come August, the only tournaments I had played in Europe were the Open in Sandwich and the Scandinavian and French Opens, which were allowed to pay me appearance money because we'd signed contracts the previous year before they changed the rules. It was a very dangerous situation for me, because my selection for the Ryder Cup team was under threat – a threat that was then carried out – and I had no exemptions to allow me to play on the American Tour. And I was

There are two quite distinct issues, although they've been confused. I think I have already responded to the first, namely about whether they would give me permission to travel to Japan. I will now respond to the second issue, the matter of financial guarantees on the ETPD circuit.

It is often said I have said that 'golf owes me half my life'. I dedicated my entire life to golf from the age of nine and thus missed out on my youth. I have no doubt my many successes are more than generous reward for this devotion, and I'd like to make it clear that that quote comes from a television interview on ITV: 'Do you think that golf owes you half a life?' was the question I was asked, to which I replied: 'I think that golf owes me something or perhaps we are at peace'.

My only quarrel with the ETPD norms on guarantees from sponsors is that they were changed without warning and seem to have been made expressly to exclude me. The previous specific norms were formulated in order to take in British golfers who'd been exceptionally successful. I would rather not think that the ETPD's attitude derives from the fact I am Spanish, because it is difficult to find any logical reasons to justify their attitude. I didn't invent match fees; they are an invention of the ETPD and the sponsors. As far as I am concerned, financial guarantees are not crucial; they are merely a sign of the sponsors' recognition of my successes and the added value I bring to their tournaments.

I have played in many ETPD tournaments for minimum expenses and little or no financial guarantees. However, I don't think it is right for the sponsors to pay large amounts to foreign players and then try to create a situation where ETPD professionals with equal or better credentials play only for their expenses.

There has been a lot of confusion in the last six months and many changes to ETPD rules that only impact on me. After each of my victories in the Grand Slam tournaments I always remained loyal to the European Tour. This hasn't always been the case with other ETPD players who have had a certain level of success.

After being the target of manoeuvres aimed at depicting me as disloyal and mercenary, and then being discriminated against by specific changes to ETPD rules and even excluded from the ETPD Order of Merit while other players were being incorporated who weren't even members, the least I can say is that I feel deeply hurt. The way some individuals have acted now makes me feel very unwelcome in a place I previously felt was like home.

At the present time I am not a member of any formal organisation on the circuit. In what remains of this year I intend to play in four to six European tournaments, in three tournaments on the American circuit and three to five tournaments in Japan, Australia and hardly delighted by the prospect of spending all my time flying between Spain and Japan. Given this gloomy panorama, I had to find a solution and repair the short circuit in my relationship with the ETPD whatever way I could. I re-joined the European Tour on 11 August. I had no choice. They had defeated me in this battle.

probably in South America or South Africa. Together with the tournaments I've already played this year this represents a packed programme. As I am not a member of any golf circuit and have won top-level tournaments on the five continents I think the best way I can serve the interests of golf and my own career objectives is to play on the international circuit. Consequently, I don't intend to become the member of any organisation in what remains of this season. I regret this because it excludes me from the Ryder Cup, but I can't see any alternative.

I would like to express my gratitude to the representatives of the media, fellow members and sponsors who have stood by me during this difficult period and who have not let themselves be influenced by distressing rumours and insinuations. Your support has been a real lifeline for me.

As far as I am concerned, the matter is now settled. I will be more than happy to respond to the press on any other issue but I will make no further comment on the issues I have detailed in this letter. It is now your responsibility to ensure that the true facts are aired. I feel no resentment towards the ETPD or the sponsors who have intervened; I really admire the efforts they are making to establish golf as a sport in Europe. At the same time as I believe that a real injustice has been committed, I think this has simply been the product of the growing pains inherent in such a development and in the creation of more sophisticated ETPD regulations. I sincerely hope that the outcome will be a set of useful regulations that will protect the best interests of all members, even those whose success deserves special consideration.

My recent level of play is a real incentive for me and I trust that with your help we will put this matter behind us so that the second half of 1981 brings us all progress and success. Yours sincerely, Severiano Ballesteros.

Chapter 24

Cruyff's Bread

Although I lost my battle with the European Tour and the issue was never satisfactorily resolved, I feel that my side finally won the *war*. In 1992, the Tour announced that it would penalise tournaments that paid appearance money, but at the same time it redefined the term. According to the new norms, a player could not earn anything by simply participating in a tournament, but if he did something special while participating – like giving a lecture, inaugurating a new wing of the clubhouse or holding a clinic – he could justifiably be paid a fee. Something similar had already been set in motion in the USA.

On the other hand, match fees *are* still being paid, although they are hidden under other names or concepts, and it reminds me of what Prince Salinas, the character played by Burt Lancaster, says in the film *The Leopard*: 'Something must change so everything stays the same.'

Those who manage the Tour know that it owes its establishment and development essentially to appearance money. If there were no appearance fees, the Americans would never have left their Tour. Years later, the guarantee of appearance money meant that the main figures in European golf were more predisposed to play on the European Tour than to chase after the succulent cheques and superior treatment offered in the United States. The introduction of appearance fees created a positive dynamic in Europe that made the Tour an attractive product for promoters and sponsors alike and at the same time a place that enabled less skilled players to earn a living. All this helped to promote golf as a sport.

One of the things that most annoyed me about the European Tour's behaviour in 1981 was its clearly damaging, discriminatory decision in relation to European golfers, who couldn't earn fees while non-

Europeans could. I think that the best players in Europe at the time – Langer, Lyle, Faldo, Woosnam and myself – were decisive for the Tour's development and we deserved all the fees we managed to negotiate from tournament organisers. Once we had contracted to take part in a tournament, we never tailored our degree of involvement to the fee agreed. The same cannot be said of all the players who came to Europe from the USA in those years. I won't give any names, but I knew some who only came for a holiday with their families. I don't mean they deliberately failed to make the cut, but they didn't lose any sleep if they did.

This kind of behaviour frustrates me. It is very unprofessional and bad for the sport, and it seemed to mock European golfers, for whom the doors to the American Tour were shut. When we *could* cross their doorstep we didn't expect the fees the Americans easily obtained here. I now know that appearance fees don't officially exist in the United States, but I also know there are many ways to define them and make them stick. Sometimes it's enough to go to a reception or a dinner, to give an exhibition round on a Monday, add your signature to the design of a course, or even agree sums of money in a contract with a sponsor, as Tiger Woods has done with Buick cars, one of the main sponsors of the American Tour.

I still don't understand the problem the European Tour has with appearance money. If a sponsor is prepared to pay €50,000, €100,000 or €150,000 or more to a player in order to use his name and image in advertising material for its tournament, I can see nothing wrong in that. It is not true that the money the sponsor has set aside for fees will be added to the prize money if fees are not paid. A player who says or thinks that is simply deceiving himself.

When the conflict arose in 1981 over appearance money, there was a lukewarm reaction from players and practically no support for my demands. The reason was obvious. Although up to that point fees were recognised in the ETPD regulations, I was the only one being paid any and so everyone else felt they weren't directly affected. Many thought it was a matter of greed, when in fact appearance money is like a royalty, a payment which recognises a leading player's rights in terms of image and presence in a particular framework, in this case a sporting one.

We must not forget that a high-level sportsman is a key element in the show business that sport has become, since he generates a valuable economic cycle that benefits the sport as well as the sponsoring institutions and companies. The working life of a sports figure is relatively short compared with those in other professions and an accident, injury or any other imponderable can deprive him of his usual source of income. When Johan Cruyff played for Barcelona, he said that he wanted to make the most of his talent and his reputation because, 'When my career finishes, I won't be able to go into a bakery and say, "I'm Cruyff, give me a loaf of bread."'

I now grasp that there was nothing personal in Ken Schofield's decision to ban appearance money for European players. He was no doubt trying to protect the integrity of the Tour, as he conceived it, without realising to what extent he was endangering its very survival and that of the Ryder Cup too. If I'd gone to the States at that time, I'm sure – and I don't say this arrogantly – the European Tour wouldn't be as important as it is now. And if I had stood by what I said in a moment of gloom – that I'd never return to the fold – nor would the Ryder Cup.

Ken Schofield inherited a promising legacy from John Jacobs, his predecessor, and he built on that to modernise the Tour. Since 1976, it has grown into a very profitable business. Nevertheless, the policy followed to create this growth almost cost us players our livelihood and almost destroyed the Tour itself.

In 1994 I played an exhibition match with Jack Nicklaus to launch the London Club, in Kent, a course he had designed. On the flight to Turnberry where the Open was being held Jack and I discussed the respective styles of management of the European and American Tours. We agreed that Deane Beman and Ken Schofield had done many good things alongside many others that I felt were mistaken. I remember that I went further than Jack: I made a few comments to the effect that I believed some of Schofield's decisions had had such a negative impact that he should perhaps be thinking of retirement.

One of the problems the Tour has – and that was made clear in the 2001 Arthur Andersen audit – is a lack of communication and slowness of response. I believe the chief obstacle was that Ken didn't listen to the people you might imagine he ought to be attentive to, namely the most experienced players on the Tour. It's true there have been many improvements, but they have almost all come late and as a result of conflict. During a tournament being played at Sunningdale, I told Schofield: 'Ken, we players need proper transport and the practice ranges should be improved.'

Both things were done, but amazingly slowly. Perhaps the reason for these delays is the Tour's incredible bureaucracy. There are too many people on the payroll: some aren't necessary and are not even qualified for what they are doing, and they are all on very high salaries. I have told Ken to his face: 'I don't think it's right your staff create so much expense and enjoy so many privileges.'

'Sure, I agree, but they can't play golf and earn the sums you earn,' was his meaningless reply. Ken was like that.

Of course people have a right to earn a living. But it's ridiculous to put an administrator and a tournament player on the same level. Such mistaken ideas generate expenses that could be avoided. Better control of the Tour's income and expenditure could have allowed for the creation, for example, of a pension fund for players, as exists on the American Tour.

You might imagine that we players are the 'owners' of the Tour, yet we aren't consulted about plans for the future, have no influence or power with the management and no economic interest, unless we are among the administration's favourites and have a secure job or a juicy contract to design a course or a Tour project.

The Tour's organisational structure has many weak points. One example is that although players are seen as individual agents free to do whatever they want, they are subject to the Tour's regulations, according to which they cannot play where or when they want to. The arbitrary behaviour of those at the top is based on this very contradiction.

But we players must also bear some responsibility for the deficiencies in the Tour's organisation and management policies. We are all represented in the organisation, through a system of committees, yet most of us pay little attention to what is said or decided at a meeting. As you can imagine, most golfers are only interested in playing and don't want to know about complaints or demands from other players relating to the conditions in which tournaments are played.

I think that players have enough on their plate just playing and training to keep at the top, and the Tour's present organisational structure doesn't favour the defence of their interests to the extent it should. That is why I believe there should be a person who closely follows what the Tour is doing and takes a constant interest in the players, someone like an ombudsman, a 'defender of the players', who can talk to them and the promoters, to everyone and ask 'How did it go this week? What do we have to do to improve this tournament? How would you solve that problem? What do you think about this?' – in a nutshell, somebody with up-to-date information about the real situation. None of this happens at the moment. There are neither questions nor answers. There is no communication.

In a discussion of the way the Tour functions you also have to take IMG into account. IMG is an organisation that not only promotes a number of tournaments, but, in my view, exercises an unhealthy degree of control over the way the European Tour itself operates. A highly significant example was the contract between the IMG and the Tour in relation to television rights. IMG, through TWI, its television arm, was one of the main independent producers and distributors in sports programming. This contract's existence guaranteed IMG's control of the sport.

It is my impression, although I can't be definite because I am no expert on the legal issues, that a contract of this one-sided nature cannot be legal. In any case it was, or is, (if it is still in place) a scandalous contract that many of us players denounced because none of us likes to feel controlled. Today, George O'Grady, who succeeded Ken Schofield in January 2005, sets out clear, concrete objectives he must realise, both for the good of the players and the Tour itself. I believe in George, because he is a person who likes dialogue; he is very professional and extremely familiar with the Tour. I am sure he is a good leader, and his ability to deal with people is beyond doubt. This became obvious just after he took up the post when he closed the file on the problem I had had with José María Zamora, a European Tour director and umpire, after our argument in Pedreña.

Chapter 25

The Stone in the Shoe

The conflict with the Tour over appearance money had immediate, damaging consequences for me. I must have felt like a stone in Ken Schofield's shoe and it seemed to me that the Tour's chief executive tried every means to stop me from playing. The first, most direct blow I received from Schofield was when I was left out of the 1981 Ryder Cup team. Although I hadn't officially qualified because I'd missed half the season, other doors existed for me that were shut without further ado. What made this decision even more frustrating was the failure to take into consideration the real situation in the Ryder Cup at the time – namely, the lack of commitment on the part of some players.

Nobody had better expressed this lack of team spirit at the previous Ryder Cup, in 1979, Mark James and Ken Brown. James has given his version of what happened in his book, *Into the Bear Pit*, and others have done so in other media. My view is that Mark and Ken could have done more preparation. I felt neither was as committed to the team as he could have been, particularly Mark. John Jacobs was a good captain and in every sense a gentleman, but they gave the impression that they couldn't have cared less.

As I've already said, as a result of the upset provoked by my conflict with the Tour I refused to play in Europe and went to the United States. While I was there one day in July, the telephone rang in my hotel bedroom. It was John Jacobs.

'Seve,' he said, 'I want you to come back to play in Europe. I can't guarantee you will get one of the two Ryder Cup places that are up for grabs – the organising committee can fill them as it sees fit – but I will be voting for you.'

I understood this to mean that if I made the effort, I'd have a place in the team. I was under the impression that two places were still nominated by the team captain, as the committee had agreed two years earlier. For this reason, I paid little heed to John's warning about the weight Schofield's opinion had on the committee, alongside those of Neil Coles and Bernhard Langer, who represented the players.

I returned to Europe and re-joined the Tour twelve days before the team that would play in Walton Heath was announced. The announcement was to be made in Fulford, on 23 August, after the Benson & Hedges International had finished. I felt calm enough because, despite all the conflict, I was still number one in the European and world rankings.

But things didn't follow the course I'd anticipated. Although I won the B&H, they considered the fact that I had missed a tournament in York reason enough not to vote for me. I felt I was being persecuted when I saw how influential Ken Schofield was, even though he didn't have a vote on the committee. I then saw that bad feeling towards me had weighed more in the final decision than the good of the team. The other candidates to fill the empty places included Tony Jacklin, Peter Oosterhuis and Mark James. Surprisingly, in spite of what had happened in 1979, James was given one of the places and Oosterhuis the other. Peter hadn't played on the European Tour that season; he belonged exclusively to the American Tour. The consequence was that the Americans gave the Europeans one of the biggest hidings in the Ryder Cup's history, and won by nine points.

It is regrettable that the Tour didn't put forward its best possible team. I felt so bad and so let down at the time that I decided never to play in the Ryder Cup team again, a pledge I unfortunately didn't hold to.

The incident of my exclusion from the Ryder Cup was the first in a series that made me feel I was being persecuted by Ken Schofield. In 1996 the Paris Trophée Lancôme was played at Saint-Nom-la-Bretèche. We found the course in such a bad state that Nick Faldo and I called a meeting with the players: we didn't want to introduce ourselves like that to a new sponsor interested in backing the European Tour. The meeting concluded that the situation was a result of bad management, and the majority of players thought Ken Schofield should resign. Everyone had the impression that the board was largely comprised of people who were on good terms with him and would have been reluctant to criticse or undermine his position of strength on the Tour. One of those people was Mark James, who turned out to be Schofield's staunchest supporter.

A few days after our meeting, Bernard Gallacher, future captain of the European Ryder Cup team, declared, according to the British press, that 'those clandestine meetings' damaged the Tour. Gallacher was always Ken's man, and it was no surprise that that meeting really annoyed Ken. We didn't speak for months, even though he was the Ryder Cup team captain. Later, José María Olazábal and I experienced a revealing moment at a dinner for Masters champions: Tim Finchem, the new executive director of the American Tour, was walking round the tables and talking to players, while Ken Schofield stayed at his table the whole night contemplating his glass of wine. Such different attitudes!

I believe that most European players considered, as we saw at the 1996 Lancôme meeting, that the European Tour was being managed very badly, or at least not as well as it should have been. However, many players didn't want to speak in public about this because they were afraid of reprisals. Ronan Rafferty is a case in point.

In 2000 Rafferty was one of those who signed a petition asking for the Tour's accounts to be audited, something that was done during the Volvo Masters. A few days before this request was made, Rafferty was relieved of his position on the committee. On more than one occasion players who have complained to the Tour management have felt that they curiously begin to get the worst playing times, incomprehensible problems with umpires, and suchlike.

When they told me, I knew what they were talking about, because I'd borne the brunt of Schofield's interventions since 1981. In 1994, during the third round of the Volvo Masters at Valderrama, Miguel Ángel Jiménez and I were fined by umpire John Paramor for slow play after Bernhard Langer had complained. Two months earlier, the umpires had also warned me about slow play and, though they didn't fine me on that occasion, they went after me in Valderrama thinking the Volvo Masters gave them a good opportunity to do so.

I may not be the quickest player in the world, but I'm certainly not the slowest. On that occasion I didn't deny I was playing slowly, but the officials refused to take into account the extenuating circumstances, as they normally would have done. The crowd of spectators following us were being very boisterous and the stewards could hardly control them. In the end I lost to Langer by one stroke, after leaving my ball behind a tree at the last hole. As I wasn't sure whether I could drop the ball, I consulted Paramor and he wasn't sure either. In cases when there is real doubt about dropping, ethics indicate that the officials must decide in the player's favour. Paramor ignored this and didn't allow me to drop my ball; thus any chance I had of winning disappeared.

Maybe I was worrying too much, but I even began to think my relationship with Ken Schofield coloured my relationship with the Tour officials, especially when it came to Madeira and Italy in 2003. In Madeira the chief umpire, José María Zamora, reprimanded me several times for slow play. He'd done this in other tournaments, but this time he was very aggressive. In the customary press conference, I explained what happened and said that some of the umpires were past it. To everybody's surprise, and although he was prohibited from making statements, Zamora intervened to contradict me. I was extremely annoyed and we had a big row in the car park. There was an enormous to-do. I was really disappointed that Ken Schofield, as the Tour's chief executive, didn't ring me. If he had then some of the bad feeling would not have persisted.

Months later I had more problems with officials. I felt they'd never let up. In the Italian Open, when I was playing in the first game on the morning of the second round, my opponent had to drop a ball at the 2nd because he'd put his shot in the water. He then lost his ball at the following hole. These incidents slowed us down, and umpire John Paramor appeared to be timing our game. Paramor, of course, was the same umpire I'd had a conflict with in the Volvo Masters two years before. With three holes to go he informed me he was giving me an official warning for slow play and that I would be in danger of incurring a penalty if the situation continued. I carried on with my game but when I put the ball on the tee at the 16th I realised I'd damaged it when I had put it in a bunker. I saw Paramor scrutinising me, watch in hand, but as I wasn't infringing any rule, I asked my caddie to give me another ball, placed it on the tee and drove off. As I was walking down the fairway to make my next shot, the umpire told me I'd just wasted more time and that he would be giving me a one-stroke penalty.

'Did you see what happened?' I asked angrily, because I knew he was gunning for me.

'Yes, I did, but it makes no difference,' came his reply.

When I'd completed the 18th hole and went to give my card in, John Paramor said: 'The card's not right. You didn't get four at the 17th, because you got a penalty stroke.'

'I can't accept that,' I replied, highly irritated. 'I will sign for no penalty,' I signed the card as it was and handed it to him: 'Here you are, you can disqualify me if you want.'

When he disqualified me there was a big fuss – because I was the star of the tournament at that time.

'The Tour is a Mafia and Kenneth Schofield a dictator!'

As you can imagine, my words fell like a bombshell and Schofield's relationship with the media meant they sided with him. Sam Torrance, whom I'd considered a friend, and Bernhard Langer also took Schofield's side. Given the way things were going, the Tour committee decided to meet me. We discussed the matter during the Volvo PGA. The committee listened to my version of the facts and surprisingly a Spanish member didn't make the slightest comment. That really upset me – theoretically he was a very close friend – but in the end I decided it was irrelevant.

When I was informed that the committee had fined me £5,000 I realised it had all been a farce. There was no reason to fine me given that, although I'd rejected the penalisation, I had accepted the fact I'd been disqualified, so I had already been punished for my so-called infringement. Because of this upset I didn't sleep at all that night and I was out of sorts psychologically for some time afterwards.

In September 2004, during the Spanish amateur championship for the over-35s, I bumped into Zamora at the Royal Club of Pedreña, where we had another very angry exchange, as a result of which he sent a complaint to the Tour. George O'Grady, who was already *de facto* executive director, replacing Kenneth Schofield, avoided sanctioning me as Zamora wanted and declared the matter over and done with.

In order to put an end to a heated situation, I made a public apology to the Tour for my bad behaviour. I apologised effusively to all and sundry. José María Zamora for his part admitted that none of this should have happened. 'Seve and I had our differences in Madeira, because we weren't in agreement in terms of the rules for that tournament but it was a mistake to have had that row,' he told the press. It's not for nothing that he's called 'the Fox'.

The way O'Grady intervened in this case was exactly what I'd always wanted from Schofield: decisive action that showed he could give leadership to the Tour; an open, efficient way of working to benefit players and Tour alike in a climate of harmony. If I criticised Schofield's management, I didn't do so to protect my own interests. I was always committed to the European Tour and wanted it to be the best and most powerful. It's true that Schofield did many important things for the Tour, but he also made mistakes that had negative repercussions on the way it functioned and developed. That's why I had reached the conclusion back in 1996 that it was time for him to make way for new people, as Deane Beman had done two years earlier by handing the leadership of the USPGA Tour to Tim Finchem.

It was never my intention that young players should turn everything upside down: that's hardly the point. Starting from the base that good tournaments with good prize money are organised to guarantee everyone's livelihood, I sincerely think the Tour in Schofield's hands could have become much stronger. He only had to listen to and act on advice given by players like Bernhard Langer, Sandy Lyle, Nick Faldo, Ian Woosnam, José Maria Olazábal and myself, winners of Grand Slam tournaments and architects of impressive Ryder Cup victories.

Among other measures, Schofield should have arranged for UK tournaments to be played between the end of May and beginning of September and I say this as someone with the greatest respect for Britain and its people, who have always given me wonderful support. But such a thing was impossible because the contract he'd signed with Sky wouldn't allow it. True enough, this contract represented a large amount of money that the Tour needed, but perhaps the need would have been less if Schofield's management of the Tour had taken tighter control of administrative expenses. It should have occurred to Schofield that many fans in continental Europe didn't have the opportunity to watch golf on satellite television. He didn't listen when some of us suggested that footage of golf tournaments should be given free to certain countries to promote the sport. Many of us were convinced that, if this or something similar were done, more people would watch the tournaments, which would benefit players, sponsors, the manufacturers of equipment and the sport itself.

The Tour grew and modernised itself considerably between 1976 and 2004. I don't doubt this. But it could and should have developed much further. In some aspects, even the progress it did make is linked to the American Tour. For example, the increase in prize money is directly related to the World Golf Championships, world tournaments that attract a lot of money. From time to time those are played outside the United States, but they are an American concept. Obviously this is only my opinion. But viewed retrospectively, and leaving aside any opinions on Ken Schofield's management as the Tour's chief executive – if I have anything personal to reproach him for, it is the way he treated me during a large part of his mandate.

If being a rebel means not accepting authoritarian decisions, then I'm certainly one. I have always defended the interests of the Tour and its players, facing up to problems and never hiding behind others. Consequently, I haven't always behaved like a politically correct person.

Chapter 26

The Unknown Charms of the Ryder Cup

My record of achievements – even with all the major titles I have won – wouldn't give a full perspective on my professional career if it didn't include the titles I won with the Ryder Cup team. In fact, I would go so far as to say that from 1979 the Ryder Cup and I grew together.

It's strange, but I knew nothing of the Ryder Cup until 1976 when I came second in the Open in Birkdale. I didn't see any particular reason why I should know about it: as a Spaniard I couldn't play in it. At the time, the competition was the preserve of the British.

The Ryder Cup has a long history. It was first contested officially in 1927 as a biennial competition between the Americans and the British. Although the British team included Irish players from 1973, American domination was overwhelming. Previously the British had won only in 1929, 1933 and 1957. Three victories in four decades! Even if you take into account that the competition wasn't played during the Second World War, the statistics were devastating.

My Ryder début was in 1979, when it was decided to create a more competitive team by bringing in players from continental Europe. I don't think I felt anything special in my first match, but I was clearly receptive to its hitherto unknown charms. If I hadn't seen its fantastic potential to help establish the Tour, I wouldn't have been so pained by my exclusion from the next contest.

My passionate enthusiasm for the Ryder Cup surfaced in 1985 and 1987 when the competition opened a new era in European golf. The Cup has given me many intense moments of both glory and despair since then, with the 1997 victory perhaps one of the most beautiful high points in my whole sporting life, because it was so important for me and for golf in Spain. But before reaching that stage lots of water had had to flow under the bridge, carrying with it the frustrations of the British.

In 1977, after the British–Irish team yet again lost its Ryder Cup encounter with the USA at Royal Lytham, Jack Nicklaus wrote a letter to the British PGA dotting the i's and crossing the t's. Jack said that although he still felt that the Ryder Cup was a great competition, and one he enjoyed playing, it ran the risk of dying through lack of interest if it was always so one-sided. Jack recalled that the British had managed just three victories since 1927 and a draw in 1969 – which served no purpose because the US retained the title. As a consequence of these wretched results Jack called for the team's strength to be boosted by players from continental Europe.

For the reasons aired by Jack, the idea that the team should include players from the Commonwealth had previously been discussed. Despite their evident weakness compared with the Americans, the British had always rejected the idea of incorporating continental players because they considered this went against the traditional spirit of Samuel Ryder's creation. Nonetheless, the defeat suffered in 1977 meant that the criteria maintained by the British could be defended no longer. The president of the British PGA and the descendants of Samuel Ryder accepted Jack Nicklaus's suggestion. In parallel, the fusion of the British and European Tours, which had been independent to that point, and the establishment of a single centre of operations in Wentworth favoured the changes. The British agreed to exclude golfers from South Africa, Australia and other Commonwealth countries and accepted the inclusion of golfers from continental Europe. From then on, the Ryder Cup would be a contest between the United States and Europe.

The first players from the continent to be summoned to play in the 1979 Ryder Cup were two Spaniards, Antonio Garrido and myself. How ironic! Thirty-five years earlier, in a Spain devastated by civil war and poverty, there had been no more than a couple of dozen professional golfers and they had so few resources that they had to petition the British PGA for clubs and balls to play with. In 1979 it was the turn of the British PGA and European Tour to call on players from that country to play in its most prestigious competition.

Our involvement wasn't unanimously welcomed in the UK. In the opening dinner at the Greenbrier, West Virginia, a manager of the European team ignored us and kept talking about the Anglo-Irish team. 'What the hell is this guy up to?' Antonio and I wondered, annoyed. It was obvious they were still in the same mindset and that the rest of the team thought we were a couple of upstarts. Although I didn't really know what the Ryder Cup was about, it made me think that we'd gone there to lose. Which is what happened.

I had won the Open two months before and was very unhappy with the idea of playing in a tournament where victory was a mirage. When I saw the attitude of the British players and reviewed the history of the Cup I realised the Americans were as used to winning as the British were to losing.

In 1979 Antonio Garrido and I played the four-ball games against Larry Nelson and Lanny Wadkins – each player uses his own ball throughout the game and the team of the player who cards the least shots wins the hole. We lost both matches because our adversaries played wonderfully well. We also lost one of our foursome matches, but we won the other, rescuing a point for Europe at the expense of Hubert Green and Fuzzy Zoeller, the Masters champion at the time. Nelson won his singles match against me.

The foursomes match in which we were victorious ended at the 16th, where there was an incident – the first of many I was to experience in the Ryder Cup. Garrido conceded a putt to Green, after hitting his ball with the back of his putter. Green, no doubt annoyed because he was losing, made a sarcastic comment that provoked a reaction on Antonio's part. Before things got out of hand I managed to put myself between them and impose peace.

The set-to between Antonio Garrido and Hubert Green gave me a clue to what was special about the Ryder Cup. There were no cash prizes, but those who participated felt that their honour as sportsmen was at stake; as representatives of a Tour, of countries or a continent, we were defending something more than a trophy. On this occasion, at that moment in the tournament, it was obvious the Americans were going to win, but winning that point was more important for Hubert Green than I had imagined at the time.

In the 1979 Ryder Cup I also discovered how much I enjoyed playing matchplay tournaments. I've always approached this form of the game with the philosophy that if I'm two in the lead I want to be

On and off the course…

(*Above*) Johan Cruyff and I swap sports

(*Below*) Me and Chema (José María Olazábal). Together we formed one of the greatest partnerships in golfing history

(*Above*) With my father at my second Masters victory, 1983

(*Below*) My son Javier caddying for me at my final Open, 2006

(*Above*) With my driver

(*Right*) An iconic photograph and my company logo. Birdying the 18th hole at St Andrews in 1984

(*Left*) On my way to another Open title, 1988

(*Below*) European Masters champions at Augusta: (*from left*) Sandy Lyle, Bernhard Langer, Ian Woosnam, José María Olazábal, me and Nick Faldo

(*Above*) Me and my dad

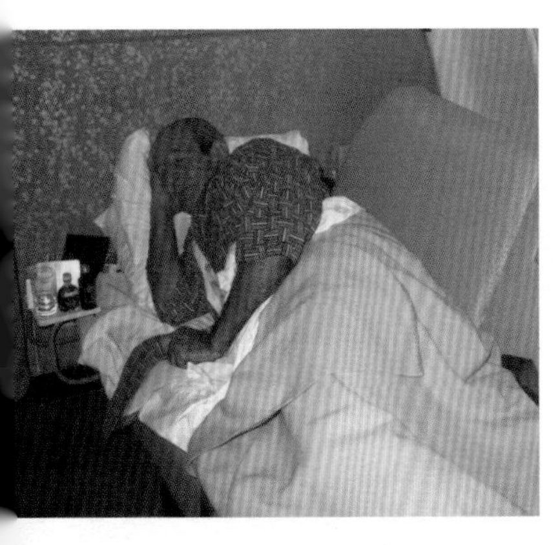

(*Above*) My father asleep on the aeroplane: 'This is the life, Seve, this is the life!'

(*Right*) My mother with her three grandchildren: (*from left*) Miguel, Javier and Carmen

With my collection of clubs

three ahead. I walk on to each tee as if I'm level. You can never weaken and say: 'I'm four ahead: even if I lose this one, I'll be three in front.' It's a big mistake to think like that. Always go out thinking you're all-square and must win the hole. When you don't think like that and you lose a hole, it's very likely you'll lose a lot more, almost without noticing.

One of the things that makes matchplay more interesting for me is that you don't tot up all the strokes but have to win one hole after another. It's not like a medal competition: you don't worry about pars, birdies or bogeys. When I realised this I knew that I'd learned more losing than winning in that 1979 Ryder Cup.

The subsequent changes in the competition have been astonishing. First of all, as regards spectators. In 1979 there were few fans on the course. Four years later, there was a big increase and the number has grown continually until enormous crowds now watch every tournament. I remember how in 1985 at the Belfry the passion with which the spectators followed each game was there for all to see. Since then, the emotional pitch has continued to rise and sometimes, as at Kiawah Island in 1991 and Brookline in 1999, it almost went beyond the bounds of what is sporting. But whatever your views on the behaviour of the crowds at each contest, you cannot deny that the Ryder Cup is now one of the world's major sporting events.

Chapter 27

The Return of the Prodigal Son

My unfair exclusion from the 1981 Ryder Cup team and the memories of the lack of commitment and competitive spirit shown by some team members at the Greenbrier were intolerable as far as I was concerned. I couldn't understand how a chief executive seemed to put his personal phobias before the common good, in this case the consolidation and prestige of the European Tour and its pre-eminent tournament.

I felt really upset and decided never to play the Ryder Cup again. As I've already said, I focused on my career as an individual in 1982. I began the following season in a similar vein. Early in 1983 I found out that Tony Jacklin had been appointed captain for the upcoming Ryder Cup at Palm Beach Gardens, Florida. Just after his appointment, Jacklin came to see me at the Belfry where I was playing in a tournament. I was eating my breakfast and he came straight to the point:

'Seve, I've just been appointed Ryder Cup captain; as you know, it's not an easy job and I need your help.' I think I made a negative gesture to cut him short. 'Seve,' he went on, 'I think you are indispensable . . .'

'Tony, I know where you're coming from, but stop right there. After the damage they've done to me I don't want to play ever again in the Ryder . . .'

'I know all about that, from my own experience, but you must have a rethink. If you keep this attitude up you'll only end up hurting yourself,' he said very seriously.

'All right, Tony, I promise I'll think it over.'

Which I did, but I still had my doubts, so when I returned home I consulted my brothers: Baldomero mainly, because Vicente was working as the professional at Zaragoza and Manuel at La Manga. Baldomero's advice was that I should have a change of heart and play in the Ryder Cup again. If I didn't it would damage not only my image but golf as a sport and, naturally, the Ryder Cup itself. I didn't want to do that.

'If there's anyone who can give this tournament a lift,' Baldomero declared confidently, 'that person is you. You should give a lead to the European team for the next few years.'

I rang Tony Jacklin a few days later and told him he could count on me. He was grateful and pleased, because he was convinced we could win now. He was right, although on that occasion we managed only to come very close. Tony paired me with Paul Way, who was making his début, and commented: 'Seve, you are the hero of our team, you've just won the Masters, you are the best and the one with most experience. There's nobody better than you to play with this new lad, right?'

I was surprised by Tony's decision but I went along with it, because he was our captain and I was prepared to play with whichever player he suggested. However, until then I'd been sure he would pair me with José María Cañizares, the other Spaniard in the team. I think if I'd said 'Tony, I don't want to play with Paul', he'd have paired me with somebody else, but it would have been a display of disrespect on my part. Anyway I thought it was fine to play with Way, as I would in the 1987 Ryder Cup at Muirfield Village, when I was paired with José María Olazábal, who was also making his début in the competition.

To begin with things didn't go too well. We lost the first foursome to Tom Kite and Calvin Peete, then recovered to win two and a half points from the next three games. Nick Faldo and Bernhard Langer also won three of their four games to give us a one-point lead at the end of the first day. We were tied level at the end of the second and for the first time in the history of the Ryder Cup we prepared to play the singles level-pegging with the United States.

I went out to play the first game on the Sunday against Fuzzy Zoeller. Tony came to see me when there were still seven holes to go and, as I held a three-hole lead, he went off sure my point was already in the bag. But Fuzzy won four holes on the trot and I had to win the 16th to tie level.

When Tony came back I was level and on my second shot, from the bunker of the 18th fairway. I looked a certain loser, as my drive had left me so badly placed it seemed I couldn't get out of the bunker even if I used a sand wedge. I looked at Jacklin at that exact instant and from his expression I imagined he must be thinking: 'That blasted Spaniard was all set to win and now we're going to lose his point.' He looked so angry and disappointed, I pledged to myself that I wouldn't fail him.

Even with the game going my way I would never normally have attempted the stroke I eventually made. The ball had lodged in an elevated position, making it easier to lift, but also more difficult to gauge the distance it had to carry. The wind was blowing from left to right and I had no choice but to aim out of the left side of the bunker and to really dig the ball out, making sure it shot up straight away to avoid the slope. In normal circumstances I'd have chosen a 5 iron, but as it was matchplay and the last hole I took a big risk and opted for a 3 wood. The ball flew some 225 metres to the edge of the green. From there I two-putted for a 5 to tie with Fuzzy.

Jack Nicklaus, captain of the American team, was rubbing his hands when he saw I was in the sand, but later he came over and said, 'Seve, that's the best stroke I've seen in my lifetime.'

What a compliment! I don't know whether Jack said that from his heart or because he was pleased because he'd won. I do know that, unlike my friend Gary Player, Jack Nicklaus isn't a man given to over-generous praise. If I had to choose one stroke from all the good shots I've made in my career, it would be this one without a doubt. I think it's superior to my chip at Birkdale in 1976 for many reasons, and better than my second stroke on the last round in the 1983 Masters, as well as the chip at the 18th in the 1988 Open.

As the afternoon proceeded, it became clearer that my half-point could prove vital, but at the end of the day it was a half-point lost. With two games to go the teams were level. But the United States won by one point and retained the Cup.

It's painful to lose, but losing by one point is dreadful. On the way to the closing ceremony my colleagues were downcast at the defeat. The truth is, we all felt frustrated because we'd had victory in our grasp and felt we'd deserved to win. It was similar to what you feel when you lose a playoff in a major tournament. At that moment I was walking with Nick Faldo and I turned round and told them: 'I don't know why you're all so sad and miserable; you ought to be thinking we almost won for the first time, and on their home ground at that. They aren't unbeatable and we'll win the next time round.'

I think that the team then realised the magnitude of what had happened. Tony Jacklin had performed magnificently as our captain. He managed to get us thinking we could win, even though we were playing in the United States. The Americans had lost only once, in Great Britain, since the Second World War. At the time, there was a lot of talk about Tony insisting his team flew by Concorde, that they wore cashmere sweaters – although they were not much help in Florida – and that all our kit was top quality. This helped to create a team image, but Jacklin's greatest achievement was to ensure all the players respected him as captain. He called on his firm, elegant manner and experience as the winner of two Grand Slam tournaments. Tony Jacklin knew what he was talking about and what he wanted. He was a born captain and knew how to lead. He made me feel at ease, confident and able to summon up all my golfing skills and he got the others to overcome difficult times and believe in their potential. In his début as Ryder Cup captain Tony Jacklin showed he was an inspired leader. As far as I was concerned it was because of him that my return to the Ryder Cup as a prodigal son was such a great spur to my game.

Chapter 28

An Historic Victory

Though the 1983 Ryder Cup was a defeat by the smallest of margins it marked a turning point in the dynamics of the European team in its struggle against the United States. Tony Jacklin's leadership as team captain became decisive and there was a radical change in attitude of the majority of players. Greater commitment to the tournament was a key element in helping to show that the US team was vulnerable and that we didn't have far to go to give them a fright and beat them.

In 1985 the Ryder Cup was played in Europe, at the Belfry. The outlook for that year was extremely promising. The European team, captained again by Jacklin, was led by Bernhard Langer, the current Masters champion, and Sandy Lyle, the reigning Open champion. On the eve of the match, our captain made us very aware of our potential.

'Lads, as you know, we've got a very good team this year and I think we have a great chance of winning.'

We started out as favourites and that can be counter-productive, but, as Tony Jacklin had said, we were a very good team and hungry for victory. After what had happened in 1981, Jacklin made sure the team was selected according to the rules, and that in 1985 the captain was responsible for choosing three members of the team. The idea that it was the committee that made the selection had to go – and it went. Jacklin selected Nick Faldo, Ken Brown and Pepín Rivero; the choice of Pepín caused a stir because it was at the expense of Christy O'Connor Jr.

Just as he paired Paul Way and Ian Woosnam, who were then dubbed 'the tiny tots' by the British press, Tony put me with Manolo Piñero. I should point out that for the first time in its history, the Ryder Cup European team included four Spaniards: Manolo Piñero, José María Cañizares, Pepín Rivero and myself.

At the end of the first day we were trailing by two points and we were all quite clear we had to change the rhythm of our game and play much better. We did just that. We progressed steadily through Saturday and by lunchtime were level. Sandy Lyle and Bernhard Langer played the last match of the morning against Curtis Strange and Craig Stadler. With two holes to go they were two behind, but at the 17th Sandy raised our hopes when he holed a twelve-metre putt right across the green for an eagle. Stadler missed a one-metre putt at the 18th: if he'd holed it, it would have tied the game and won it for them. But our luck held: he didn't, and we were tied at six points apiece at the end of the morning.

The Americans were agitated because they weren't used to being in this situation and they complained that the spectators had applauded Stadler's miss. This is common in the Ryder Cup, but I think the spectators weren't applauding that player's miss as such; they were cheering because things were going well for their team. The reaction of the Belfry crowds was actually quite understandable: they hadn't had anything to cheer about in the Ryder Cup since 1957, the year I was born.

We were told about Stadler's miss while having lunch and we realised at once that it was a huge psychological blow for the Americans, as well as a huge boost to our morale. What happened soon after raised our morale even further. The afternoon games finished 3–1 in our favour, and that gave the European team a 9–7 advantage to take into the singles.

The events of Sunday are etched in the memory of European golfing enthusiasts. I was up against Tom Kite, and he was three in front with five holes to go. But I won the 14th with a twelve-metre putt for a birdie; the 15th with a six-metre effort for another birdie; and I managed a third birdie at the 17th with a four-metre putt. By this stage Kite was in an evil temper. Unfortunately, I didn't make my putt at the 18th and so we ended tied. My missed putt was even shorter than the one Stadler had missed the day before.

With my half we only needed one more point for victory. Piñero had already beaten Wadkins, a real heavyweight; Paul Way had beaten Ray Floyd; Lyle, Jacobsen; and Langer, Sutton. Howard Clark had to play O'Meara while Sam Torrance was facing Andy North. Everybody was very tense.

Clark teed off at the 17th holding a one-stroke lead, but missed a putt of under two metres. Torrance, who was two behind at the 14th, managed to catch up and reach the 18th level. Perhaps Sam's recovery had got under North's skin, because while our colleague made a splendid drive, the American hit his ball into the lake. Sam's second shot was also very good. He left his ball six and a half metres from the pin, and holed it for a birdie, giving victory to the European team. It was an unforgettable moment. Spectators and players were jubilant – history had been made!

This was the starting point for a new era for the Ryder Cup and for European golf. It was at that instant, when I saw the euphoria of the spectators and my colleagues' display of emotion, that I understood the real meaning of the Ryder Cup. I can say quite candidly that I felt as if I'd won another Open title, although if possible I was even more excited and emotional. The July afternoon in St Andrews had made me ecstatic, but on that September afternoon at the Belfry we were all extremely happy and proud, for the victory we'd won was the result of everybody's effort and commitment. We won that Ryder Cup because we played better golf than the Americans, but also because the spectators cheered us on at every stage. It was fantastic.

The European team's victory wasn't only historic because it ended the unchallenged domination of the USA, but also because it resulted in a huge leap in quality in the Ryder Cup itself. Our victory meant that it was now the biggest event on the international calendar. Thanks to this change, the Ryder Cup entered the twenty-first century as a tournament that received tremendous media coverage and generated incalculable sporting and economic rewards.

After that great 1985 triumph, two years later we went to Muirfield Village in Columbus, Ohio, all set to become the first European team to beat the Americans on their home territory. And we did just that.

Not everyone will agree, but I think the 1987 Ryder Cup team was the best Europe has ever had. It's true that when I was captain in 1997 I said the team that year was the best ever and I wasn't lying, because it was in a way. Up to then, no European team had had to play outside its birthplace, Great Britain, and this gave the team a special additional quality. However, in a broader sense the 1987 team was the best. Unlike the 1979 team, which flew by scheduled flight to the slaughterhouse, the 1987 team flew by private Concorde to victory.

In support of such a claim, I would say, even though it may seem arrogant, that week saw the birth of the most brilliant partnership in Ryder Cup history, namely that of José María Olazábal and myself. I've often thought that what motivated us and pushed us into playing as well as we did in the Ryder Cup is the fact that Chema and I have so much in common. We were both born and grew up next to a golf course: I grew up next to the Pedreña club and Chema beside the course in Fuenterrabía. Apart from this and independently of our qualities as players, Chema and I are extremely fierce competitors. We are ambitious and have similar styles of play, as we both rely on a very strong short game. Consequently we each understand how the other approaches every shot. It just takes a single glance.

In 1987 all the stars in the team were on best form. Nick Faldo was the reigning Open champion and Sandy Lyle, Bernhard Langer, José María Olazábal, Ian Woosnam and I were playing our best golf; our other teammates were at the height of their powers too. As usually happens, it was the latter – Eamonn Darcy, Howard Clark, Sam Torrance and Gordon Brand Jr – who gained the vital points, when it seemed that all the effort we'd put in on the first two days had been for nothing.

Another factor that contributed to making us a great team and winning that first away victory was the terrific good feeling and atmosphere among and around us. Many UK fans came to cheer us on. When Jack Nicklaus saw the support we were receiving, he was forced to call for greater backing for his team on the Saturday morning. The organisers distributed a consignment of small American flags they had brought along. The Americans waved their flags, and it was the first time we'd seen them identify so strongly with their team. They applauded, shouted and generally spurred them on. As Jack said later, until then it had felt as if they were playing in Europe and not at Muirfield Village.

Despite all that, we beat them and did so because we had the best team. Although their team of twelve was almost always potentially superior to ours, there was barely any difference between the top six on each side. At the beginning of the 1980s you could have argued whether the Americans were or weren't superior to the Europeans, but in 1987 there was absolutely no doubt we were the best.

Despite this, many commentators thought the Americans would win because they were playing a course they all knew well. They said we would find it tricky whereas they'd have no problem: American golfers played at Muirfield Village every year, in the Memorial Tournament. Moreover 'the Jack factor' had to be taken into account: the Americans were captained by Jack Nicklaus, the best golfer of all time, and – if that weren't enough – the man who'd designed the course.

I personally think these factors that were *a priori* in the Americans' favour benefited us in the end, because they lifted our game to a higher level. Far from feeling ill at ease at Muirfield Village, the European team enjoyed the opportunity to play in the sort of perfect conditions that they would never find on a European course. And it is reasonable to conclude that these extraordinarily good conditions helped the team that was best equipped technically. Also – as had happened in 1983 at Palm Beach, although we had not been able to take advantage of the situation – Jack as captain overawed his players. I wouldn't have been surprised if on more than one occasion a player about to hit a long iron hadn't faltered when he saw Jack watching him.

These reflections aside, it was the best Ryder Cup encounter ever because of the quality of play and the emotions it stirred up from the very start. When we began off so spectacularly, the Americans showed signs of being jittery and worried. At the first hole of our fourball on the Friday against Tom Kite and Curtis Strange, Chema was on the green in two, although a long way from the pin, and I was 14 metres adrift and off the green. Chema's putt left his ball less than a metre from the cup. So that he wouldn't disturb my stroke I spoke to him in Spanish, asking him to hole it. Kite intervened: 'What was that you said?' he rasped, giving me a suspicious look.

I repeated what I'd said in English and Strange immediately objected.

'He can't finish now because he'd walk over my line,' he added solemnly, as if we were trying to set him a trap.

'Don't worry, mark it,' I said. 'I'll play anyway.'

Chema marked his and I holed my putt to win the hole.

The tension on the course was such you could have cut it with a knife. Consequently, it was predictable that we should have another incident later. It showed how edgy the Americans were and that they were looking for any excuse or slip on our part to steal a march on us. This time I was walking along the fairway at the 11th after holing a 13-

metre putt at the 10th to put us four ahead, when I heard Strange tell Kite that Olazábal was about to play out of turn. I realised they were going to let him get on with it so they could complain to the umpire. Luckily that didn't happen because I warned him in time and avoided any future wrangles. They won the hole, but we won the game by 2 and 1 to complete a European whitewash at the fourballs.

Later on, when the tournament was over, Jack Nicklaus explained the American team's defeat by saying: 'Our golfers haven't played so much together as the Europeans. The problem is down to the American system. As it's so difficult to win, our golfers aren't used to competing as if their lives depended on it. Instead of playing attacking golf, they ration the percentage of effort they put into each game. On the European Tour, on the other hand, there is "less competition", and so players have more opportunities to attack and that makes them better players; they finish tournaments on the offensive. They're simply more used to fighting than ours . . .'

I confronted Curtis Strange again in the singles. It was a charged, tense atmosphere. At the 10th, Strange hit his third stroke out of turn and I had to ask the umpires to warn him, although I didn't ask for the redress within my rights. After two more holes he'd reduced my lead from two holes to one. I looked at the scoreboard and realised I couldn't afford any loss of concentration: the way things were going my game was crucial. We had to forget any idea that the lead we'd built up over the first two days would give us a comfortable victory. That was pure wishful thinking.

I won the 14th to regain my lead of two, then I tied the 15th with a two-and-a-half metre putt for a birdie. I drove perfectly at the 16th to leave the ball two metres from the pin. By the time I got to the green I'd found out that Eamonn Darcy had made his par putt to beat Ben Crenshaw, which showed he had lots of spunk. Europe now had 13 points, so we needed just one more to draw and retain the Cup, and one and a half to win. I told myself yet again that my victory was crucial. I knew I couldn't let Curtis take two holes and that I had an opportunity to clinch the match. I putted . . . but my ball hovered on the rim of the cup.

At the 17th I learned that Langer and Nelson were level at the last hole. As I was two up with two holes to play, if Bernhard drew his game – something I knew might happen – I only had to beat Curtis for Europe to triumph. My second shot was an 8 iron which left the ball in the centre of the green, a good seven metres from the pin. Strange could only make a par and my putt left the ball half a metre from the hole. I had the game in the bag. In the meantime Langer had tied with Nelson in very strange circumstances. Each man conceded a one-metre putt for a draw. This agreement benefited us more than it did them, since it was in the Americans' interest to play to the last shot to win the point.

For my part, I holed my putt and immediately discovered that that shot had given us 14.5 points. My putt at the 18th to win the Open in 1984 is undoubtedly the happiest stroke I've hit in my whole career, but this shot to win the Ryder Cup on the Americans' home soil isn't far behind. The great pleasure I derived from winning the Ryder Cup again was complemented by my pleasure at defeating Strange, then considered by the Americans to be the best player in the world. A few moments after my ball went in the hole, Tony Jacklin, Nick Faldo and I hugged each other on the edge of the green. The three of us cried. We were so excited!

In the final game, Gordon Brand Jr and Hal Sutton drew and our victory was sealed with a score of 15 to 13. It was the first time the Americans had lost the Ryder Cup on home territory – in their backyard. After what had happened to me in the previous two Masters, winning four out of a possible five points was a great boost to my morale.

Chapter 29

Remember the Alamo!

The appointment of Tony Jacklin as captain was the key to the radical transformation of the European Ryder Cup team. Thanks to him the team became united and competitive; the results are there for all to see. We had shattered the United States' domination of the sport and spread disarray in American ranks, to the extent that many were quick to resort to a cheap show of patriotism. The next Ryder Cup match – the Belfry – was heralded almost as an avenging crusade.

Eight months after the victory at Muirfield Village we suffered a great loss; a misfortune that saddened all those connected to the European Ryder Cup team. In April 1988, Vivien Jacklin, Tony's wife, died in their house in Sotogrande on the Costa del Sol. All those who knew her were very fond of her and we knew how much she had supported Tony as captain and the important role she'd played in maintaining the team's high spirits. In spite of this desperate loss and the impact it had on him, Tony Jacklin agreed to continue as Ryder Cup captain for the last time, and re-stated his genuine commitment to the contest and the players.

One August Saturday in 1989, the day before the team was due to be announced, I was playing in Germany when Tony called me. It was to tell me that the three players he'd thought of selecting in his capacity as captain were Howard Clark, Bernhard Langer and Sandy Lyle, who was then playing in the United States. I was in agreement, but when I'd finished my round on the Sunday, Tony called me again to say Sandy had declined the invitation to join the team because he was very unhappy with his game and said he couldn't play the Ryder Cup. Tony understood Sandy's state of mind and had thought of Christy O'Connor Jr as an alternative, which I felt was a good choice.

Sandy Lyle never returned to the Ryder Cup team, which was a great loss.

We started the tournament badly, losing in the morning, but we recovered in the afternoon. Chema Olazábal and I crushed Watson and Mark O'Meara 6 and 5. I remember that I finished them off with one of my best runs in the Ryder Cup – an eagle at the 10th followed by three birdies. When we got together at the end of the day, we all reckoned our 4–0 victory in the afternoon's fourballs had been the best possible response to the provocative declaration made by Raymond Floyd, the new USA captain. In the opening ceremony, still bleeding from previous defeats, Floyd had said his team comprised 'the best twelve players in the world'. Jacklin reacted brilliantly and asked, 'Where does that leave Seve, thirteenth? What about Nick Faldo? And Bernhard Langer? And while we're about it, what about Greg Norman?'

The Americans persevered with their policy of contempt and provocation. Apparently they'd already forgotten Jack Nicklaus's words at Muirfield Village, when he said we were more used to fighting and winning. More than one person doubted this could be true, so someone consulted the statistics the Americans were so fond of: the European team had accrued a total of 195 victories between them; the Americans only 121.

In a climate the US team had been set on making ever more heated, Europe held on to its two-point lead throughout the Saturday. In the morning Chema and I played Curtis Strange and Tom Kite, who drove off at the 1st, turned to me and said: 'Remember the Alamo!'[1] I didn't really understand what he was saying, but guessed that perhaps he wanted to unsettle me. I thought he must be referring to the bellicose incident between the United States and Mexico. Right then I didn't understand why he said that to me. I thought perhaps he was wrongly

[1] The Mexican army besieged Texan rebels of United States origin entrenched in the fortress of the Alamo, San Antonio, Texas, from 23 February 1836 to 6 March 1836. North American settlers had been illegally colonising the Mexican territory of Texas for years. When the Mexican government abolished slavery, the American settlers rebelled to proclaim the Republic of Texas and keep their land and their slaves. The Alamo is an episode in this war that has been cleverly manipulated to promote American heroism and change a defeat into a victory – something that many Americans have finally come to believe is true. Perhaps Tom Kite was one of them. 'Remember the Alamo' was the war cry that Texans later used when taking part of Mexico from the Mexicans.

informed about the Alamo and had got his Mexicans mixed up with his Spaniards. Well, like the Mexicans, we beat them when I sank a two-metre putt for par at the last hole.

We had no difficulty beating Mark Calcavecchia and Ken Green in the fourballs, but the big victory for Europe that afternoon was Mark James and Howard Clark over Curtis Strange and Payne Stewart. Mark and James recovered from one down with three holes to play. Poor Curtis, the world's best player in the Americans' book, had drawn his first game and lost his next three at the final hole.

We began the last day with a lead of 9–7, which by the end of the first eight games had been extended to 14–10. We couldn't lose now. Nonetheless, we relaxed and allowed the Americans to draw level. My game with Paul Azinger is one to forget. It was full of incident and he even dropped the ball at the 18th, where he was in the lead, although I've never found out why. When I saw him doing that, I said to my caddie, Ian Wright: 'Ian, what the hell is this guy doing? He's playing a wood from those trees! I don't understand him!'

I walked across the fairway to find out what was happening, but Paul and the umpire, Andy McFee, were on the other side of the lake. To get to them I would have had to go back to the tee, which I couldn't do, and so he played his stroke. I turned round to take my second shot, only to find the water. Even though I had to take a drop I still hoped to leave the ball near the hole for a five to put pressure on Azinger. I took a 9 iron and made perfect contact, but over-hit. The ball was seven and a half metres past the pin; literally above the hole, on the crest of the second ridge on the green. This meant that not only did I have to putt down a very fast slope but that, rather than pressurising Azinger as intended, I had given him a break. This break enabled him to hit a terrific shot to within a metre of the pin.

Given where I was, Azinger thought I was more likely to finish with a six than a five. I studied my putt very hard. It was a very fast putt and I had to get the ball from the edge of the green to the left of the cup. I sent it in. It was one of the best putts I have ever made when I really needed to. It was spot on and gave him a fright.

'A great putt,' Paul Azinger said as he patted me on the back when I plucked the ball out.

But despite his scare he also sank his putt, tied the hole and won the game.

When José María Cañizares holed a one-metre putt at the 18th to beat Ken Green, everyone ran to congratulate him, including the captain. Both Tony and myself should have run off to encourage those still playing, but rather than do that we stayed and waited at the 18th. Only Olazábal showed himself able to maintain his game to the end and he finished the week with more points than anyone, four and a half of a possible five.

The 14–14 draw enabled us to hold on to the Cup, but we were disappointed because we'd had the chance to deliver a fresh blow to American morale and pride. But if they'd come intent on revenge for the defeat we had inflicted on them in their fortress at Muirfield Village – as we can deduce from Tom Kite's 'Remember the Alamo!' – they didn't come out of it very well. It was evident that among Raymond Floyd's 'twelve best players in the world', there was no John Wayne acting as Davy Crockett.[2]

The warlike spirit displayed by the Americans at the Belfry, epitomised by Tom Kite's absurd cry, exceeded the bounds of sporting ethics in 1991. What happened at Kiawah Island, South Carolina was deplorable. The press talked about 'The War on the Shore' because of the level of aggression, which was something I'd never experienced in any previous outing in the Ryder Cup.

David Stockton, the American team captain, and several of his players acted in a most regrettable fashion, as if they'd really been possessed by the spirit of the Alamo and winning was a matter of life or death. It was all so exaggerated and jingoistic that several players wore military caps and incited the crowds as if the Europeans were their enemies in the Gulf War.

You can understand that the Americans wanted to recover the trophy they had lost in 1983 and didn't want to suffer a second consecutive defeat at home but you can't understand or justify their going to such extremes in order to win. We had already sensed the climate they'd created at the 'welcoming' dinner.

'Ladies and gentlemen,' announced one speaker, 'we're going to show you footage of the most recent Ryder Cup contests.'

[2] In the film *The Alamo* (1960), John Wayne plays Davy Crockett, one of the heroes who defended the fortress and who according to legend died beating Mexicans with his gun when he ran out of bullets. According to historians, Davy Crockett surrendered and was executed by the Mexicans.

Then they showed the video and, although Europe had held the Cup since 1985, the only images on view were of American successes. Ken Schofield, then executive director of the European Tour, who was sitting next to me, couldn't restrain himself. 'How shameful!' he exclaimed. Immediately he got up and presented a formal complaint to one of the directors of the American Tour. This was the preface to a very hard week in a very hostile climate. If things didn't get even worse, it was down to the political skills shown by our new captain, Bernard Gallacher.

To begin with, as some of the facilities were still under construction we were forced to change in a trailer. But the crowds of mosquitoes that attacked us were small beer compared to the people we had to put up with. For me the strangest event of the whole four days occurred after the Saturday fourballs, when Steve Pate, who was due to play me in the singles, said he'd badly strained his wrist in an accident. As a result of this Pate and David Gilford, designated by Gallacher as our 'spare',[3] shared half a point. Considering how things were going it was hard not to think that something underhand was going on. And the Americans were right to be afraid of me, for I was playing at my best and finished this Ryder Cup with more points than any other player. In the end, I faced Wayne Levi rather than Pate, who had initially been designated by the Americans to oppose Gilford.

On the first day, the game that created most expectations was the foursome I played with José María Olazábal against Chip Beck and Paul Azinger, he of the mysterious drop at the Belfry. Before we began we had a meeting about the rules, at which it was made very clear you couldn't change the type of ball you were using in a game in order, for example, to take advantage of a following wind or to make up for a headwind. In a foursome a player can use a different brand or compression to that of his colleage, but he can't exchange balls with him in an attempt to exact some hypothetical advantage. This meant that if I was playing with a 100 compression ball at the even-numbered holes and Chema with a 90 compression on the odd-numbered holes, we always had to use the 100 ball on evens and the 90 on odd. Gallacher made a big point of this and we thought it perfectly normal, because it was a rule we were used to.

[3] This expression is used to describe a player who is left out of the singles on the Sunday when a player in the rival team is unable to compete.

When we reached the 7th, Chema heard Azinger and Beck arguing about which ball they were going to play, because they had the wind at their backs and wanted to keep the ball on the green. Unfortunately Chema gave me the news too late – we'd already played the 8th – and I didn't see Sam Torrance, one of Gallacher's aides, until we got to the 9th tee. We lost that hole and were three down when we met Gallacher and the umpires at the 10th tee. We told them what had happened. Beck said nothing, but Azinger denied he'd changed balls. The umpire's decision was that as we hadn't objected when the supposed infringement took place no penalties could be incurred for any previous hole. The moment he heard they couldn't be penalised, Azinger admitted he'd changed balls, but said he hadn't done it to play any dirty trick. Azinger emphasised he was no cheat.

'Nobody is saying you're playing dirty tricks, Paul,' I told him. 'We're not talking about dirty tricks, because dirty tricks and ignorance of the rules are two different things.'

I genuinely believe that Azinger and Beck really weren't familiar with the rules and that when they changed balls they did so not realising they were committing an infringement. However, it wasn't this mistake that upset José María and myself, but the fact that Azinger denied it up to the moment he was sure they wouldn't be penalised. He didn't act honestly when he denied what happened. That was a fact; and it was a fact that we were three down. So Chema and I pledged to beat them, changed balls or not.

'Let's play the back nine really well. Whatever they do, we're going to beat them.'

When we reached the 12th, I could tell the Americans were on edge because Azinger moved away from his ball looking at me when I coughed. I often cough and sneeze because I have allergies, but Azinger looked at me as if I'd done it on purpose. At the end of the game, he went round saying 'Seve is king of the cheats'.

Nothing could be further from the truth for I've always respected the rules – to the extent that I've penalised myself when I've committed an infringement and nobody has noticed. And others do this as well. I can give examples of penalties I imposed on myself at the 1984 Sun City Million Dollar Challenge and in the 1989 German Masters. I also remember that at one World Match Play final at Wentworth, at the very moment Nick Price hit his shot I choked on a piece of banana and coughed. As Price's ball went into a bunker, I immediately asked the umpire to allow him to play the shot again. He rejected my request, so I offered Price a half for that hole. In matchplay competitions being a sportsman is a necessary part of the game and it's not right for a player to do anything to distract his opponent when he's about to play the ball. You can be sporting, however, and still put pressure on your opponent. For example, at one hole in that same Ryder Cup game my chip left the ball a good metre from the hole, while Paul Azinger was much closer. I went over to him.

'Half a point?' I suggested innocently.

'How can you suggest such a thing?!' exclaimed Paul, bouncing back at me. 'Can't you see I'm much closer than you are?'

'Of course,' I retorted and to stress him more I added, 'but I'm putting first.'

If Azinger shouted out that I was king of the cheats maybe that's what he believed or maybe he was angry he'd lost a match he'd been winning. Perhaps he even wished to divert attention from the business of the ball-changing, that is, from the infringement he'd committed which José María and I had been fully within our rights to complain about.

Paul's attitude wasn't conditioned only by what they called 'the spirit of the Alamo' but also by the advice he was apparently given when he faced me at the Belfry in 1989. On that occasion, as I later discovered, Curtis Strange, still bleeding from the wounds he had sustained in losing to me, is supposed to have told him in so many words, 'Don't let that guy pull a fast one. Don't let him do anything to get his own way. Watch out and be ready for anything.' I think he must have said something like that because when I asked to change my damaged ball on the 2nd green, Azinger refused and called the umpire, who also said no. Azinger's suspicion made no sense, because if my ball was fine, why should I need to change it? Later on I saw clearly that his attitude was determined by his need as an opponent to make no concessions to me whatsoever.

He pursued the same line of behaviour in the 1991 Ryder Cup. Right up to the point when he changed balls with Beck, he came over to inspect my ball whenever it fell in the rough.

'What an awkward cuss!' I told Chema. 'He's always coming to check on my ball and he stands a metre off every time I play. Perhaps he's worried I'm going to kick him!'

'Don't worry, just forget him,' Chema replied, to calm me down.

I think Azinger's intention from the start was to play the hard man or hero, the Davy Crockett of the American team. His behaviour was so difficult I began to think their team comprised 'eleven fantastic guys and Paul Azinger'.

Despite this, later on we met up and talked over what happened and we're now good friends. Moreover, Paul Azinger showed he was very courageous and a man of great integrity when he had to fight to defeat cancer. Although I don't believe he behaved well at Kiawah, he is now a man I respect and admire.

Over time I have come to understand that the Americans commit infringements in matchplay not out of bad faith but because they don't know all the rules, but in my Sunday singles game Wayne Levi made a mistake that in fact made me think that they do know them. But before we got to that moment, there were a lot of interesting bridges to cross.

On Friday afternoon, José María and I again defeated Azinger and Beck by 2–1, with some masterly stroke-play from Chema. Stockton was in a rage because, seeing the pair were in a bad state after the morning game, he had put them down to go out second to avoid Chema and myself. But what he didn't know was that Gallacher, whom he seems to have ignored, had also put us down as the second pair, thus anticipating his manoeuvre.

By midday on Saturday we were three points behind, but in the afternoon the team got stuck in and won three and a half of a possible four points. Astonishingly, we came to the singles on Sunday level on 8 points. That last day my game with Wayne Levi had a bit of everything. The 2nd hole was perhaps the most insane. We were all square after the first, but I drove so badly off the tee I had to take a drop. I then over-hit to the left and found the bushes. A disaster. Levi, on the other hand, was in easy reach of the green, having played just two shots.

'Seve, that's the end of that,' Billy Foster my caddie remarked. 'I'd concede this hole. There's nothing doing here.'

'Hold on for a minute,' I replied. 'Let's see what he does with his third shot.'

The pin was at the back of the green and behind that water lay. Instead of taking care to pull up short, Levi went for the pin. The ball ran off the green and into the water. Instead of dropping the ball from where he'd entered the water, he did so from where he'd played his approach – only to end up in the water again. Levi was betrayed by his nerves and I won the hole.

'Funny things can happen . . .' I commented to Billy.

There was no way Levi could catch me, but at the 9th, he, like Azinger, Beck and the American players in general, showed yet again his total ignorance of the rules of matchplay. We were both on the edge of the green in two and he putted first, leaving the ball just over a metre from the pin.

'I'm going to hole it,' he said stepping forward to do just that.

'No, no,' I responded immediately. 'Mark your ball please; this is matchplay and you can't finish without my permission.'

Levi called the umpire and, as was to be expected he didn't authorise his request. I finally won the game by 3 and 2. Nick Faldo and David Feherty won the first two games too. It seemed everything was going in our favour. The bad news was that after me only Paul Broadhurst, who beat Mark O'Meara, won a point for us. It was a real blow for Europe when Chema lost his game against Azinger. If you included the half-point that David Gilford had won because of Pate's injury, the score was 14–13 in the Americans' favour, which meant that the competition would be decided by the last game, between Bernhard Langer and Hale Irwin.

Langer won the 15th with a two-and-a-half metre putt to reduce Irwin's lead to one. From then on very strange things started to happen. At the 16th, Irwin's third shot seemed to be heading right of the green, but his ball appeared in an excellent spot much nearer than I had thought it would be. He made a magnificent pitch from there for par, but Langer holed a two-metre putt to manage a half. Irwin maintained his lead; Bernhard had to win the last two holes and the game if Europe was to retain the Cup.

The pair reached the 18th hole level and drove off in an atmosphere of great tension. Langer's drive left the ball in the middle of the fairway, whereas Irwin's was so bad we all reckoned it would end up in the thick rough that runs down the side of the narrow fairways at Kiawah. However, as strangely as it had at the 16th, the ball appeared on the fairway. Irwin was not at all implicated in this, but it seemed to me he'd received unsporting, gratuitous help from a spectator. The behaviour of a sector of the American public had been deplorable throughout the week.

In spite of this assistance, the second shot from an Irwin who was wilting under the pressure was also mediocre and left the ball to the right of the green. For his part, Bernhard was on the green in two, but at the back rim, from where he had to play a very fast 13-metre putt. When he played the shot I thought he was going to leave it very close but it rolled a metre and a half past. The spectators crowded in and we all held our breath. Irwin had a six-metre putt for a par four, but he was too soft on the stroke and the ball rolled short, about half a metre from the pin. As things stood, he could have missed his next putt, even though it was very close. But Langer, to everybody's surprise, gave it to him.

Everyone knows what happened next. Bernhard made a perfect putt but it didn't go in. As was to be expected, the Americans went mad. They'd had to wait a long time for this victory – but they'd won it by making golf pay a high price as a sport.

Corey Pavin capped this lack of sporting behaviour when he turned up at the end wearing the military headgear of an officer in the battlefield. He wanted to make it very evident that they, the Americans, had won 'The War on the Shore'.

The euphoria of the American public and players alike drew a curtain over the aggravations, including Steve Pate's strange injury which meant he could avoid facing me and got half a point at the expense of David Gilford, the changes and mysterious movement of balls and so on, as well as the provocations from the spectators.

If anything good can be rescued from this Ryder Cup it is perhaps the fact that the Americans were able to recognise how well Bernhard Langer had acted. When our captain, Bernard Gallacher, pointed this out in the closing ceremony, they all followed our example and gave him a standing ovation. Though he'd missed that crucial putt, Bernhard Langer had given a masterful lesson in sporting behaviour and courage. That's why his name has remained linked for ever to the story of the 1991 Ryder Cup.

Chapter 30

The Rollercoaster

My victory at the 1988 Open marked the high point of my sporting career. From then on the ups and the downs, the former particularly represented by my Ryder Cup successes, followed each other as if I'd been riding a rollercoaster. That year, I won seven of the twenty-four tournaments I played in seven different countries – the same as in 1978 – and finished in the top ten in eight, which put me in first place in the European and world rankings.

In the next two years the downs rushed in, for I only won three times in 1989 and once in 1990. In the August of 1990, my first son was born twelve hours after I missed the chance to win the Open at the Belfry. We named him Baldomero Javier after my father, although we all call him Javier. His birth was the first of the three triumphs that blessed me as a father. The others would be Miguel and Carmen.

My previous successes kept me at the top as a golfer and in 1991 I won the Order of Merit for the sixth time, even though I only won two official Tour tournaments, the PGA Volvo Championship and the Dunhill British Masters, and, for a fifth time, the World Match Play. At the beginning of May I'd also won the Chunichi Crowns in Japan, my first international victory after fourteen barren months, and I would go on to win the World Match Play title for a fifth time. But problems, both physical and external, that would prevent me from maintaining the edge and concentration in my game worryingly recurred.

Shortly after my victory in Japan, I lost a playoff in the Spanish Open to Eduardo Romero after frittering away a lead of three in the last round. I couldn't understand why and was in a real rage, which meant I was hugely motivated for the PGA at Wentworth. I won, but not without a scare, a playoff and surliness towards me from some of the officials that made me feel I was the target of someone out for revenge.

I suffered the main attack when I was about to tee off at the 14th. An umpire approached Bernhard Langer and me.

'Gentlemen, you are playing so slowly you are two holes behind,' he said. 'You must play more quickly.'

'Where are the players behind us?' I asked from the middle of a thronging crowd. 'I can't see anyone behind us. Why the hurry if no one is coming behind us and we've only five holes to play?'

Nick Faldo and Colin Montgomerie were two holes in front. Monty finished 16 under par for the tournament, after two birdies in the final holes, which meant that after my bogey at the 16th we were level. I could see I faced an uphill struggle, and more so with the huge crowd milling around the edge of the fairway of the 17th and invading the course. None of the Tour officials seemed able to control the spectators. I couldn't concentrate on my next shot.

'I can understand why you're so excited. I am too!' I told the people crowding around.

It sounded like a joke, but I was in fact angry: no official was controlling the situation, and to cap it all, the scoreboards were malfunctioning. Predictably I bogeyed the 17th too. I needed a birdie at the 18th to force a playoff with Monty. The tension was so palpable that for a minute it seemed as if the crowds had stopped breathing. To make my birdie I had to hole a two-and-a-half-metre putt. I could have been overwhelmed by the situation: the satisfaction at getting it right would always be less than the damage to my morale if I missed. Later I thought the heavens would have crashed down upon me if I'd missed, because people would have started thinking my nerve was beginning to fail me at crucial moments. But at the time you don't think like that: the one thing in your mind is the line of your putt. Despite all the chaos, I holed my putt and it was a short-lived playoff. At the 1st I hit a magnificent second shot with a 5 iron to leave me a metre from the pin for a birdie and the tournament, and that's how I frustrated Monty's bid for the second victory of his career.

This triumph boosted my morale and my game was almost perfect the following week at Woburn, where the British Masters was held. On this occasion at least I was in no danger of being up against the ropes, although I let a seven-stroke lead dwindle to three.

The rollercoaster I was riding, partly because of my physical problems and the change in life that comes with marriage and children, peaked several times in 1992, the year of the Barcelona Olympic Games, when I won the Dubai Desert Classic, the Five Hundred Years Anniversary Team Cup in Argentina and the Balearic Islands Open.

My victory in the Dubai Desert Classic that February marked my fiftieth win on the European Tour and meant I had now won the most prize money of any player in golfing history. This kind of measure doesn't necessarily help to judge a player's quality or his achievements. But in my case it was significant, because I'd won a large part of that money in Europe, where prizes are much less handsome than in the United States.

My next victory was at the Balearic Islands Open in Majorca, which I won in a playoff against Jesper Parnevik. I seemed to be on a roll – I'd won two out of four tournaments and the season's prospects looked good. Nonetheless, it all suddenly went pear-shaped and my year ran out of steam. The downs on my rollercoaster were marked when I made the top ten in only one of the twenty tournaments I contested. I missed seven cuts, played a mediocre Masters which included a round of 82 and finally sank myself by coming last in the Johnnie Walker Championship held in Jamaica.

Having hit rock bottom, I thought things could only improve. But Murphy's law asserted itself and it wasn't to be. The descent of the rollercoaster was longer and steeper than I'd imagined possible. In 1993 I didn't win a single tournament on the European Tour for the first time in seventeen years. I fell to 42nd position in the European rankings, my worst position since turning professional.

My only consolation that season was the European Masters in Crans-sur-Sierre in Switzerland; I didn't win but at least my game showed promise, and it deserved the runner-up slot. I reached the last hole still in with a chance of winning. I had to get a birdie, but I drove very poorly, sending the ball into the thick rough in the woods to the right of the fairway. The shot looked so bad that, just in case it had gone out of bounds, I drove a second time. However, my first ball was in play: it had rebounded and dropped next to a cement wall separating the course from a swimming pool.

To begin with I thought I could only slice it, but I reflected for a moment and glimpsed another, albeit very risky solution. There was a space between the trees through which I could reach the green, although I'd have to lift the ball very quickly to miss an almost two-metre-high wall, and fly through the branches of the trees, over the swimming pool and the press centre. The problem was that if I didn't dig the ball out sharply, it would rebound and perhaps hit me, which would give me two penalty strokes and an injury. I hit the ball perfectly. I think it was one of the best recovery shots I've ever played.

As I'd had to use the wedge to dig the ball straight out, it fell 20 metres short of the pin. I had no alternative but to make my birdie, and I did. I used the wedge once more, and it worked again.

Regrettably it wasn't enough and Barry Lane beat me by one shot. Despite that, and my bad run of results, my finish in Crans gave me a high I'd never experienced before simply from coming second.

The absence of victories extended for more than two years until I won the Benson & Hedges International held at St Mellion in Cornwall in May 1994. When I reached the course, one of the Bond brothers (the course's owners) greeted me warmly, but in a tone of voice that revealed a degree of reticence over my potential. 'So delighted to see you again, Seve!' he said as he shook my hand, adding, 'I hope you make the cut!' I just smiled back at him.

It was obvious that few people were expecting me to recover my old form. Luckily for me, they were wrong. I held the lead for the first two rounds until I gave way to Gary Orr on the Sunday morning. It was very bunched at the top, but I maintained an excellent rhythm and was par for the first fifteen holes, made birdies at the 16th and 17th and another par at the final hole to give me a three-shot victory over runner-up Nick Faldo.

That was my first victory in twenty-six months, since the Balearic Islands Open. I'd played fifty tournaments in this disheartening period, had failed to make the cut sixteen times, and only finished in the top ten four times. I seemed a completely different player to the one who'd dominated the European Tour for twenty years.

At the end of that same month I came sixth in the PGA Volvo Championship, where a birdie on the last round gave me an accumulated record of 1,000 sub-par rounds over the 261 tournaments I had played to date on the European Tour. My ascent was reaffirmed at the beginning of October when I won an exciting victory in the German

Masters in Berlin. I defeated two tough and magnificent rivals in the playoffs, José María Olazábal and Ernie Els, then champions respectively of the Masters and the US Open.

I recall that in the game with Ernie when I was preparing for my second shot, my caddie began to calculate the distance; but when I saw where the ball had dropped I told him: 'No, don't bother counting, I know how far it is . . .' The reason was quite simple. My ball had dropped in exactly the same place as it had half an hour earlier during the fourth round. So I picked up my 6 iron again and left the ball even nearer than the first time.

A fortnight later I found myself playing Ernie Els again in the World Match Play. I played some good golf but it wasn't enough this time and he beat me 2 and 1. The irony was that I played only because IMG had been forced to invite me after John Daly withdrew. Perhaps the fuss the press kicked up when they found that my name wasn't on the list of those invited had had something to do with it.

Chapter 31

Future Promise

At the beginning of the 1990s my problems with those managing the European Tour, my new family situation and my back pains comprised a set of negative factors that ushered in the twilight of my golfing career. I could no longer dominate the European Tour and at the same time I started to feel pressure from a new generation of players and the accelerated changes golf was undergoing as a sport.

As I've said, I won two tournaments in 1994 – the Benson & Hedges International and the German Masters – with patches of good play. But the reality was I had more and more bad weeks and I'd never experienced that before. I won my last victories in the 1995 season, which I now see as my swansong.

Apart from the 'Oak Hill miracle' in the Ryder Cup, I enjoyed two wins that year – with Olazábal in the Tournoi Perrier in Paris, at Saint-Cloud, and in the Spanish Open at the Club de Campo in Madrid, where I beat Pepín Rivero and Nacho Garrido by two shots.

The Perrier was a team tournament, in which Chema and I, who many had seen as the best partnership in the world ever since the battle of Kiawah Island, finished on a total of 24 under par, giving us victory by three strokes.

I played the Spanish Open the next month, in May, and I genuinely don't know how I won. I went into the last round with a one-shot lead, but I felt so uncomfortable and out of sorts that I made three bogeys in a row. The ball seemed to have a will of its own. Luckily for me no one could take advantage and a birdie at the 14th put me level with the leaders. I suddenly seemed to have wings and at the next hole my sand wedge shot left the ball a metre and half from the pin for another birdie. I played practically the same shot at the 18th and that's how I managed to win the Open. It was the first time I'd won it in ten years and the third victory of my career.

I had caught a glimpse, confirmed with the passage of time, of the rise of a new generation of players; I also noticed that the technological changes in the game were having serious repercussions for more senior players. Nick Faldo, Sandy Lyle and I had begun to lose tournaments, something that places in greater relief the performances of Bernhard Langer, who still plays very well, and Ian Woosnam, who achieved a fantastic win in the 2001 World Match Play Championship.

I know that the sceptics thought my career as a tournament winner was over by this time. Even the best critics doubted I would ever again make the cut. However, up to 2005 I still thought I was capable of winning a major tournament – the Open or the Masters – if I could manage to overcome my physical problems and recover my game. Nonetheless, despite my enthusiasm, I recognised that my best period as a professional golfer had more of a past than a future; however, I could feel proud of my days of glory.

As far as I'm concerned, the changing of the guard began when José María Olazábal and Colin Montgomerie reached the Tour. These representatives of their generation have reached an outstanding level of play. I have no doubt that from among the younger players Sergio García will make it and, after him, probably Paul Casey and Luke Donald, together with other promising players, including some of the Swedes. The European Tour, now under George O'Grady's leadership, must do everything in its power to ensure that these young players commit themselves to Europe. If they play more in the United States, as has been happening with Olazábal, Jiménez, Parnevik and García, the European Tour will become weakened.

One of the problems golf is experiencing in the first decade of the new century is that all the attention is focused on Tiger Woods. He is of course an extraordinary player and the one who has contributed most to the new popularity of golf throughout the world. The danger for Europe lies in the fact that these virtues act as a magnet: when Tiger plays he attracts all the best golfers in the world to the American Tour because they want to defeat him, as is only natural.

From a European perspective, it is vital that the best golfers play more on the European Tour. Nonetheless, they can hardly be reproached for playing in the USA if that helps them establish their careers. When I opted to support the European Tour I did so realising that it was a personal gamble on European golf. Nobody can deny that by not going on the American Tour I gave up considerable winnings. If I had done so, I might have earned less in appearance money, but I would have more than made up for that with sponsorship deals. Just look at Greg Norman, a golfer who wouldn't be what he is now if he hadn't gone to live in the United States.

It's true that money isn't everything and I say that from experience, because even before Langer, Lyle and Faldo erupted on the scene, I had decided to stay and play in Europe. But it's equally true that until they appeared I felt as if the whole weight of responsibility for promoting the European Tour lay on my shoulders. It doesn't mean somebody else now has to feel that; it's about creating favourable conditions so that the European Tour is strong and resilient. In this sense, the new management would do well to avoid complacency and give strong support to the careers of budding stars. This is what Tim Finchem, the director of the American Tour, does, and American domination will go unchallenged in the future if the European Tour doesn't react. If it does so and supports young promising players, we could see a new Tiger Woods or even an Arnold Palmer emerge in Europe.

Chapter 32

The Load on My Back

The weight of responsibility I first felt on my back when I decided to play on the European Tour was quite pleasurable. It was a weight I could tolerate as a reminder of my hope that golf would become strong enough in Europe that players could earn a good living and not have to live or spend long periods in the United States. But the real burden for my back was a physical pain that became increasingly annoying and even crippling.

My physical problems were getting more and more unbearable, so between November 1993 and January 1994 I took myself and my family off to Scottsdale, Arizona, to undergo treatment to strengthen my muscles and hopefully put an end to my aches and pains. Carmen's grandmother died before my treatment ended and she and the children had to return to Spain, leaving me alone. I stayed because I was optimistic about the impact of the strengthening exercises on my muscles, but in the end my hopes were in vain.

My back problems go back to my adolescence. I've always enjoyed playing every kind of sport, and next to golf, my favourite sport was boxing. I admired Muhammad Ali and enjoyed watching Ken Norton, Joe Frazier, George Foreman, Lennox Lewis – in a word, all the greats. But my favourite was Ali. I was fourteen years old when I injured my back in a way that tortures me even now. When your adversary throws a punch at you, a blow to the body, you naturally step back to avoid being hit. That day, my friend threw a punch, stepped forward and quite accidentally stamped on my foot as I beat a quick retreat. I fell backwards and banged my lumbar region hard against the floor. I limped badly for a fortnight.

As a result of this accident, and because I had carried bags for members of the club when I was a kid, my back began to react badly until I developed an injury that turned into a chronic problem. When you are a child you don't realise that some of your excessive displays of strength to show you are 'a man' will cost you dear as an adult. I learned much later that it is better to spread a heavy burden over several journeys and that you should never carry big loads without bending your knees and keeping your back straight.

I never had the proper conditioning to be a professional golfer. The intensive training I underwent for the Spanish Under-25s Championship in 1974, also impacted badly on my back and it began to hurt a lot. In the hope that I'd play well and win the championship – which I did – I hit as many as 700 balls the day before the tournament, ignoring the cold and the damp of the Cantabrian spring. I seized up and even thought I wouldn't be able to play the following day. The pain was so bad that my back had to be injected with cortisone in the morning so I could participate. I played an excellent round but I've probably been paying for it the rest of my life.

I've spent many seasons suffering tremendous pain; it comes and goes but usually appears when I practise very hard, and that's why I've often been unable to train as I would have liked. When I decide to train hard, I always know that I run the risk of finishing up in pain and stiff for the next twenty-four hours. My injury doesn't allow me to remain seated for long periods, as when I'm flying, or to stand for a long time. It's one of the reasons I hate cocktail parties, where you have to stand still for hours on end talking to people.

After the Under-25s tournament, I began to suffer sharper, more frequent pain. In 1977 I visited Dr Carbajosa in Madrid to see if he could find a solution. After taking X-rays, he advised me to stop playing golf for a year and to sleep with a wooden board under my mattress. As it was unthinkable I should give up golf for a year, I went to see another specialist, who also had no answer. It's likely that if I'd followed Dr Carbajosa's advice I wouldn't have suffered so much – but I wouldn't have had the career I had either.

That same year when I was in training for my Masters, I tried seeing an osteopath to relieve the pain. Shortly afterwards I went to Houston, Texas, to see Dr Antonio Moure, the surgeon who'd treated Lee Trevino. Lee had had lots of back problems ever since he was struck by lightning when playing the Western Open in Chicago in 1975. Dr Moure examined me and recommended an operation to repair a damaged disc. However, I didn't have the operation because I was afraid it might damage me permanently.

Predictably, my back pain had a big impact on my participation in tournaments. For example, in 1978 I was forced to withdraw from the Dunlop Masters, and the following year I had to turn down the invitation to play in the American PGA Championship. Around this time I realised this new opponent of mine wasn't going to go away. I tried to get rid of it by using Gravity Gym apparatus I had set up at home, as I had managed to reduce the pain with workouts. Later on I tried acupuncture, desperate to find a solution.

Whether it was because of pressure on my discs or some other reason, the pain grew more and more unbearable. It was even bad enough to make me cry. Nevertheless, I resisted explaining or mentioning it in public. I remember that during the 1980 Masters, when I'd finished the Saturday with an eight-shot lead, a journalist asked me about my back during dinner and I told him: 'If you talk to me about my back, it reminds me that it hurts. So I'm not going to talk to you about my back. Sorry.'

I managed ten years at the top in golf putting up with constant pain. Only someone who has suffered or suffers pain of this kind can understand how difficult it is to make a good swing when you know that it will up the level of pain.

In 1995 I had to apply all my willpower and desire to win in order to play well in the World Match Play Championship and the Volvo Masters. The following year, after I was forced to withdraw from the PGA Championship, I had a back operation. I was in so much pain that I went to see a doctor in Tampa, Florida, and was operated on there. Very few people knew about this.

I thought the operation would cure me for good but it wasn't to be. In March of the following year I consulted a German homoeopathic doctor who had successfully treated José María Olazábal. Dr Hans-Wolfgang Müller had also treated Boris Becker, Linford Christie, Michael Owen and the football team of Bayern Munich, the city in which he had his clinic. After two weeks of treatment with homoeopathic products I abandoned his clinic and treatment because I could see no improvement. They say you have to have faith in them for the medication to work. I had none.

Ever since I have continued with my workouts, because my back has continued to hurt. As times passes, the physical problems worsen, because your body loses its suppleness, your bones stiffen up and new pains appear, something that only multiplies the symptoms of chronic pain when you're in my state.

When I work out I do notice some improvement, particularly if I swim backstroke. There are times when the pain and discomfort affect everything I do. I know I could have looked after my back much better when I was young, but it's also a fact that advances in sporting medicine are a relatively new phenomenon. Nowadays, the treatment of back trouble is reinforced by considerable therapeutic resources to prevent injury and by exercises designed to strengthen muscles in the lumbar region. I often think that, considering my natural talent as a golfer, if I turned professional now I'd play much better because I'd have the opportunity to get the right treatment at the right time.

It's stressful to coexist with permanent pain and very hard to get the better of it day in, day out. It's annoying to feel discomfort, because you can't enjoy anything to the full and relax. Knowing what I know now, it's likely I'd have played far fewer tournaments and travelled much less. From a very young age, my back has had to bear the brunt of the same sort of misfortunes we all have to bear, but all the same I am and have been a lucky person. I enjoy the gift of three children and have more time for other activities, like my business ventures, which give me great satisfaction.

Chapter 33

1993: A Horrible Year

My back pain struck hard in 1993. It affected my game and I didn't win a single title. For the first time in my career, I had a completely blank year. I wasn't able to help recover the Ryder Cup, something I found even more painful.

In July of that year, the day after Greg Norman won the Open, José María Olazábal and I played an exhibition game at Pedreña. We faced Tom Watson, who had been made captain of the American Ryder Cup team, and Payne Stewart, one of the team members. This game was very important for us, as there'd been a lot of press speculation, particularly in Britain, about whether Chema and I would be in the European team. The game was of so little significance to the club that not a single photo exists to record it. There are no photos of the Spanish Open played here in 1988 either. Given the circumstances, my inclusion depended on whether the captain, Bernard Gallacher, would select me. Chema wasn't definitely on the team either, because, although he was eighth in the rankings, he was only going to play two of the last few tournaments that offered Ryder Cup qualifying points. This meant he would also have to be a captain's pick. The biggest problem was that, for various reasons, neither of us had won a major tournament in sixteen months and, since the spring, each of us had only finished once in the top ten.

'If Gallacher chooses the two Spaniards and they play well,' Peter Allis, the BBC commentator argued, 'it will be obvious it was the right step and his decision will seem a stroke of genius. But if they don't play well for the team everyone will say "why did he choose them when we all knew they were playing badly?"'

Such comments didn't make Bernard's job any easier. Nonetheless, before the Open, he'd told me he was counting on me, unless I refused to play, as Lyle had done in 1989. After this conversation, Gallacher and I didn't mention the subject for several weeks. Chema's place in the team was in no doubt, because Gallacher was well aware of our record in the last three Ryder Cups: nine victories, two draws and one defeat in twelve games. It was difficult to ignore that.

As was now the tradition, the team list was finalised at the German Open at the end of August, and the only novelty was the inclusion of the Italian Constantino Rocca. Gallacher confirmed my selection, and that of Olazábal. That left him one last place to decide on. The candidates were Joakin Haeggman, who was 10th in the rankings and might now be the first Swede to join the team, Ronan Rafferty or Sandy Lyle.

At the end of the Düsseldorf tournament – Langer won his home country's open for the fifth time – we had a meeting to discuss the final member of the team. As I had to catch a plane back to Spain, I left before the meeting ended, but I was sure that after our debate, the captain's third choice would be Ronan Rafferty or David Flaherty, who had won his singles game in the 'War on the Shore' at Kiawah. However, when I got home, I discovered that neither had been selected and Haeggman had been chosen. I was very unhappy at this as we already had three first-timers, Constantino Rocca, Barry Lane and Peter Baker. The task of a captain is not to reward the first in the queue, but to strengthen the team with experienced people. The selection of Haeggman couldn't even be backed by his record, because he'd only had one victory as a professional.

I've always thought the reasons for including Haeggman were more complicated that just sport. Sweden had been producing good players of late, and some had been knocking on the door of the Ryder Cup team since 1985, but Volvo was the Tour's main sponsor. I'm not saying the company put pressure on for a Swede to be chosen but, knowing Ken Schofield, I could imagine him summoning Gallacher and making a recommendation that Haeggman would be good on the team.

As we saw in the tournament at the Belfry, the inclusion of the Swede didn't strengthen the team one bit, especially as Chema and I weren't playing at our best. This was obvious from the start. On the Friday morning we lost a foursome for the first time in six years. Davis

Love and Tom Kite beat us 2 and 1. The game began strangely, because Love, who was down to play first, was so nervous he told his colleague: 'Tom, you better drive off first.'

So I played with Tom Kite. At the first hole I had a petty argument with Kite, which was becoming a bit of a habit. He had a very short putt to halve the hole. He put his ball back on the green expecting I'd concede the shot. But I let him look at his line then, when he was about to putt, I said: 'That's OK.'

Kite picked up his ball, but looked at me suspiciously because I'd taken so long to concede the shot. This kind of thing is quite usual in the Ryder Cup, where each player tries to pressurise his opponent and undermine him psychologically. It's part of matchplay strategy. Perhaps because of that or simply because we played better in the afternoon we managed to reverse the trend and win the fourballs.

We did the same in the foursomes on the Saturday morning, but I knew that, despite my two wins, my game left much to be desired. After the foursome we'd lost the previous morning, Chema and I had changed positions. I teed off at the odd numbers, leaving him, given his great mastery of the medium irons, to lead off at two of the three par-3 holes on the course. Apart from Olazábal's magnificent play, we had great mutual understanding and our short games were in excellent shape. We both showed that when the ball is in a reasonable position, it's possible to make a par or birdie from anywhere. That's how we won.

Nonetheless, I was getting more and more concerned because if I kept playing as I had been I'd get crushed in the singles. To make matters worse, my back really hurt. I decided it was better to rest than to play in this state. But, before I said anything definitive, I spoke to José María.

'Whatever suits you, Seve; you know how you are better than anyone else,' he replied.

I told Gallacher, when he came to see me at the 12th tee: 'I think you should play Joakim Haeggman with Olazábal this afternoon. He's yet to play and I don't feel very well. I'd prefer to rest and concentrate on the singles tomorrow.'

'Agreed,' Gallacher responded swiftly.

I may have decided not to play, but I thought my absence wouldn't matter so much in the fourballs. After three series of games we were three points in the lead and that Saturday afternoon we should have managed to keep our lead, if not increase it. But we only took one point out of four that afternoon. My decision not to play because I didn't feel sure of my game impacted negatively on the team, and undermined its confidence.

On the way to the 10th tee, I saw Chema looked very worried and started to cheer him on: 'Come on, Chema, take it calmly, concentrate on playing as only you know how to . . . sure you're going to win.'

It was then that María, Raymond Floyd's wife, came over to me, throwing her hands up. 'Seve, I understand Spanish and you can't say that; you know it's not allowed.'

'For heaven's sake, María! What do you mean? I'm only cheering him on!'

She half turned before going off in a huff. The following day Raymond apologised to me on the practice range: 'I'm sorry for the bad time you had yesterday, Seve. I know María was totally out of order and now she doesn't know what to do to say sorry.'

'Thanks, Raymond,' I replied. 'Don't worry, we all know our nerves play bad tricks on us.'

After I'd lost my singles match his wife came over again to apologise. 'María, please forget it –' I cut her off because I wasn't in the mood after just losing the Ryder Cup. 'You've won, go and celebrate.' That was the end of the matter for me, because I am particularly fond of Ray and María.

As in the previous Ryder Cup, we had another 'spare' come into effect. This time it was in the second singles game. Sam Torrance had a very painful ingrowing toenail that had only allowed him to play the first round of foursomes. He dropped out. To counterbalance this absence, on the American side Lanny Wadkins, who'd already experienced the excitement of winning a Ryder Cup, nobly volunteered to drop out so Watson didn't have to leave one of his débutants on the bench. I am sure Watson hadn't intended to keep Lanny out, but he accepted his offer.

The last day was full of ups and downs; unfortunately our team had more downs than ups. Barry Lane lost to Chip Beck, after being three up with five holes to go; Rocca fell to Love as Olazábal did to Floyd. And Nick Faldo could only tie with my old friend Paul Azinger.

As the afternoon advanced, all the games were on a knife edge and

Gallacher didn't know which to go to. At that time, without a doubt, Rocca the débutant would have been grateful for his advice. He was one up and putting for a birdie that would have won him the game. In the end, he three-putted from six metres. Love won the hole. At the last hole, when Gallacher was waiting for him at the green, the Italian missed his second shot and the American won the game. We lost by 15 to 13.

At that crucial moment in the game Constantino Rocca shouldn't have been abandoned to his own devices: if Bernard couldn't go, he should have sent me or someone else to keep Rocca calm and his spirits up, so he felt the team was behind him.

At the press conference later, Bernard Gallacher congratulated the Americans on their victory, but the feeling that prevailed in our camp wasn't that they had won but that we had lost it. And I mean we all lost it because it wasn't down to any one individual:

'I had the impression that the encounter and the Ryder Cup all hung on Rocca . . .' Gallacher even said.

'Don't say that, Bernard! This is a team competition! Just drop it!' Woosie, as we affectionately called Ian Woosnam, interjected swiftly and sensibly.

That Sunday night I felt very frustrated, as Constantino Rocca probably did too. I'd lost my game against Jim Gallagher. I think it was my worst game ever in the Ryder Cup. Wadkins's withdrawal had at first seemed advantageous for me as I then had to play Gallagher, the 'spare', but I played so badly that to this day I feel ashamed of my performance. It was as if all my expertise had suddenly vanished. But the saddest moment of all was seeing our fans departing the Belfry downcast and in a silence that hurt me more than if they'd insulted us. I found it hard to hold back my tears.

Chapter 34

All in a Day's Work

When a lad who's waking up to life sees pretty girls following him on the course while he's playing a tournament, it is a fantastic source of extra motivation. More than once I've showed off playing for them. Models, actresses, writers, journalists and princesses would approach me and I let them seduce me, but never to the point where I became distracted from my real love, golf.

Before getting married I had relationships with girls from the most diverse social backgrounds, but I never felt I was being a Don Juan or a playboy. I wasn't the seducer, but the seduced. I sensed they were attracted by what I represented. They didn't see me as a man they wanted to start a serious relationship with, because there wasn't time to develop a friendship or get to know one another. I think all these fleeting relationships were happy and even positive and healthy, because they didn't cause either me or them problems of any kind. I treasure many pleasant memories and amusing anecdotes.

In 1982, during my stay in the United States, I went out with a girl who'd been selected as Miss Texas. I met Christy in Miami, where I had a house at the Doral Country Club. She was an incredibly beautiful woman and, being a great swimmer, had a spectacularly athletic body. As the football World Cup was being played in Spain that year, I invited her to come and see some games with me. When we reached Madrid, we were waiting by the carousel when our luggage emerged at the same time as that of the Mexican team, who'd come on the same flight.

'Seve, I didn't think you were so famous. It's incredible how all these footballers are looking at you,' Christy said.

'Christy, I don't think you've got it right,' I replied, looking at the faces of the Mexicans. 'It's you they're looking at, not me.'

There was also a princess from northern Europe who virtually wore a crown on her head. I have wonderful memories of her, because she was beautiful and a charming, straightforward person. We got on very well. There was a special chemistry at work between us, partly because she was quite unpredictable in her shows of affection. Once our schedules coincided in Barcelona, where I was playing a tournament, and we spent a great day together. As she had to return to her country that evening, I accompanied her to the airport. She took out her boarding pass and I said goodbye. I returned to my hotel with her image in my eyes and a pleasant feeling in my body. At about ten o'clock I went to bed. I hadn't fallen asleep when there was a knock at my door. I was surprised. I opened the door and there she was.

'Did you miss your plane?' I asked her, rather taken aback.

'No, I just decided I didn't want to leave,' she replied.

She went to her room and we spent the next day visiting all the sights.

As everybody knows, I lived in Monaco for five years. The principality was a place that favoured all kinds of relationships. There, in a kind of fairy tale, I had a very friendly, warm relationship with the ruling Grimaldi family, whom I hold in the highest regard. I cherish very fond memories of them.

My relations with girls never impacted on my behaviour on the golf course. I was always clear that golf came first and that I could never allow myself be to sidetracked. I've never liked parties and receptions because – apart from having to go to bed early – I feel oppressed by so many people.

My socialising stopped the moment I got married, because I was with Carmen, who I believed was the right woman for me. Things didn't turn out as I'd imagined, but that doesn't mean we didn't try and aren't still trying to give the best upbringing and education possible to our three wonderful children. I agree with Carmen that the best schools in the world are in England. That's why we decided to send Javier, Miguel and Carmen to school there, just as we've made sure that they share our beliefs, tastes and likes.

When you travel the world, as I've had to, you often have to give up doing a lot of things. One thing I stopped doing was going to Mass; like most Spaniards, I'm a non-practising Catholic. When I was a child, I went to Mass every Sunday like all the village children, but when I joined the Tour it was very difficult to continue doing so. Partly because Sunday is the day final rounds of tournaments are played, and also because the sermons given by priests in other countries are very different and difficult to understand. I've never gone to Mass just so people can see me going. When I was at home, Carmen and I tried to attend church with the children, so that they would have a spiritual reference point. I've always thought it important to believe in something, because it gives you peace of mind. But horrific events fill me with doubts and questions about the existence of God. When things happen like the terrorist attacks of 11 September in New York, 11 March 2004 in Madrid and 7 July 2005 in London, and the massacres and hunger in Africa, you wonder if God really exists or, as Pope Ratzinger asked when he visited Auschwitz, 'Where was He?' Why didn't He intervene to avoid humanity suffering so much sorrow?

I understand the idea that God has given us the freedom to decide our behaviour, but I can't help feeling deeply confused on this issue. I want to believe there is someone above us, but when thousands of children are dying in the world every day, starving to death or victims of war, you ask yourself: why doesn't God do something for those who are completely innocent?

It's painful to see how religions that have presented themselves as ways to salvation over the centuries have more often than not been a source of damnation. Fanaticism and religious intolerance are at the root of much of the sadness, misery and death in the world. When the most important thing in life is existing safely in peace togther, I can't understand why people kill each other, whether it's terrorists, whatever their label, or armies, or those who kill their partners simply because they can't live without them.

From the moment I considered having a family, I've wanted them to be straightforward individuals sensitive to what is happening around them; and to understand that the fact they've some wealth behind them doesn't make them any better than anyone else. They have to be able to develop themselves as individuals.

From the time I could be at home more, I've tried to spend as much time as possible with those who are close to me. While Carmen and I were together, I loved to go out with her for a stroll through the village, and for us to go and have dinner by ourselves or with friends. It's much easier here, because Pedreña is an extension of my home. Everyone knows that I am Seve the golfer, but they know me and treat me as Seve the villager. These are ways of behaving and looking at the world that I try to get my children to take on board, at the same time as valuing what they have. You achieve nothing without putting in the effort.

Chapter 35

Hobbies

In my view, we are partly defined by our outlook on life, what we enjoy doing, our hopes and fears. As I've mentioned, I am very fond of hunting, probably because it's a sport practised in the north of Spain, and also of boxing, because it requires skill, good physical shape and an ability to withstand the blows. It's a tough sport where you can't whinge. Another of my great likes is football, and in that I'm like most Spanish males.

I'm a fan of Racing Santander, because it is the historic Cantabrian club. Dr Santiago Ortiz de la Torre is partly to blame, as I've said, for occasionally giving me tickets when I was young. When I started to follow Racing they were in the second division, which is where they end up from time to time. As a team with modest resources, they find it hard to stay in the first division, where they have to compete with many similar clubs as well as with big teams like Barcelona, Real Madrid, Athletic Club de Bilbao, Valencia or Atlético de Madrid.

I am also a great fan of Barcelona but I like Real Madrid too and enjoy good relations with their team. I have a delightful memory from the end of 1997, when I played in a charity match in the Santiago Bernabeu stadium for a campaign against drug addiction. Once on the pitch I felt what Jorge Valdano described as the 'stage fright' that the stadium provokes in rival teams; when it's full, it's intimidating. One memory triggers another – I've just remembered something that happened to my brother Manuel at the Bernabeu.

Manolo was the first of my brothers to play golf professionally, influenced, as we all were, by the local club and by my uncle Ramón Sota, who in the 1960s became the best golfer in Spain and one of the best in Europe. Manolo was also the first of us to play abroad. When he had to play in the Italian Open he didn't have the money for his airfare. My father sold two cows at 10,000 pesetas apiece and we gathered in the kitchen to count out the 1,000-peseta notes, one, two, three . . . under my mother's reproachful gaze as she shook her head as if to say: 'My God, after all the effort it takes to earn that money . . .' When my father finished, my mother couldn't restrain herself:

'Mero, why are you giving our son 20,000 pesetas? Do you realise how much money that is?'

'You be quiet, woman, it will be all right in the end and he'll be a great champion!' my father retorted, looking at Manolo, as if to warn him: I'm giving you this money, but don't fail me, or your mother will never stop going on about it.

Manolo drove off to Madrid with my uncle Ramón Sota and with 20,000 pesetas in cash in his pocket to pay for the flight to Milan. As it was a night flight and Real Madrid was playing Valencia in the afternoon, he and my uncle went to see the match. The telephone rang at home that night, my father picked it up and almost immediately I heard him shout: 'My God!'

'What's wrong? What's wrong, Mero?' my mother cried.

'What's wrong? Only that our son had nothing better to do than go to a football match and let somebody steal his money!'

As my father could do nothing to help, Uncle Ramón lent Manolo 20,000 pesetas and he caught his plane. Luckily he finished fifth and recovered the money, but my father had to stomach the annoying fact that he'd sold two of the fourteen cows from his stable only to have his money stolen.

I suppose such things happen anywhere in large crowds. The worst thing in a football stadium is the violence from groups of intolerant fans. I can't understand why people do such barbaric things. We all want our team to win, but it's not a big deal if it loses; it's only a game and, as in any competition, someone has to lose, win or draw. I get very annoyed and shocked, because I can't understand why some fans go wild even before the game has started. There's nothing more uncalled-for than insults directed at a referee. When I take my children to watch Racing play, I tell them they can get excited but shouldn't lose their temper: it's too easy to move from verbal to physical violence. Whether you are a fan or a player, it's vital to respect everybody else; when you do so, you can coexist with anyone, because you yourself feel respected. It's what living in a democracy is all about.

One of the main roads in Pedreña is now called the Avenida Severiano Ballesteros. I'm very proud that a street in my village carries my name, because it's a sign of respect and affection from the community. Under the Franco dictatorship nobody would have thought of giving a village street a golfer's name – perhaps a footballer's or bullfighter's, but never anyone who played golf.

Much has changed in Spain since democracy was established. In the first place Spanish society transformed itself from a backward, eminently rural society into a modern, advanced democracy. My generation has been lucky to experience this radical, positive transformation of our country in such a short space of time. This exemplary change is the result of the effort and will of the majority of Spaniards, from King Juan Carlos and a political class that knew how to manage the historical situation to ordinary citizens of every social class. I think King Juan Carlos has played a crucial and decisive role, especially in the difficult years of the transition to democracy. It's not surprising that he is loved so much in Spain.

Democracy has brought many benefits to every Spaniard. I only have to remember the days when I was a caddie: I wasn't even allowed to walk in front of the clubhouse because I might annoy the members. In such a social climate, and with the laws governing us at the time, it was unthinkable that one of us would ever be allowed to become a member – even supposing we could find the money to pay the membership fees. It wasn't just a financial issue: it was a question of social status.

But my fondness for golf and affection for the Royal Club of Pedreña go beyond social prejudice or personal grudge. The recognition I have received and the affection displayed by the community has confirmed to me that I made the right choice. Now that playing can no longer give me the satisfaction it once did, I find that the effort I've made to popularise golf, my first and great love, has prospered. This has gone a long way to compensate for the back pains, the headaches caused by my business affairs, and the days when I've played badly.

I'm really thrilled that my children like golf and seem talented. I like to teach and accompany them. In 2001, one week before the British Open at Lytham, I was very happy to act as caddie for Javier, when he first used his first full set of clubs. That day, as I accompanied him, I told him about my victories in the Opens in 1979, 1984 and 1988, and the way I had hit such and such a stroke. Javier hit a terrific 170-metre drive as if inspired by my talk, although his forte is his short game, which is full of character.

I don't think it will surprise anybody if I say that one of the reasons I tried to end my golfing career on a high is because I wanted Javier, Miguel and Carmen to watch me win a tournament. I would rather they hadn't had to depend on video footage for proof that their father was a very good golfer.

Chapter 36

The Miracle of Oak Hill

After our disappointment at the Belfry, we won the Ryder Cup back in 1995 with an impressive display. It was so fantastic that the only way I can think of describing it is as 'the miracle of Oak Hill'. Each European player contributed at least one victory to the final result. Many of these came in the singles on Sunday. Quite frankly, it was a real eye-opener. Even today I find it difficult to believe I won the points I did because I was playing so poorly at the time.

Before the match started I asked Bernard Gallacher, our captain, to let us reverse the order for our outfits, and wear green sweaters on Saturday and blue on the Sunday. (Blue is my favourite colour. I've always felt at ease dressed in blue.) On Saturday we drove off wearing a hopeful green and Sunday in navy blue in search of miracles.

On the first day we had some bad results. David Gilford, our 'spare' in the battle of Kiawah, and I were the only ones to win our fourballs in the afternoon. Although I was all over the place during the game, I believe I helped David's confidence after the disappointment he'd had when he was left on the bench in 1991. After the game I told the press we'd agreed our tactics before the start: we decided we would approach the course from different angles and that this would be the key to winning. However, what really gave us victory was the lack of communication between Brad Faxon and Peter Jacobsen at the 7th. We went one ahead because Jacobsen made a mistake: he picked his ball up when he still had a metre-and-a-half putt for par because he thought Faxon was already safely home. Nobody had told him his colleague had had to drop his ball, thus receiving a penalty stroke. After this, we only had to keep control of the game to win it by 4 and 3.

On Saturday, although Europe began the day trailing 5–3, we

recovered in the foursomes to draw level. The afternoon fourballs were fiercely contested and by the last game the US had a minimal lead, with Nick Faldo and Bernhard Langer level with Corey Pavin and Loren Roberts on the green of the 18th. Unfortunately Faldo and Langer couldn't get their half, and the day finished 9–7 in favour of the US.

The scoreline was a great blow and few thought Europe could recover the Ryder Cup. Several of our players and even our captain already seemed defeated. We were so out of sorts that we didn't even have a meeting. Each player simply went to his locker to change his shoes. While we chewed over the desperate situation, Bernard Gallacher just read out the order in which we would play. And that was that. It was the first time there'd been no meeting since I'd been playing in the Ryder Cup. In such circumstances a reasonable tactic on the part of the captain would have been to forget his own feelings and say something like, 'Lads, it's a pity we haven't played better, but all is not lost. This is the order of games for tomorrow and I want you to go all out to win every one.' But he didn't say that or anything similar. This pretence of a meeting was as gloomy as the atmosphere and our own expectations.

It shouldn't have been like that. After all, we'd won in 1985 and 1987 and drawn in 1989 when we'd been two points behind, as was the case now. Everyone seemed consumed by a peculiar form of pessimism. Many later said they were hoping things would turn out as they did, but that's not true. Nobody had a clear view of what was happening until almost the last game.

To be quite frank, even now I wonder how we managed what we did on that Oak Hill course in Rochester, New York. It was simply miraculous. But there's no miracle that can't be explained, and the explanation in this case is that of the five games that went to the 18th hole we won four and drew one. What is more mysterious is that at one time or another, all of these games looked lost.

As I imagined the Americans would put one of their best down to go first – Tom Lehman as it turned out – I asked Gallacher to put me down first as well. I was playing so badly, I thought I could sacrifice my point to a player who could beat any of us, so that one of our team might win his game against a less powerful opponent.

I lost the 1st but then recovered at the 2nd. Much to my surprise and even more so to Lehman's, I managed to stay level, even though my game was erratic. My driver wasn't working well, but I managed some extravagant recovery shots and excellent putts, while Lehman missed birdie chance after birdie chance.

Lehman won the 8th but I managed to halve the next two holes in our tug-of-war. It was then I told my caddie, Billy Foster: 'If we can stick it out for two or three more holes, we can start thinking we're going to win. He realises he should have won this game by now and if it continues like this he'll lose.'

I didn't think I could win the way I was playing but my idea was to stick it out as long as possible to encourage my colleagues coming up behind. Unfortunately I made a bogey at the 11th to give Lehman a lead of two. But then the heavens began to favour Europe and on our way to the tee at the 12th we heard a great shout go up – Howard Clark, who was playing against Jacobsen, had holed in one at the 11th. This decisive strike enabled him to draw level and win on the green of the 18th. As for me, at the 12th, which is a par four and uphill, I finally managed two good shots to leave the ball just over two metres from the cup. It was Lehman's turn to play and he left it very close for par. It was obvious I would concede that putt, so he went to pick his ball up. I asked him to mark it, because the mark would help me find my line, but he didn't take any notice.

'Tom, mark your ball, please mark the ball,' I insisted but he didn't hear and sank the ball. 'What are you doing?' I asked. 'Why did you hole out? I'd asked you to mark your ball.' Lehman became angry. 'Tom, I wasn't trying anything on, I just wanted you to mark your ball.'

The spectators started to crowd round and the hubbub grew. Lehman called the umpire. The crowd was protesting because they thought it was a trick of mine to undermine their player. The umpire who arrived was a very correct young man. He listened to Lehman's protest and then spoke loudly to the spectators:

'Ladies and gentlemen, Mr Ballesteros only wanted Mr Lehman to mark his ball. That's all there is to it. Please stay where you are, and be silent.'

After all that fuss I was the one who was upset. I didn't hole my putt and Tom Lehman won the next two holes and the game.

Immediately I went back to look for Gallacher and follow the other games with him. If Howard Clark's hole-in-one had been the first hopeful sign, David Gilford's game against Brad Faxon left us in no doubt that we were on the verge of the 'miracle of Oak Hill'. At the 18th, Gilford, who was one up, hit his second shot past the green and the ball landed in very high, thick grass near the green. We all knew that chipping wasn't one of Gifford's strengths but I was dumbstruck when I saw him pick out a 7 iron. It was an impossible shot surrounded by that grass.

'Bernard, you've got to tell him he can't play that kind of shot, he'll get stuck in the rough before he reaches the green or he'll over-hit by miles; tell him if he plays that iron there's no way he'll get the ball on the green. Please tell him to use the sand wedge.'

'Seve,' replied Gallacher under the watchful eye of Ken Schofield, who was listening to our conversation, 'You know how bad David is at listening to advice; I can't do what you're asking me to do.'

'You've got to!' I insisted. Only a captain is allowed to give a player advice. I was powerless and incredulous when our captain, Bernard Gallacher, refused to give him any.

As I'd predicted, Gilford hit the ball into the rough and needed a fourth shot to get within four metres of the pin. He then holed the putt for the game, after Faxon missed his from under a metre. It was incredible – despite Gilford's serious error, Lady Luck had smiled on us. I was very pleased for him and I have often thought that victory of his was the key to our overall triumph.

In the game after Gilford and Faxon's, Colin Montgomerie beat Ben Crenshaw at the 17th to leave Europe with four and a half points after seven singles had been played. This meant we needed three points from the last five games. The situation was still on a knife edge, because although Sam Torrance had a commanding lead against Loren Roberts, Langer and Johansson looked certain to lose theirs against Pavin and Mickelson respectively. The last cartridges in our belt were Nick Faldo and Philip Walton. The latter was dormy three against Haas; Nick Faldo was level with Curtis Strange at the 18th, but in difficulty.

Nick showed his class in what was a very charged atmosphere. If Nick could finish with a birdie four, he would win the game. He made a great champion's approach shot to leave the ball a little over a metre from the hole. Nevertheless, it was far from over. The tension was unbearable. Strange missed his putt, as he'd missed at the two previous holes, and Nick holed his, as you would expect from a winner of six majors. I ran to embrace him and we were so excited we started to cry, even though we hadn't yet won the Cup. At that precise moment Philip Walton and Jay Haas were coming up to the 18th, with Walton leading by one. He only had to halve the hole to win the game and bring the Ryder Cup home, but I didn't even want to think about what must have been going through Philip's head right then.

Haas sliced his drive into the rough on the left and Walton went into the rough on the right. The American played his ball on to the fairway, hoping to match what Nick had just done, and Philip sent his ball into the thick rough on the bank beneath the green. Jay Haas didn't emulate Nick Faldo: his ball dropped short, rolling back into the rough on the edge of the green. With the pressure he was under, it looked very unlikely he would finish the hole in five, as Walton seemed likely to do. But the latter's nerves were on edge too. He struck his chip shot – and for an eternal second we thought it was too soft to get over the edge of the green. But the miracle was happening. Walton's ball kept rolling to leave him with an uphill putt. Haas's chip went three metres past the pin. Philip had two putts to guarantee victory. It was wonderful to see him leave his ball only a few centimetres from the cup. The 'miracle of Oak Hill' had occurred. We had won the Ryder Cup.

The colour blue had again brought luck to me and to the rest of the European team. In the midst of all our celebrations and the Americans' misery I realised a despondent Jay Haas had been abandoned. I went over, put my arm round him and said all you can say at such times: 'Jay, it's sport . . . you've played well, but sport's like that.'

Chapter 37

Against the Windmills

From the end of the 1980s there had been a lot of talk on the European Tour about the need to take the Ryder Cup out of Britain to other European countries. It was a reasonable suggestion and was bound to help develop and popularise golf on our continent. But it was a long, difficult process bringing the plan to fruition. On more than one occasion I felt like Don Quixote tilting at windmills in the belief that they were giants: those of us fighting to take the Ryder Cup away from its birthplace met with a lack of understanding and support – and even subterfuge – even though the Cup undoubtedly owed its current prestige to the priceless contribution made by leading European Tour players.

In May 1990 it was announced that the 1993 Ryder Cup would be played at the Belfry. This meant that the Belfry would stage the competition for the third time running. The idea of playing on the European mainland had been rejected. As Spain had presented the candidacy of the Club del Campo, I felt especially disappointed, as did many other people close to the project. The committee's vote had ended in stalemate: the representatives from the European Tour voted in favour of Spain but the three representatives of the British PGA voted for the Belfry, its headquarters. Predictably, the PGA president, Lord Derby, used his casting vote for the British course.

Many Tour members were indignant at the result of this vote and many questioned the Ryder Cup's future if the British PGA wouldn't agree to share ownership of the tournament with mainland Europe. For my part I told the press I thought it was a wrongheaded decision to continue playing the match in England, since the Cup would very probably have disappeared years before without the participation of continental players, in particular the Spanish. I also said that my involvement had been decisive in bringing the Cup visibility and prestige and that I thought I had the right to call for the Cup to be played in my own country – to help develop the sport there, not from any individual whim of mine. After we'd lost the chance to play the 1993 Ryder Cup in Spain, we weren't going to miss out in 1997. I concentrated my efforts on making sure that didn't happen. I insisted the Royal Spanish Federation kept putting the pressure on. I went to several meetings in London, and spoke personally to Ken Schofield and other influential people.

The proposal that the Ryder Cup should be played in Spain was finally approved. For the first time in its history, it would be staged outside the UK. However, I don't wish to claim this as a personal success.

My idea was that the 1997 Ryder Cup should be played on the Galapagar course which I was designing near Madrid. Ken Schofield visited the site and stated that it was outstanding. Regrettably, the project was never carried through because of the countless objections that were raised by the authorities: a real obstacle race where the hurdles got higher and higher. The situation became so discouraging that I came to believe I had powerful and well connected opponents totally opposed to a new golf course being built in Madrid to host the Ryder Cup.

I even discovered that someone was making fun of the idea of attempting to take the Cup to a course that was yet to be built, as if it were all a fantasy. That 'very serious' person ignored what had happened in 1991. Initially that Ryder Cup was to be played on a course in California, but the company that had signed the contract with the American PGA to stage the tournament decided it should take place at Kiawah Island, South Carolina, on a course that was still under construction when we arrived.

I felt it was all for show. I believe that Schofield and the Ryder Cup Committee had decided the tournament would be played on the course which they preferred. But instead of stating their preference, for reasons I cannot fathom they seemed to be flirting with everyone. That was what really offended me. It made me think that the course selection process had not been truly open to other possibilities and that a lot of people had ended up wasting their time and money.

When Galapagar was rejected, my brother Baldomero suggested

we should try to get the Cup played at Novo Sancti Petri, a course I'd designed near Cádiz, on the Atlantic coast of southern Spain. I didn't and don't have any financial interest in this course, but as its designer it was obviously important for me that it should host the Ryder Cup.

Alongside Novo Sancti Petri, La Moraleja, El Saler, La Manga and Valderrama seemed to be in the running. Around that time, Jaime Ortiz Patiño, Valderrama's owner, asked me to redesign its 17th hole. He also asked me to back Valderrama's candidacy. To try to put an end to all the manoeuvring, Baldomero and I met up with Ken Schofield, George O'Grady and others. Turning to Ken I said at an appropriate moment, 'I'm going to back the Novo Sancti Petri course and I want you to support me.' They looked at each other, but nobody said a word. For my part, I was determined to put pressure on all sides and in November 1993 I formally announced my support for the Novo Sancti Petri course as a candidate to host the 1997 Ryder Cup.

I was now offered a place on the Ryder Cup Committee, I think to give the process a Spanish voice. It's possible – although this is pure conjecture – that I was given this responsibility to prevent me from personally defending any of the candidates. In due course, as a member of the Committee, I received several reports that discounted the suitability of various courses but I felt their merits and failings were never sufficiently analysed. Given the situation, a month before the decisive meeting I decided to resign from the Committee in order to defend my favoured course.

Some days later, at the beginning of May, after the second round of the Benson & Hedges International at St Mellion, Bernard Gallacher, then Ryder Cup captain, asked me to have lunch with him. During lunch I asked for his support, but he said the course I was backing didn't have the necessary facilities, which was untrue. I prepared a statement that was distributed while I was playing the last round of the Spanish Open. In this I clearly set out my point of view on the course selection process, including Jimmy Patiño's proposals.

It was the last card I could play: I thought that if the matter were aired someone would react. I felt the way everything was being dealt with was unfair because the Novo Sancti Petri's infrastructure was much better than Valderrama's. For example, there were two good hotels next to the course, and several that were on the point of being built. Valderrama had none nearby. Valderrama was and is one of the most elitist private clubs in the whole of Europe and, as people know, I've always defended public courses. If the idea was to promote the golf in Spain, it wasn't a good idea to stage the Ryder Cup on an elitist course like Valderrama. I don't mean that the course isn't very good and that Patiño hasn't contributed a lot to the development of the Tour by hosting the Volvo Masters since its inauguration in 1988. I don't deny this. I merely want to underline the lack of coherence and openness on the part of some people during the negotiations. As far as I was concerned, all they had to say to me was: 'Seve, don't put yourself out and waste your time, because we don't want to consider different options. Valderrama is our favourite. We think it'll be impossible to persuade us otherwise.'

I feel I was badly treated in all this. Many people agreed that the two reasons why the Ryder Cup should be held in Spain were the large number of tournaments this country contributed to the European Tour, and my own participation in the Ryder Cup. Our aim was fulfilled, but it left a sour taste.

On 26 May 1994 it was announced that the Ryder Cup would be played on the Valderrama course. Inevitably.

Chapter 38

A Captain's Labours

Once Spain was designated host country for the 1997 Ryder Cup, everybody took it for granted I would be team captain. However, I wasn't so sure. I was keen to play.

Two years before, on my way to the Far East, Ken Schofield had met me at Heathrow airport to ask if I would accept the captaincy. I didn't give him an immediate answer. I wanted to wait until I'd returned to Spain and had a chance to consult my brothers.

'I don't think I want to be captain, it's not a good idea. I'd rather do all I can to play,' I told them.

'You don't have any choice,' they replied there and then. 'You're the best possible captain now that the Cup is going to be held in Spain.'

I thought it over and saw they were right. Then I went back to see Ken and told him I'd accept. For a time I toyed with the idea of being both captain and player, two roles that Ken told me could be combined. In the end I concluded it was impossible to be a good captain and to play golf at one's best. A Ryder Cup captain has lots of duties; they take up all his time. Besides, as this was to be the first Ryder Cup played outside Great Britain, I would have more work to do than any previous captain. Looking after the social side of the competition – the welcoming party, the opening and closing ceremonies and the gala dinner – is enough to ensure the captain can't play. Then you have to add on the press conferences, interviews, team meetings, rules meetings, etc.

As soon as I took up the captaincy, I stated my view that all this was excessive and that, as far as social gatherings were concerned, the gala dinner and opening and closing ceremonies were enough. I was also opposed to the holding of a 'victory dinner'. Although there are twelve players who are happy because they have won, there are twelve others who aren't. It shows a lack of consideration to expect them to attend such a dinner when they are in that frame of mind. I'm not against a dinner to celebrate victory, but it's one the winning team should organise itself.

The Ryder Cup committee readily accepted my views on these matters. The social occasions were reduced to a bare minimum and no 'victory' dinner was held. But the committee did not accept the idea that I should choose four members of the team. 'I'm sorry, the captain will only receive two picks,' I was informed by Ken Schofield after he'd consulted the committee.

The following spring, I asked once more for the number of my selections to be increased and the majority of players backed me in this, but it was all to no avail. The committee wouldn't yield.

If this wasn't the source of enough tension, in August 1997 Ken Schofield suggested Jesper Parnevik shouldn't be one of my picks, arguing that he didn't support the Tour. Parnevik, Olazábal, Faldo and Langer were on the list of players who possibly wouldn't qualify and whom I wanted to include in the team. But I could only choose two. Langer subsequently qualified and that left me with three options. Chema was in twelfth place and very unlikely to qualify. I spoke to him during the European Open in Ireland. 'I'm counting on you,' I told him. 'You should go all out to qualify, but even if you don't, you'll be on the team.' I phoned Nick in the United States and told him he would also be one of my choices. I told both Nick and Chema these were confidential conversations, because it was very important that all the players in with a chance continued to be motivated to fight to qualify. You always have to be prepared for the unexpected. This time was no exception.

Miguel Ángel Martín, one of the players who had qualified for the team, injured his wrist. He had to have an operation at the beginning of August. He wrote a letter informing the committee he wouldn't be fit enough to join the team. As soon as I found out, I rang him to see how he was.

'What's wrong, Miguel Ángel?'

'I've had a wrist operation and I don't think I can join the team.'

'I'm sorry, it's a real shame, because if I'd known earlier I'd have chosen you as vice-captain,' I replied.

I genuinely regretted Martín wouldn't be in the team: it was a great opportunity for another Spanish player to take part in the event when it was being staged in Spain for the first time. And I couldn't make Martín vice-captain because I'd already offered that position to Miguel Ángel Jiménez. Martín's withdrawal opened the way for Olazábal – the man immediately below him in the rankings – and meant I could invite Parnevik. Consequently, once I had spoken to Martín, and once the committee had sent him a fax informing him he wouldn't be playing, I rang Parnevik in the United States to tell him he would join Nick Faldo as my captain's pick.

At the end of August, during the BMW International, I was preparing to announce the Ryder Cup team when David Garland, one of the Tour umpires, asked me to send a fax to Miguel Ángel Martín to confirm he couldn't possibly play. It was a mere formality and I complied. To my great surprise, Martín replied that he was now ready to join the team. He'd clearly had a change of mind. I discussed his response with Colin Montgomerie, Bernhard Langer and José María Olazábal. All three agreed it would be difficult for him to be fit enough for a major match at the end of September so soon after such an operation. They felt the best he could do for the team was to withdraw, as Sandy Lyle had done in 1989 and Olazábal in 1995. However, the fact remained that Martín – who had stated he wasn't fit to play a few weeks ago – now wanted to take part. That meant I couldn't name the full team yet. It was a really absurd situation. Moreover Martín's attitude and the way the matter was handled by the Ryder Cup committee led to a series of misunderstandings that could have been avoided.

I'd been on very good terms with Miguel Ángel Martín up to that point and, if he'd been in good health, I'd have been delighted to include him in the team. He knew that. Before I had found out about the wrist operation, I'd visited Valderrama to check on the preparation of the course. I had asked for a few changes, such as moving the tee forwards at the 10th because I knew that Martín wasn't a long hitter.

Having created a messy situation, Martín stuck by his wish to play, and told people he believed an attempt was being made to exclude him in favour of Olazábal, who was eleventh in the qualifying list. Many people fell for this line of reasoning, because they knew that whoever held the eleventh spot in the rankings could expect to fill the last place automatically if it became vacant.

Three days after the BMW International, Ken Schofield asked Martín to provide medical evidence for his claim that he'd recovered from his operation. I contacted Martín myself. He told me he wouldn't undergo the necessary tests, because they might affect the outcome of his recovery.

While I was in Switzerland, where I'd gone to play the European Masters, I discovered that Schofield had sent Martín a very friendly fax on 2 September inviting him to join the official team delegation. Almost simultaneously – I don't know why – he sent him another fax threatening to expel him from the team if he didn't present himself the next day at the 1st tee at in Valderrama to demonstrate whether he was or wasn't in a state to play. I found out that the fax in question also informed him that the captain and the committee were considering excluding him because he was unfit to compete. As soon as I realised all this was going on I rang Richard Hills, the Tour's manager for the Ryder Cup, and he read out the text of this second fax over the phone.

'Richard, this isn't right!' I told him indignantly. 'Why am I being quoted when I wasn't even at that meeting?'

It was reasonable enough for Martín to think I was behind the fax, but rather than ringing me and asking for an explanation or returning the calls I made to him, he decided to call a press conference in Madrid and finger me as the person responsible for his exclusion from the team. At the height of the controversy, a Spanish radio programme interviewed us together and the first thing Martín said was something like this:

'Seve, you're to blame for my exclusion, because you're on the committee.'

'Miguel Ángel,' I replied, trying to keep calm, 'I've not been on the committee for years.'

I then explained that if we aspired to win such an important and demanding competition as the Ryder Cup, our players had to be in the best possible physical and mental state.

'That may be an issue with you and Nick Faldo, but I'm fit enough to play,' he answered in an offensive tone. To prove it, a fortnight before the Ryder Cup, he took part in the British Masters. His belief in his fitness was quite mistaken. Nonetheless, my brother Manuel, then president of the Spanish PGA, asked the committee to reconsider its decision on his participation. The committee decided conclusively not to include him in the team. Martín, who threatened to go to court to recover his place, didn't understand that a Ryder Cup team has to have enough time to train properly. No one can expect, as he did, that the team can wait on a player's recovery until a week before the tournament starts. It wasn't fair on Jesper Parnevik who in the meantime had to keep his own diary of commitments on hold.

All the complaints he listed in a further press conference upset me a lot, for there were journalists who were unsparing in their criticism of me because of the way the team selection had been conducted. I'm quite sure I acted correctly all the way through, but the experience was sufficient to ensure I didn't continue in my post as Ryder Cup team captain. And that wouldn't be the end of my troubles.

Chapter 39

The Storm Before the Match

The first half of the 1997 Ryder Cup week was marked by a series of wrangles that I found very distasteful. They showed that not everyone had approached the event professionally. Then the weather almost washed out our party into the bargain.

Apart from a succession of small problems magnified by people who didn't want the Cup to succeed in Spain, from a sporting perspective things looked unpromising. The predictions of the experts who'd analysed the statistics and world rankings of the players were clearly favourable to the United States. Nonetheless, I was confident of the European team's potential. My task as captain was to ensure my players were equally confident, and that's why I gave several of them firm advice. I mean that I didn't hesitate to intervene in a game when I thought it was necessary. During the first fourballs, Jesper Parnevik was in the centre of the fairway of the 4th, ready to make his approach to the green. His colleague, Per-Ulrik Johansson, was lining up his second shot. I saw him take his sand wedge.

'What are you doing, Per?' I asked him.

'I'm going to pitch it short just to be safe, and then Jesper can go for the green.'

'No, let Jesper play first and, depending where his ball lands, you can either lay up or go for the green as well,' was my advice.

Jesper over-hit the green but landed in a good position, allowing Per to go for the green as well.

I believed I had to be close to these players because many were inexperienced and lacked tactical sense. They knew that and felt more at ease when they saw me around. Obviously the odd one, like Colin Montgomerie, felt that I was treating him like a child. Colin didn't like being given tips. I remember going over to him to discuss the tricky 17th. Before I could open my mouth he shouted angrily: 'Seve, I know what to do! I really do!'

'Colin,' I replied also angrily, 'I know you do. I only wanted to remind you.'

The spectators around us laughed, but Monty was in no laughing mood. As I've said, Monty is a great player, but he tends to react stormily.

Ian Woosnam criticised me as well, this time on more serious grounds. He told British journalists that 'Europe has a captain who goes around as if he were playing blind man's buff'. I imagine he said this because I drove around the course encouraging everyone, even on practice days.

Much of my advice centred on the way to play the 17th, a hole that some of the Americans were extremely rude about: they said it wasn't fair after driving your ball 270 metres to find yourself in the rough that crossed the whole fairway. I knew they'd protest about that and was glad when they did.

My view was then and is now that it's no different finding yourself in a stream or in a bunker. The main issue is that as long as there's an easterly wind blowing, you expect the hole to play like an easy par 4; that bit of rough turns it into a tricky par 5. You may fear it will be difficult to find the green, like at the 15th in Augusta, but the danger at the 17th in Valderrama is actually from the water. Players who are ill at ease with this hole are those who don't understand the need for strategy. Tiger Woods couldn't work out how to play it.

I should say that we won the point we needed to guarantee a draw and hold on to the Cup at the 17th.

Another aspect of this hole is worth explaining. The 17th hole is a fantastic natural amphitheatre, because the slope behind the green can accommodate a large number of spectators, with spectacular views of the action beneath them. After the Ryder Cup, the unfounded criticisms of this hole from some players arose because Tiger Woods, the world's best golfer, insisted on making life difficult by attempting inopportune exhibition play at the 17th. In 2000, the year he found the water three times in four days, the 17th at Valderrama was played in an average of 4.817 shots, that is, under par.

★

The opening day of play finally arrived, and I must have been the first to jump out of bed. It was about 6 a.m. on Friday morning. I peered out to see what the weather was doing. It had obviously been raining for a while and it was still pouring down. I felt incredibly frustrated.

'For God's sake! Look at that rain; we've been waiting two years for the Ryder Cup, we've moved heaven and earth to bring it to Spain and when's it's finally all about to happen, we can't get on the course! At this rate it could take a fortnight to get it done! We're really doing ourselves proud!'

I immediately called all the players and told them it was pointless to go out on the course and that I'd call them when we might be able to. I then spoke to Miguel Ángel and asked him to find videos, films or whatever to entertain the players.

At midday, we could at last get outside. The staff worked incredibly hard to get the course up to scratch. Given the amount of water that had fallen, I don't think there's another course in the world that could have been rendered playable in such a short time. I haven't changed my opinion about the unfair treatment of Novo Sancti Petri, but I genuinely accept that Valderrama coped with the deluge quite magnificently.

One of the things I'd decided on as team captain was the need to change the order in which the foursomes and fourballs were played. I'd put this change to the European Tour in the spring, and, much to my surprise, after I'd spoken to Tom Kite, the American captain, it got the support of the American PGA.

Quite apart from the stress and mental pressure which the competition subjects you to, the Ryder Cup is physically very draining. The changes I'd suggested were designed to save our team physical energy – the loss of which would also drain our mental power as the encounter proceeded. I knew from the statistics that the Americans had historically failed to make full use of all twelve team members. My plan was to ring the changes more frequently than Tom Kite. The fourballs tend to wear a team down more quickly, so if we played those in the morning and the shorter foursomes in the afternoon, the players would be fresher the next morning. They'd also be less tired when it came to the singles on Sunday. Equally, playing the fourballs in the morning would give my men a bit of a cushion. The foursomes risk exposing a pairing and making it vulnerable if one player isn't playing well or seems under stress. In fact, the changes we introduced worked so well that they were retained in subsequent Ryder Cup encounters.

Something else I did was to narrow the fairways in the areas where the drives were going to land, something that didn't go down well with Tiger Woods or Fred Couples. But we had no reason to set up the course to suit them. We'd seen what Tiger was capable of at Augusta, so we prepared our terrain carefully. I think he could only use his driver once, at the par-5 11th, and it's not even a great help because if you end up on the slope, the ball can roll back down.

I was amused at the welcome reception when Fred Couples said: 'Seve, it's not fair; I've always thought the further you drive the ball, the better your chances in golf, but that's not the case here.'

'Well, Freddie,' I responded, 'you must take the course as you find it.'

Naturally enough, all home captains try to make sure the course suits their team best. Our players were very familiar with the Valderrama course, because they'd played the Volvo Masters there every year since 1988 and knew the likely pin placements. All I had to do was to make the most of the resources at my disposal.

It was my aim as captain to make us all feel like a team and committed to the tournament. With this in mind I gave the players a very clear message when we arrived at Valderrama:

'On the first two days there'll be eight players on the course and four in a temper because they're not playing, but you know you can't all play and that this is a team effort. I'm not worried about your individual performances because our mission here is to win fourteen and half points. If we can do that, we will all have won.'

I set out the strategy that we would follow, which meant I had to take difficult decisions during the encounter. The players didn't always understand. For example, I only played Ian Woosnam and Darren Clarke once, aside from in the singles, because I opted for the players I thought were on best form. I put both of them in the second fourballs on the Saturday – Woosie with Bjorn and Darren with Monty – and they won. On Friday evening I'd told myself that 'if these two want to show me they're playing well and that they should have played today, they now have their opportunity'. As I'd imagined, they both played fantastically well and I was very pleased for both of them, but my primary concern was always to do what I thought was right for the team.

One of the most demanding moments for the captain is when he has to nominate his pairs, especially for the foursomes. Individual players need to have a close understanding of and sensitivity to their partner's game. As far as is possible he should look for players who like playing together, for it's next to impossible to win points when partners don't get on. Similarly it's a good idea if players are very consistent in foursomes and bold and imaginative in the fourballs.

I am sure the main reason Olazábal and I were so successful in the Ryder Cup was because we got on well on and off the course; there was a great understanding between us and we shared similar perspectives. For me, Chema was central to my being able to attain a Ryder Cup record of twenty victories, five draws and only twelve defeats.

Prompted by this need to make sure my pairings were compatible, I asked everyone at the beginning of the week to name two teammates they'd feel comfortable with playing foursomes and fourballs. I recall that Lee Westwood named Darren Clarke and Nick Faldo, who in turn had named Westwood. I put them together on all four occasions, with good results. I also asked each how many rounds he felt he'd be able to play. Langer said he couldn't manage five, so he played four. Rocca, Faldo, Westwood, Montgomerie and even Olazábal, who'd returned to competitive play only that March after a serious injury to his feet, put themselves down for five. Ignacio Garrido and Jesper Parnevik also volunteered for all five, although they only played four. In Jesper's case that was because his foursome on the Friday afternoon was held over until the next day; it meant he would have had to play forty-four holes on Saturday, a tremendous effort I didn't feel able to ask of him.

The captain is the one who has to make all the decisions, and he must do so in line with the strategy he's elaborated, the way the match is going and the mental state of each member of his team. It's important for him to assert his authority over them while not getting anyone's back up. Good communication between captain and team is essential to weld the team together and make it strong. And the captain must never take decisions unilaterally or on a whim; they should arise from taking into account the views of the team, in particular those of the most experienced. Nonetheless, some decisions are very difficult and I avoided doing anything hasty during pre-competition practice. There are personal situations that require firmness and understanding.

For example, as Darren Clarke, Woosnam, Bjorn and Garrido hadn't played the first fourballs on Friday morning, I asked Mark James and Tommy Horton to go to the practice range to tell me who they thought was shaping up best to play in the afternoon's foursomes. Mark soon started to insist over the walkie-talkie that I should put Darren Clarke's name down, because, so he said, he was on top form and hitting some terrific shots. I felt that Mark might have been influenced too much by his friendship with Darren, and that might be preventing him seeing the situation objectively. I couldn't take personal relationships into account. As I said Miguel Angel Jiménez, 'I'm only interested in the team working perfectly and winning this match.'

By Friday lunchtime Darren Clarke knew I hadn't selected him for the afternoon either. I picked him for a game on the Saturday. (Sorry, Darren, I didn't do it to annoy you. I just did what I thought was right.)

Despite all the problems, the team worked worked very well. They would give me my best possible prize, both as captain and as a Spaniard.

Chapter 40

Victory in Spain

The fact that the Ryder Cup was played in Spain was a triumph in itself, but the European team's victory in 1997 made it unique. It was the crowning achievement of my long sporting career and it was all down to the team's commitment and competitive spirit.

As scheduled, the opening ceremony took place the day before the competition started. King Juan Carlos and representatives of the central and Andalusian governments, as well as leading international figures were in attendance. There were interesting contrasts on the first day, when in the morning fourballs we watched Chema Olazábal, partnered by Constantino Rocca, hit a magnificent shot at the 14th for an eagle. By the end of the afternoon, when play was suspended because of poor light, the scoreboard showed the teams level on three points each.

After the torrential rain that delayed the start, Saturday began with the foursomes that were left over from the Friday. The final two games saw Nick Faldo and Lee Westwood beat Justin Leonard and Jeff Maggert – Westwood decided it at the 16th when he sank a magnificent six-metre putt for a birdie – and Jesper Parnevik and Ignacio Garrido halve their contest with Tom Lehman and Phil Mickelson.

The bad light and weather meant that only seven of Saturday's scheduled games finished on the day, but we performed spectacularly. For the first time in sixty years of Ryder Cup history, the United States had gone a whole day without winning a single game. Despite the storm clouds the sun shone on the European team. But the games had been generally much tighter than the scoreline reflected. Half-way through the fourballs we were behind in all three of the games that we eventually won. Two of our victories came at the 17th and two at the 18th, which showed yet again that Europe was the stronger team at the final holes, when the tension reached its height. That Saturday Nick Faldo achieved his twenty-third victory in the Ryder Cup, thus beating Arnold Palmer's record, and his colleague Lee Westwood made five birdies in seventeen holes playing against none other than the formidable Tiger Woods and Mark O'Meara. Montgomerie and Clarke beat Fred Couples and Davis Love, and Woosnam and Bjorn beat Leonard and Faxon.

In the final game of the morning Olazábal and Garrido managed a draw that felt like victory against Lehman and Mickelson. With two holes to go they were level, but at the 17th Nacho Garrido was in a bunker whereas Phil Mickelson was only two metres away from the hole and looked set to make an eagle. Nacho played with incredible sangfroid and surprised everyone by digging his ball out of the sand to leave it two and a half metres from the cup. He made his birdie whereas Mickelson missed his putt for eagle. The two teams were still level. The tension didn't diminish at the final hole. Chema was left with a seven-metre putt to halve the game. Obviously if anyone was going to hole one of the most difficult putts in the world, it was Chema Olazábal. And he did.

Lehman and Mickelson were the strongest American pairing in this round of the Ryder Cup, since Woods and O'Meara didn't play together as well as people hoped. Nobody could believe their eyes. In the afternoon a distraught Tom Kite declared that the pairs he had selected were 'his A team, and they've been massacred'. The European team wound up that sensational Saturday almost in the dark with a magnificent 9–4 scoreline.

The team was really on a high that night but I warned them that, although we'd done very well, the tournament wasn't finished. I reminded them how we'd won at Oak Hill in 1995 because the Americans' complacency had cost them dear. We couldn't make the same mistake on the Sunday. I also told them not to look at the scoreboards – they shouldn't be worrying about other people's game; they needed to concentrate on winning their own.

I was so tense I took some sleeping pills. Like everyone else I felt the Cup was ours, but I also thought we could have a bad day and throw the whole thing away. If we let slip a five-point lead it would be very bad for the team, for European golf and for me, the team's first non-British captain. What's more, the match was being played in my own country. Defeat would be a real disaster. Already I could feel the weight of responsibility and criticism raining down on my head, especially the criticism that would arise in Spain, which didn't have the golfing culture that existed in the United Kingdom or Ireland. I finally went to sleep with all these worries going round and round in my head.

Early next morning, while I was having breakfast and reading the newspapers I discovered that some very important people had arrived in Valderrama. George and Barbara Bush and Michael Jordan were there. When I saw Jordan I gave a start. The previous morning, a few minutes before handing in the list of pairings for the afternoon games, I had been sitting on a buggy at the 10th jotting the names down, when I'd looked up and seen a giant next to me wearing shades, a hat and a scarf round his neck.

'Hi!' he greeted me.

'Hi!' I answered, not paying him any attention. (In fact I thought 'Fuck, what's this guy doing in the middle of this fairway!')

Now that I saw him in the newspaper I realised the huge fellow whom I'd treated so offhandedly was none other than Michael Jordan. 'Hell! What can he have thought when I ignored him?' I thought. I'd played with him a few years previously in a Pro-Am in Los Angeles and he'd shown me he wasn't a bad golfer. Three years after the 1997 Ryder Cup, Jordan came to Cheste, near Valencia to watch a motorbike race and he said he wanted to play a round with me. I accepted and apologised for my rude behaviour when he'd greeted me that morning in Valderrama. Jordan burst out laughing; he was amused that somebody hadn't recognised him.

The sun was shining brightly on Sunday morning. We got the final series of foursomes out of the way, which left us leading by 10½ to 5½. Faldo and Westwood had lost to Hoch and Maggert; Garrido and Parnevik forced a draw with Woods and Leonard, to the surprise and incredulity of the Americans; Montgomerie and Langer had beaten Janzen and Furyk; and Olazábal and Rocca smashed Couples and Love 5 and 4.

Despite all my fears we'd got through this first phase much better than I'd hoped and we now prepared to play the singles with a clear five-point lead. My night-time anxiety began to fade and I told myself, 'It's now almost impossible for us to lose this Ryder Cup. It's a big lead and we're playing in Spain, on a course that our team is very familiar with; we're home and dry.' After all the rain that had poured down, any dryness was purely rhetorical.

Everything seemed to indicate that the road to victory would be straight, but that wasn't the case. It was still very possible we could face disaster. I was a nervous wreck the whole afternoon, because as the match proceeded I could see that not only might we lose the odd game, but we might lose the tournament. Suddenly, our team was under fantastic pressure, and the Americans, with nothing to lose, started to pepper the board with red numbers, the colour used for recording US points.

In the morning, when I was deciding on the order of play for the singles, I was sure that the Americans would put their best players in the first games, since they needed to win points immediately to reduce our lead. Therefore, I wanted to keep back our best players for the final games. Before making a final decision I consulted with the players and everyone was in agreement. Except for Woosnam, who wanted to play in the first game – perhaps he was impatient because he'd only played one game so far – my four most trustworthy players – Olazábal, Langer, Montgomerie and Faldo – were in the second half of my list. I didn't want to put newcomers in a position of being able to win or lose the Ryder Cup.

We got off to a rocky start, but then managed to steady the boat. For the third consecutive time in the Ryder Cup Woosnam faced Couples, who overturned the previous run of results to win 8 and 7. Woosnam's defeat was followed by victories by Johansson over Love and Rocca over Woods, a terrific point to win. I remember I'd asked Constantino before the start, 'Who would you like to play, Constantino?'

'Tiger,' he replied without a moment's hesitation.

After seeing who was playing whom, I went back to him.

'Constantino, guess whoe you've got?'

'Who?'

'Tiger.'

Constantino's intuition had been right. His win put Europe two points from victory. As the sky became overcast and it rained harder and harder Thomas Bjorn got us a surprise half when he drew a frantic game with Justin Leonard, the then Open champion. Thomas was extraordinarily tenacious and fought back having trailed by four after the first four holes.

By this stage we needed one point to retain the Cup and one and a half to win. As I went round the course I saw that Olazábal was one up against Janzen; Langer was two in front of Faxon; and although Faldo and Montgomerie were trailing Furyk and Hoch, they were still in with a chance of getting a point.

Then – as is invariably the case in the Ryder Cup – things changed. Olazábal was on the 17th green in three, as was Janzen. The latter was less than five metres from the cup; Chema not much further. Unfortunately for us Janzen holed and Chema didn't, so they reached the final hole level. Given the extraordinary way José María had returned to competitive golf at the beginning of the season it would have been wonderful if he, a Spaniard playing in the first Ryder Cup to be held in Spain, had won the point to retain the Cup. But it was not to be. This honour fell to Bernhard Langer, who hadn't won a singles game since 1985 and who had borne the brunt of the 1991 defeat at Kiawah Island.

Faldo lost to Furyk and that left only Colin Montgomerie and Scott Hoch, who came into the last hole level pegging. We went to watch. Monty had to get at least a half to ensure he won the game and the match. With great self-control and mastery of the game, Monty dominated the hole from the start. He reached the green with two good shots, which left him six metres from the pin. For his part, Hoch had found the rough and took three to reach the green. He faced a putt of over seven metres. Monty's putt left the ball very close to the cup and Hoch didn't make him play again. I suggested to Monty that he should do the same to give us an elegant finale. There was no point forcing Hoch to putt just to see whether we could extend our margin of victory. We had won the Ryder Cup!

Then it started to pour down. The European players and spectators danced, laughed and exulted in the rain. We let out our accumulated tension and drenched ourselves in champagne to hide the deeply emotional tears we were shedding. The party went on until 2.30 a.m. It was well deserved: we'd crowned with success a long-pursued project to bring the Ryder Cup, the world's most prestigious team tournament to Spain, and win it.

As I have said, victory in my home country was the crowning achievement of my career. I felt incredibly happy and relieved, but I also felt that I didn't wish to continue as team captain. But before I pursue that thread, I'd like to say that the most moving moments for me in the packed press conference after our victory came when José María Olazábal spoke. As captain I had asked all the players to describe in turn their impressions of that rainswept week. Chema, who was at the end of the table, was the first to speak.

'It's been more or less similar to the other occasions when I've played the Ryder Cup but this time it was very special for me . . . a year ago I couldn't even walk . . .' he said and then burst into tears.

Chema had suffered a bad injury and he didn't play competitive golf for eighteen months from September 1995. Three weeks before his return to the Tour at the Dubai tournament in March 1997, he drove two hours from his house near San Sebastián to Pedreña, where we played eighteen holes and then had lunch. We talked about everything under the sun. I told him I was already counting on him and was very aware he had withdrawn from the team in 1995 and he must be sure to tell me if he didn't feel well. When he expressed his fears I advised him to go and play in Dubai, as it was the ideal place for him. It was the right thing to do, because he finished twelfth. He then came fourth in Portugal and first in his next, the Turespaña held in Gran Canaria. He didn't disappoint at Valderrama and made a great contribution, winning two and a half of the four points he played. José María Olazábal has been and will continue to be one of the great Ryder Cup players in the modern era.

The day after our victory, I lay in bed mentally reviewing everything that had happened both before and during that week. I felt exhausted by the enormous efforts I'd expended in organising the tournament. I thought the most sensible thing I could do was give up the captaincy. I had had to sort out so many things, deal with the politics, put up with players' complaints, attend to the press, and, to top it all, endure the ridiculous business over Miguel Ángel Martín's injury. I felt I'd returned from the battlefield. We'd won in the end and, I thought, 'I've done my duty by the Ryder Cup'. I had no wish at all to continue, at least not for the moment. 'Perhaps later on,' as I said at the press conference. But I felt very happy, because all the effort to persuade the Ryder Cup committee to play the tournament in Spain had been rewarded with success. It proved that taking the Ryder Cup away from the UK to the European mainland was good for Spain and European golf.

I believe Mark James generally conduced his captaincy in a very praiseworthy way in the next Ryder Cup at Massachusetts in 1999. I would perhaps just question his choice of players. When a captain directly selects a player it means he thinks that player vital for the team. You don't pick someone to leave him on the bench until the Sunday, as he did with Andrew Coltart. I didn't object to Mark's selection of Jesper Parnevik, but I did to his choice of Coltart, given that Bernhard Langer, a hugely experienced major winner and an excellent four-somes player was available. To choose a newcomer and leave him on the bench until it's time for the singles is really quite incomprehensible. I think it was insulting not to select a distinguished player like Bernhard, who had done so much for golf. Not only was he playing well, but was only two behind Coltart in the rankings. If there was a reason for not wanting Langer there, it's unknown to me; perhaps Mark may have thought the German's prestige might undermine his authority in the eyes of the team. I also think it would have been better to choose Robert Karlsson, who was in the top twelve in the points list. I wonder what qualities James thought Coltart had over Karlsson to warrant his selection rather than the Swede's.

I should also say that I think it's quite unfair that the Ryder Cup captain isn't paid for carrying out his duties. It's right that players should not be paid for participating in the tournament and that the profits made should go into promoting golf for young people or some other charit-able endeavour. Nevertheless, the captaincy takes up an enormous amount of time and requires more work than any other position in the organisation: if anyone deserves to be paid, it is the captain. Apart from the responsibility he has in choosing players and shaping the team's strategy, he must also see to everything from the clothes, food and hotel to following the players' form and course preparation, to dealing with the press. The committee should consider compensating the captain for the hours he spends on his team in the world's most prestigious tournament.

My long, close commitment to the Ryder Cup also allows me to suggest other radical changes that would benefit the Cup and indeed the sport of golf in Europe. In the first place, the tournament should belong to the European Tour, because it was the inclusion of players from the European mainland in 1979 that enabled the tournament to develop the prestige and global profile it now enjoys. It is a question of principle that the great amounts of money it generates should be distributed throughout Europe and that the tournament should be rotated between the countries of the mainland. Sweden, Germany, France and Italy, among others, are countries that should have the opportunity to host a Ryder Cup. I'm glad that the 2018 tournament will again be held on the mainland, but that will be twenty-one years after Spain showed that the Ryder Cup is a powerful weapon to promote golf in European countries where it has not yet become properly established.

Chapter 41

The Ryder Cup: From the Ringside

If the 1997 Ryder Cup was special since as captain I was top *torero*, in recent years I have had to watch the bulls from the ringside rather than from the arena's sands. But I have always been the European team's biggest fan and the truth is I have derived great satisfaction from being a spectator. These bullfighting expressions come to me via my close friend Enrique Ponce, a great fan of golf and an occasional pupil of mine, and a genuine number one in the world of bullfighting.

Excepting 1999, the Ryder Cup has continued to wear European colours since our victory at Valderrama. Our team spirit, outstanding captains and excellent players have demonstrated time and time again that Europe isn't second best.

Ryder Cup 1999

The 1999 Ryder Cup, held at the Country Club in Brookline, Massachusetts, is perhaps the most controversial of recent confrontations. The American team made an almost miraculous recovery to win the tournament 14.5–13.5, after coming into the final day trailing 10–6.

The Americans, captained by Ben Crenshaw, won 8 points from the 12 singles games on the Sunday for the first American victory since 1993. The key moment took place in one of the final games. Olazábal was dominating his match against Leonard: he was four up with seven holes to play. The American won the next four so they teed off at the 17th level. As the rest of the games stood at that moment, a half-point would have been enough for the American team to secure victory.

Olazábal's approach left the ball some seven metres from the hole. Leonard's landed only three metres from the flag, but rolled away to leave him a birdie putt from 13 metres. Although holing out in such circumstances was difficult, Leonard had already made putts from 7 and 11 metres that day. He found the hole, and US players, wives and fans erupted in wild celebrations, jumping on the green to celebrate. Olazábal knew that he had to make his putt to extend the game. If he missed, victory would go to the United States (the Americans required 14.5 points to win the tournament because of the 1997 European victory in Valderrama). Olazábal tried to concentrate as best he could, but he missed. Victory went to the American team.

Although the American team's celebrations broke no rules, the game of golf is considered to be a 'game of gentlemen', and there exists a series of unwritten norms and codes which were ignored here, in the opinion of the European players. After the tournament, many members of the American team apologised for their behaviour and both teams made a concerted attempt to reduce the tension the contest had provoked. Mark James, the European captain, became the centre of attention and criticism because of the way he made up his pairings. Three players (Jarmo Sandelin, Jean Van de Velde and Andrew Coltart) made their débuts in the singles on Sunday without having played matches on the previous days. This had the additional misfortune of meaning that many of the European players were very tired when it came to playing the final decisive games.

As I previously commented, it's always a good idea if every player can play a game – at least one – before the Sunday singles.

Ryder Cup 2002

The Ryder Cup was cancelled in 2001 for fear of possible terrorist attacks since just before it was due to be played the horrific September 11 attack on the Twin Towers in New York took place.

In 2002 Europe succeeded in defeating the American team 15.5–12.5 thanks to good European performances in the singles on the Sunday.

The Irishman Paul McGinley managed the necessary half-point in his game against Jim Furyk to give Europe victory. It was a memorable victory because the Europeans lost only two of their singles matches, and won by three points, the greatest margin since 1985 when Europe won 16.5–11.5.

Captain Sam Torrance couldn't hold back his tears and the entire European team jumped on the turf to hug McGinley, a Ryder Cup débutant, whose four-metre putt at the 18th green will go down in history.

On this occasion the tournament was played in the most sporting of atmospheres. At the end of Saturday, when the scoreboards showed the teams level on eight points, Sam Torrance started to worry over statistics which showed that singles weren't the Europeans' forte – the United States had won six of the last seven singles encounters. But Europe took a risk in the first matches by putting forward its most experienced players: Montgomerie, García, Clarke, Langer, Harrington and Bjorn. It would be the turn of the débutants later and the Swede Parnevik would play the last game against none other than Tiger Woods.

The American captain, Curtis Strange, preferred to spread out his players, and keep his big stars to last: Davis Love III, Phil Mickelson and Tiger Woods. But he lost his wager. On the European side García lost to David Toms: the young man from Castellón couldn't reduce a minimal American lead over the last three holes. First he missed a putt to win the 16th, then another at the 17th that was even closer, and then he put too much draw on his drive at the last hole and ended up in the water.

Montgomerie, Langer and Harrington won their games overwhelmingly against respective rivals Hoch, Sutton and Calcavecchia. After García's defeat, Thomas Bjorn gave Europe the vital point, when he beat Stewart Cink by 2 and 1. At the time, Europe was leading 12.5–9.5. There were six games to play.

The Swede Fasth came to the last green with a one-hole lead over Paul Azinger. Nevertheless, the American drew on his experience and good fortune to hole from the bunker and half the game. Europe needed half a point, and McGinley was the man to do it. At the age of thirty-five the Dubliner gave the glory to Europe in his first Ryder Cup, and pushed Tiger Woods, the world's best player, off the back page.

My enjoyable experience of team competitions led me to create the Seve Trophy, a competition at the highest level that sets Continental Europe against Great Britain and Ireland. I should emphasise that

Michael Robinson and my brother Baldomero were key here, and my strongest supporters in turning this idea into reality. The tournament was first staged, with great success, in April 2000. The arrangement was that it should be held in alternate years, so as not to clash with the Ryder Cup. Consequently the 2001 postponement led to a certain disruption of dates; so although the Seve Trophy's second outing was held in 2002, the third was brought forward to 2003. Subsequently the Seve Trophy has been held in odd years.

Ryder Cup 2004

The competition took place between 17 and 19 September 2004, at the Oakland Hills Country Club in Bloomfield Township, Michigan. The European team won the tournament by a final margin of 18.5–9.5. Colin Montgomerie was the player who signed off the victory, thus maintaining his record of never having lost a singles game in the seven times he had participated in the tournament. The size of the victory was the largest recorded by the European team in the tournament's history, and the biggest since 1981, when the US team beat the Europeans by the same score (that was the year they decided to do without me).

Ryder Cup 2006

The Ryder Cup – the only sporting competition that pits Europe against the United States simply for the honour and the glory, and where not a single euro or dollar is in dispute – will remain in European hands for two more years thanks to the victory of Ian Woosnam's team, which again finished with 18.5 points against the 9.5 of the Americans, who were this time captained by Tom Lehman. Europe had now won five of the last six outings – three consecutively.

The morning began under a grey sky at a fairly muddy K Club but despite the bad weather the games began on time. The players received an astonishing welcome at the first hole. They were cheered and applauded, particularly the Irish members of the team.

The Europeans led the whole day, from the moment Colin Montgomerie took the lead at the third hole of the first game. At the 17th, Luke Donald won his encounter with Chad Campbell and got the point that guaranteed Europe a least a tie. Soon afterwards the

Swede Henrik Stenson, one of two making their débuts, beat Vaughn Taylor 4 and 3. Europe was triumphant yet again.

To sum up, I believe that the most enduring memories of all those who have won a major tournament are not of personal success, but of leading our teams to victory in the Ryder Cup.

(*Above*) At the Pedreña marina

(*Below*) Practising with Miguel and Javier!

(*Right*) In the swimming pool with the kids

The Ryder Cup.
(*Main photograph*)
Triumph in 1985:
Tony Jacklin is getting a
little wet!
(*Inset left*) Celebrating
again in 1987;
(*Inset centre*) Disaster at
Kiawah Island, 1991;
(*Inset right*) Flying the
Spanish flag in 1995

The Ryder Cup comes to Spain, 1997: (*Top*) Shaking hands with King Juan Carlos at the team presentations; (*Bottom*) A pre-tournament shot of the European team – there was no way I was going to let the Americans get their hands on the trophy!

The Ryder Cup 1997 – bringing victory home: (*Top left*) Looking on anxiously on the opening day; (*Top right*) Celebrating during the Saturday foursomes; (*Left*) With the trophy safe at Valderrama

My favourite trophies

FACING PAGE
(*Main photograph*) My five majors and the Seve Trophy. (*Inset*) At home: from here you can see the Bay of Santander and Puntal Beach

On Puntal beach

Chapter 42

Spain, Golf and Me

It is very significant that in 2001 golf was recognised as the fastest-growing sport in Spain. A crucial factor in this spectacular spurt was the staging of the 1997 Ryder Cup in our country. Among my justifications for relinquishing the captaincy immediately after our victory, were the indifference and the lack of interest shown by the government of the time and by the Royal Spanish Federation of Golf. When Spain won the right to stage the contest I felt they had no idea of the tournament's importance or what a fantastic opportunity they now had. They didn't appreciate the benefits golf could bring to Spain, or the future profile of the sport. Many didn't see that golf could be a significant engine for tourist development. It almost made me despair that – after all the effort and hurdles overcome in order to hold the Ryder Cup in Spain – they couldn't see it was important.

This negative attitude showed I could expect no support from politicians or the Federation. In the end, I received a call in the pressroom from King Juan Carlos and telegrams from Tony Blair, the British prime minister, and from several Irish ministers, but no greeting from a Spanish minister even though more than one came to Valderrama. After the 2006 Ryder Cup was held in Ireland, the accountants Deloitte and Touche were commissioned by Ryder Cup Europa and Fáilte Ireland (the body responsible for promoting tourism in Ireland) to assess the economic benefits generated by the event. They estimated that the Irish economy earned €143 million as a result of the Ryder Cup, which was 32 per cent more than had been earned in England in 2002 and 80 per cent more than had been earned in Spain in 1997.

When a country manages to attract an event of such significance, it usually sets in train a series of investments to boost the event and especially to show off to the mass media and visitors the attractions of the place, the region and the country itself. Nothing was made of this opportunity. In Spain important improvements were made to civic infrastructure at the time of the Olympic Games in Barcelona. The America's Cup – an event with a very similar profile to that of the Ryder Cup – gave rise to a series of large investments that have totally modernised Valencia. If the government was not prepared to recognise the importance and future repercussions of the Ryder Cup, you might expect that somebody – some organisation – would have pointed out their shortcomings.

Many people have worked hard in Spain to popularise the sport of golf. However, now that the results are there for everyone to see, several people have been quick to claim undeserved credit. The RFEG (the Royal Spanish Federation of Golf) has used incredible sleight of hand to promote itself as the architect of the tremendous expansion of the game in Spain, but its role has simply been that of spectator. I have encountered its president at all manner of celebrations, and I've been astonished to hear her presented at those occasions as the person who has revolutionised golf in our country. Her major contribution to Spanish golf was the creation of a National Golfing Centre which, in doubtful taste, was named after her.

Two professional golfers from the European Tour, Gonzalo Fernández-Castro and I, attended the launch of the centre in March 2006. In the course of this event I recalled meeting the then Mayor of Madrid, Professor Tierno Galván, during an exhibition game I had played at the Bernabeu stadium, on 18 April 1983, during the Madrid Open, a week after I'd won the Masters. I asked him to build a public golf course in the capital. 'One? No, two: one in the north and another in the south,' came his reply. Years later, at a meeting I had with Juan Barranco, Galván's successor, I made the same request. Juan Barranco promised me that a public golf course would be built in Madrid; successive mayors have promised the same thing. As time went by and I saw that nothing was happening I started to use interviews in the media to criticise this lack of action. I was concerned that the National Golf Centre should include a course that would be second to none.

The RFEG announced an international competition to design the

National Golf Centre. After studying the specifications for the competition and all the papers relating to the land and plans at length, my brother Baldomero sent a letter to the president in which he explained why we refused to participate in the competition. It said, amongst other things, that 'the specifications drawn up for the tender reflect most of your requirements, or what is the same, those of a big National Centre, but a problem arises because these don't match the characteristics of the land you have currently in your possession'.

After listing all the installations mentioned in the specifications, such as 'dual-use practice ranges, with a minimum size of 320 by 150 metres, a building to house machinery, maintenance and course staff, an access and parking area, as well as a lake to be set next to the entrance to the National Centre', we concluded: 'If we discount the sites referred to – which are all necessary and reasonable – we are left with a final area of less than 47 hectares (469,910 square metres) in which to place "public golf course for training and development purposes adequate for the holding of high level amateur and professional championships, of both a national and international character" . . . that is to say, the final area available is not sufficient to guarantee that the large golf course you envisage can be accommodated. And we feel we are duty-bound to state that we are dealing with terrain which in our opinion is problematic at best, because of the nearby railway and M40 road.'

The aim of this statement was to persuade the RFEG to reconsider its position and to come up with more land, or to look for an alternative location for the National Centre and the large golf course which we all wanted so much. The first time we saw the land in question, at the end of the 1980s, the area had been perceptibly bigger. Technicians from my Trajectory company had even collaborated with the RFEG in the very early days. As far as we were concerned, the aim was to create the best golf course in Spain, a permanent venue for the country's open, if that was what was wanted, like France had with its National Golf Centre in Paris, Le Golf National.

However, the competition went ahead and after a very long building period, the day came to launch the Centre. In 2006 it opened for golf. It hosted a Challenge Tour event that summer, but the RFEG technical committee concluded that alterations would have to be in place before it could host the Spanish Open in 2007. Consequently, the course was extended and new tees were built for eight holes. The green at the 18th was modified, bringing it closer to the lake, and for the Open it was decided the fairways would be narrowed and the rough allowed to grow more than 10 centimetres high. It seemed to me as if they wanted to present the course as if it were a 'links' (though it was no such thing) but they wished to employ the much-criticised philosophies used in preparing US Open courses.

After more than twenty years, in 2007 control of the Spanish Open passed to the RFEG, after the agreement with my firm Amen Corner, which had organised the Open since 1986, was not renewed. I won't make any judgement in this respect, but I feel that the treatment meted out to Amen Corner by the RFEG was as unfair as it was expected. The RFEG hoped by this change to attract leading professionals from the European Tour and take the Open to the best courses in Spain. But for the moment, we will have to await future outings, as in this first year there has been a clear step backwards on both counts.

Lastly I must report a very painful occurrence. At the Golf Gala of Cantabria in December 2005, the president made an extraordinary speech. On hearing her, I stayed in the room only out of respect for those present. What began as words of warm affection towards me turned into a series of joking comments full of gratuitous advice and opinions that would have been difficult to voice in private conversation, and should never have been expressed in a speech to a forum of four hundred people, including friends and acquaintances, many of whom – my children included – were perplexed by what they heard.

There is quite clearly a great gulf between the RFEG and professional golfers. The RFEG is a closed shop; some of its leaders are anchored in the past and fiercely defend their own privileges. Its policy focuses exclusively on amateurs, which would be a fine thing if it were a seedbed for the game, and not the exclusive preserve of a specific social and economic elite, as it is in some cases. The majority of professionals, with the exception of those who like deferring to silk ties and bespoke suits, reject it. These people listen but don't hear; they don't realise the world has moved on. Apart from being anachronistic, their behaviour is so Spanish. In countries with a golfing tradition, like the United Kingdom, association officers are there to help and don't expect a reward; in Spain you only have to give someone a position for them to think arrogantly that they are indispensable.

The American model should be the one to follow. The golfing industry there is powerful and this is because it is in the hands of professionals. In Spain the reverse applies and the amateur world tries to control everything. For example, RFEG should be replying properly to the widespread and repeated criticisms of golf courses from environmentalist perspectives that are always couched in demagogic language. The lack of precision in these attacks when it comes to the consumption and quality of the water courses use should receive a systematic, scientific and robust response from the Federation. Golf courses are creators of life, genuine green lungs, producers of oxygen and absorbers of CO_2, as well as barriers against desertification. And yet they are treated as enemies of the environment. Their water consumption is much lower than that of any agricultural concern and in any case the water they use comes from a purifying plant; it is only suitable for gardens and parks – in many cases it can't even be used to irrigate crops. Ideally, the Federation would have a specific office to systematically explain the benefits of golf courses and to defend what is in effect an entire industry. However, in the public eye to build a golf course is to launch an attack on nature.

I have a businesslike relationship with the RFEG, but it is a very cold, distant one and there is little collaboration. Proof of that is the fact that in my capacity as a shareholder of Amen Corner, I had to underwrite the Spanish Open financially both in 2002 and 2003. In the end neither endorsement was called in. I was lucky.

There exists a handful of first-rate professional golfers who have good ideas to contribute to golf and whose opinions deserve to be taken into consideration. Spanish golf requires a radical change in the Federation's structures and policies. After all, the number of participants in the sport in Spain does not much exceed 300,000 and it is rising only slowly. Golf trundles on . . . while some stand still. I can't feel proud of these figures. Sweden has 442 golf courses and 544,000 golfers; Germany has 658 and more than 500,000; France has 550 courses. In Spain we have 300 courses, 25 per cent of which are only nine-hole affairs, with 310,000 golfers. We are still a long way behind neighbouring countries, although Spain is in a privileged position as regards high-grade tourism. Obviously, in other countries – such as Great Britain, Ireland, the USA, Japan and Australia – with a much longer golfing tradition, the sport has been developed to a much higher level.

Despite the quantum leap in golf's appeal in Spain after the 1997 Ryder Cup, it is still not an enormously popular sport. Many things have changed: the higher standard of living enjoyed by Europeans in general and the Spanish in particular and the diminishment of social barriers are factors that help to make golf more popular, and this should be exploited. We should consider how much we can do for people by helping them to practise the sport – in addition to the fact that golf attracts high-quality tourism and hence is a means of generating wealth in rural areas that are greatly in need of this. On one occasion when I was going to London to participate in a programme on the BBC, I bumped into an elderly, youthful-looking gentleman in Bilbao airport.

'I'm seventy-one,' he said, charmingly coy, 'but if I'm like this it's because you've set me an example. Thanks to you I was encouraged to take up golf; and if it weren't for golf, I'd have long been in that fine hotel –' and he pointed to the sky.

A few years ago, I was training on my bike in a small village in the heartland of Cantabria when I came to a crossroads and didn't know which way to go. I met an old man walking along the road with the help of his stick. He seemed half blind and I started to talk to him. He recognised me, but what most struck me was how much he knew about golf and the European Tour. He finally said:

'Severiano, thanks for what you've done.'

'You mean my golf?'

'No. Because you've put Cantabria and Spain on the map.'

It was almost a miracle that a man who was half blind should recognise me, because few Spanish people have seen me win one of the really major championships. There was once a kind of blindness in the Spanish media, which was victim to the elitist character of the game in the past and the absence of any true golfing culture in the country. Luckily, this has been changing and Spaniards have seen José María Olazábal win his two Masters and many other tournaments. But I often think that if they had had a chance to see my many victories in my days of glory, as the British did, golf would be much more popular than it is now; just like Formula 1, thanks to Fernando Alonso; motor-cycling, thanks to Ángel Nieto; tennis, thanks to Manolo Santana; skiing, thanks to the much-missed Paquito Fernández Ochoa, who was a great individual and big fan of golf; or cycling, thanks to Pedro Delgado and Miguel Induraín.

It is difficult for people to understand and appreciate something they only read about occasionally in the newspapers. And I should also add that few of the journalists who write about the sport in the Spanish press are really knowledgeable. When I started to compete, Spanish journalists rarely covered even the major tournaments or the Ryder Cup, and they didn't begin to do so in any significant way until the end of the 1980s, when the echoes from my victories began to break down the barriers against golf.

Chapter 43

Fame

Becoming a champion depends on desire, talent, and character on the golf course. Being famous as a champion depends on other factors. These include the importance and tradition the sport has in your own country and the coverage your victories receive in the media. If a great bullfighter appeared in Great Britain, for example, I doubt people would give him the attention he deserved. Something similar has happened in my case, although I'm quite sure that I've contributed a little to the fact that the Spanish public now takes some notice of golf, and that the success of golfers like José María Olazábal, Miguel Ángel Jiménez and Sergio García gets the attention it deserves.

When I won my first Open in 1979 and my first Masters in 1980 the news received next to no coverage in the Spanish press, and even less on Spanish television. My countrymen saw none of my early successes. However, as a result of my international profile and the coverage in the British and American press, the Spanish media began to give some space to my participation in major tournaments and even to show some live action, although this tended to coincide with football and other sporting highlights. Some channels covered the 1983 Masters live, but as the final round was postponed to the Monday, transmission was interrupted before the end to show a recording of a football match or an interview with a politician.

Something similar happened the following year when I won my second Open. There were several live broadcasts from the tournament – but when I was still playing the very last hole, the transmission was again interrupted, this time to show a mediocre horse race from nowhere in particular! Someone even told me that the big news story that day was the death of a pure-blooded mare by the name of Kriti. It was really incredible. There was no Spanish television coverage in 1988 when I won my third Open title.

All this goes to show that golf took a long time to penetrate the Spanish media. Even now it very rarely makes the headlines. In contrast, it's striking that the BBC's sports department granted me the honour of giving me its Overseas Personality of the Year award as long ago as 1984, putting me in the same company as Pele and Muhammad Ali. This prize awards ceremony is one of the most popular television events in the United Kingdom.

In Spain newspaper journalists now cover my activities but golf in general still doesn't get enough space in the media. Even the Santander daily newspapers seem reluctant to write about golf – or me – and it's not as if they can boast many local sports with an international profile: not even dear old Racing Santander, which is a long way from being one of the best football teams in Europe.

I draw attention to the press in Cantabria because it has always had the typically provincial attitude of ignoring what is at hand and admiring what's far away. It's as if a Liverpudlian said, 'Why say anything good about the Beatles? I mean, they only live round the corner.' This is perhaps why I have the impression that the international media have created my image and reputation.

Public institutions in Cantabria have never wanted or tried to establish good relations with me. Aware that as part of the sporting elite I have a public profile, I've always tried to collaborate with my local region in a disinterested way in various promotional initiatives. But my wish to help has not met with the response it deserved. My gestures of goodwill don't seem to interest those of my fellow countrymen who take political and economic decisions, the ones with the power to back campaigns to give Cantabria a higher profile. I find it amazing, for example, that in almost thirty years Cantabria has seen only ten new golf courses in addition to the course I designed at San Vicente de la Barquera. Meanwhile, more than forty have been built in Andalusia. I'm not referring to private as much as to public courses, for my idea has always been to make golf a popular sport within the reach of as large a number of people as possible. To this end, when I played in a tournament organised by the American PGA to help their juniors, I made it a condition of my participation that I should receive 500 clubs which I would donate to Spanish juniors. I also interceded with Román Cuyás, the then Secretary for Sport, and as a result he allotted more than twelve million pesetas to public courses, including the one in Mataleñas.

Cantabria is one of the most beautiful places in the world. There's no pollution and hardly any petty crime; it has a strong cultural identity, magnificent food, striking natural landscapes and beaches that I think are the best in Spain – and that's not just my local pride talking. If the people of Cantabria really want a tourist industry they have in me, if they so wish, and in the sport of golf, terrific levers to raise their profile. But Cantabria is bottom of the league of Spanish regions in terms of golfing growth. It beggars belief: the region's topography and climate are ideal for the construction of courses that won't disrupt the natural environment. (Here I disagree with many of the criticicisms of ecology groups; few golf courses are built with no thought as to their future impact on the environment. In my view a course should occupy terrain where the builder can plant trees and create lakes to attract birds and other animals, and create other resources to complement the features of the local landscape. One aspect that often generates great conflict around golf courses is the huge amount of water they require. Modern courses, however, are equipped with proper recycling plants that mean they help the local environment.)

Cantabria, although a wonderful place for tourists, needs to improve its transport links with the rest of Spain. That said, it has always had good connections by sea with northern Europe. Many British tourists arrive by ferry from Plymouth and Southampton and a good number come to play golf – but soon they head south with their cars and clubs, because there isn't enough locally to lure them into staying. When they get off the ferry, the first thing they see is a sign pointing them out of the city. It's as if they are being asked to leave without visiting the cities or the beauties of our coast or mountain ranges.

I don't want to get involved in politics, for I don't understand how it works. Politicians or their parties have asked for my support many times, but I've always wanted to keep my independence as a citizen. This doesn't mean I don't have my own ideas about politics, but unfortunately I don't hold the political world in high esteem, even though I know there are some politicians who are honest and have the country's interests at heart. I hope the views expressed here are seen as an expression of my willingness – as a champion with an international reputation – to contribute to the development of Spain in general and of Cantabria, my local region, in particular.

From 1975 when I first set foot as an adolescent on a British course – Royal St George's, in Sandwich – I've always felt loved and appreciated by the British press and public. They treated me well as soon as they got to know me; they made me feel at home and let me into their 'kitchen'. I shall always be grateful. It's true I have sometimes had unfair – sometimes downright unpleasant – articles written about me, but respect and a high regard for me has nearly always prevailed in the British press.

Some UK sportsmen and women feel persecuted by the media, as in Nick Faldo's case. Nick and the others may be right but I have found that the media have generally been restrained in their behaviour towards me and generous in their comments. Maybe the fact that I'm not British has helped; perhaps, like their Cantabrian counterparts, British journalists share the view of the Beatles expressed by that Liverpudlian!

In 1991 the British Association of Golf Writers named me Golfer of the Year as the player who had contributed most to European golf. I was given the prize at a dinner held in Muirfield at the beginning of the 1992 Open week. I thanked the journalists there for making me more famous than I really was, because that was the reality of my situation in the United Kingdom. I owed the British press this recognition because it has so often interviewed me and written about me, generally in a positive way. Even though I've won five major tournaments, my name wouldn't be so well known today if it weren't for British journalists.

I've met really remarkable people in the ranks of the UK press, some regrettably no longer with us. I remember Michael Williams of the *Daily Telegraph* with great affection, and Peter Dobereiner of the *Observer* too. Michael died suddenly just after the 1997 Masters. Peter only found out he was ill shortly before he died in August 1996. I'm very happy I had the chance to write wishing him a quick recovery and to receive a reply from him that referred to me and my contribution to golf. It was a wonderful letter that brought tears to my eyes. Peter Dobereiner was a real gentleman.

The mass media, wherever they are based, are extremely powerful and influential; more so now with the new technologies. Their activities can form part of a wide-ranking marketing operation. Take Greg Norman, for example, who has created a reputation for himself that is on a par with Jack Nicklaus's even though he has only won two majors compared to Jack's eighteen. But Greg has cultivated his image and reaped fantastic benefits from the process. In contrast, Larry Nelson has won three major tournaments and almost no one mentions him.

My marketing aim has been to win tournaments and appear as myself before the media and the world. This is relevant because people called me the Arnold Palmer of European golf. In fact I identify much more with Gary Player, as I have said, but anyway, it is a compliment because it's flattering to be compared to Palmer, who has done so much to popularise golf in the United States. In this area, Arnold Palmer is much more important than Jack Nicklaus, although the latter's record is simply awesome.

I think I combine a little of both men, because I am popular like Palmer, thanks in large part to my relationship with the British press and public, and have a distinguished sporting record that includes six Order of Merits, five major tournaments and five World Match Play Championships, among my more than ninety victories.

But I like to think that there is much more to being a champion than simply being a good golfer and winning tournaments. If I had to define myself, I would say I have tried to play golf as if I were an artist. That's why the way I played excited and enthused the general public and why many became fans of the game or took it up themselves. I've always felt I should behave like an actor on the course and perform for the public. It's what Arnold Palmer did. You have to laugh, frown, and show you're happy or sad. You must display your emotions, because then the public feels close to you: that you're one of them, sharing their fears and doubts, but that you also possess attributes that allow you to do what most of them could probably never do. That's always been my style.

In England, lots of people approach me to thank me because they have enjoyed watching me on the course or on television. I think this is wonderful. When I'm in London and take a cab, it's not unusual for the driver to say, 'Hello, Seve, how are you?' People there are much more familiar with me than in Spain. The same is true of Ireland, Scotland, Wales, the United States and even Japan, the country where I am most often asked to pose for a photo. Apparently all Japanese carry a camera and large sheets of white paper that they ask you to autograph so they can hang them on their walls! I don't know if it's because they speak little English, let alone Spanish, or because they are shy, but as soon as you've done what they want, they shake your hand and run off.

Signing autographs can sometimes be a real pain. It is one of the things that makes you think there really are loves that kill. I admire Nicklaus and Palmer because of the way they organise their autograph-signing. To start with, when I was asked for an autograph I would stop and sign and I could never get to where I was supposed to be heading. One day when I watched Jack Nicklaus signing autographs for a group of children I realised that he didn't stop. He kept walking and signed a notebook, a T-shirt, a cap – whatever was put before him. I began to do the same after that, although you always have to sign for longer than you're expecting when someone pleads 'just this last one, please'.

Such anonymous affection opens many doors and facilitates many things, like getting a table in a restaurant or not having to pay the bill. But it also has its drawbacks, as when people interrupt your meal in a restaurant to say, 'Sorry to bother you, but . . .!' And after apologising for bothering you they ask for an autograph, say hello or something similar. What I've never understood is, if they know they're bothering you, why do they apologise for doing so? Apologising doesn't give you the right to do anything – even to apologise. I was once in Germany when a lady in her sixties came over and said, 'Oh, Mr Ballesteros, how pleased I am to meet you. How wonderful! Could you sign here, please?'

I had a bowl of soup in front of me and she took out a notebook and a pen so I could sign. She was so nervous that when she took the top off her pen, it fell into my soup.

'Oh, I'm so sorry, Mr Ballesteros!' the good lady exclaimed, dipping her fingers in my bowl to extract her pen top. 'What delicious soup! It really is, isn't it?'

Having something dropped in your soup is the least of it: the worst is when you're eating and they ask for your autograph, want to shake your hand and talk while your food is getting cold. You try to be pleasant, but people don't realise how much they're invading your privacy. On the other hand, I understand it's the price you have to pay, for it may be the only chance people who admire you have to greet you in person.

A typically ridiculous situation is when someone comes over smiling and asks, 'Do you remember me?'

'Of course I do, but please remind me where we met,' I tell them.

'Well, it was in Sandwich, at a pro-am we played in fifteen years ago.' Fifteen years ago – as if they'd said 'Yesterday, in the hotel bar'!

Popularity is something you have to learn to wear lightly. You may not always be in the mood to put up with its drawbacks, the worst of which is the invasion of your privacy, when people won't leave you alone at times when you most want to be. I have enjoyed being popular and famous, particularly when I started out, but it never attracted me to the extent that I forgot my real aim. I didn't want to be rich and famous. I wanted to be the best player in the world. My fame and success are the results of hard work and . . . British swing.

Chapter 44

Into the American Night

My first experience of the United States wasn't at all encouraging. Not because I played badly, but because I *wanted* to play badly. You will recall how I shot 40 over the last nine holes of qualifying for the American Tour in order not to get my card. I didn't feel at ease in the United States and didn't want to live there. I wanted to be with my family in Spain and play golf in Europe.

After this 'failure' at the Tour school I went to California with my new representative, Ed Barner. This trip finally convinced me I had no wish to live in the United States. If that had happened, I'm not sure I'd have made the same progress in my career that began when I tied in second place with Jack Nicklaus at the 1976 Open. Even so, it was clear I would have no choice but to play on the American Tour whenever I had the opportunity.

In 1976 the European Tour staged nineteen tournaments, with a total of £570,000 in prize money. (To give an idea of how the situation has changed, there are some forty tournaments in Europe now and the top players can easily earn double that amount over the course of a season.) America, with its much greater number of tournaments and far greater amounts of prize money, seemed like a different world.

The first tournament I played in the United States was the 1977 Masters. The second was the Greater Greensboro Open in the spring of the following year. I really entered this tournament only to acclimatise myself and train for my second attempt at the Masters, which was immediately afterwards. I remember I took an Iberia flight from Madrid to Miami on which Manuel Benítez, 'El Cordobés', the bullfighter, was also travelling, though he was in first class and I was in economy. We'd been in the air for two and a half hours when suddenly a voice over the loudspeakers said: 'Ladies and gentlemen, this is the captain speaking. There's no need to worry, because it's not serious, but we have a problem with one of the engines and, as a matter of safety, are returning to Madrid.'

Back in Barajas I called my brothers Baldomero and Manuel; I said the same to both of them: 'That's it. It's all off. The plane broke down and I'm here in Madrid. I'm not going to get back on that plane. I couldn't get to Greensboro in time in any case.'

I must admit I wasn't afraid. I was just making an excuse.

'Seve, you can't come home; you can't fritter away this invitation from the sponsors. You've got to play,' Baldomero responded.

'You have a mission. You've got to go, so go,' came Manolo's reply.

They gave me no option. I got back on the plane and barely arrived in time to play the tournament, although I had time for one practice round at the Forest Oaks Country Club, North Carolina.

I only just made the cut on Friday, ten shots behind the leader, but playing in quite windy conditions on Saturday I went round in 69 and halved my deficit. On Sunday morning I almost got to the tee at the 1st late, as happened to me in the 1980 US Open. I arrived in a terrific rush and I teed off without hitting a single ball on the practice range. I made eight birdies to sign a card of 66. I had to wait a long time for the last games to finish and for Jack Renner to miss a two-and-a-half metre putt at the 18th, to find out I'd won the tournament.

I would be twenty-one the following week; I'd given myself a good birthday present. I've always been characterised as being rather emotional when I win, because I build up to such a state, but I must confess that I was taken by surprise when I won the Greensboro – I think it was one of the most pleasant surprises of my career. That wasn't because it was my first tournament on the American Tour or because I was the first international player, as the Americans call us, to win on their Tour début, or even because I'd only narrowly made the cut having been ten behind the leader. It wasn't to do with any of that. It was because everybody had said it was impossible to win in the United States.

'The American Tour is another world'; 'It's impossible to win in America; you're doing well just to make the cut.' That's what people like Ramón Sota and Valentín Barrios said.

I simply went to see what would happen. And not only did I make the cut but I won the tournament. When everybody tells you it's very difficult to win and you go and win, then victory inevitably has a special flavour. This victory made me the first player to have won a tournament on his début in the past five years, the first winner not to have been a Tour member in the last twelve, and the third youngest winner of all time.

After that wonderful week, I made a succession of errors prompted by my hastiness. It wasn't very sensible on my part to reject an invitation to play in the USPGA Championship, as I was advised. I could even have made some sparks fly on the Tour when the director, Deane Beman, offered me a card without having to go through Qualifying School, but I declined his generous offer as well. The issue here was that the PGA Tour regulations would only recognise me as belonging to their continent's Tour and not to the main European Tour. Thus, aside from the Open, I would not have been allowed to play more than three tournaments in Europe. It was evident these conditions didn't suit me.

When I looked over from Europe at the United States I genuinely believed it was the country of freedom and equality of opportunity. I even believed in the good qualities of the American way of life. When I went there I saw that there was a lot of propaganda. The great players have always welcomed me, because they like competing against good players of any nationality. But everyday professionals eyed me suspiciously as I was not one of them. My victory in Greensboro upset a lot of these players. The week after the Masters I had a chance to win the 'Costa' Championship held in Carlsbad, California (I'd got my place by virtue of winning in Greensboro). I had a dreadful last round playing with Lee Trevino. But even more than my bad play, it was the sarcastic way several American players patted me on the back and said 'Real bad luck!' that really annoyed me.

However, my real problem in the United States wasn't with these 'rivals' but with Deane Beman. Beman had been persuaded by sponsors to offer me a Tour card. It was against the wishes of many of the players, and Beman seemed offended when I said no after my victory in Greensboro. Although it wasn't my intention, Beman had read my rejection as an insult. He wasn't a man to hand out goodies.

Deane Beman ran the American Tour for twenty years. His

management, which began in 1974, contributed enormously to the prosperity of professional golf in the United States – to the extent that most of the world's best players went to live there. His experience with me didn't, however, enable him to grasp that it should have been much easier for foreign players to join.

Despite what people have written and what I've said from time to time, I had no personal conflict with Beman. The problem was to do with the dynamics of the American Tour and the attitude of those players who didn't want to see me on their courses because they felt I was winning money that was rightfully theirs. One day, during a tournament, I was in a changing room when I heard one say to another: 'This Spaniard is only here to take our money.' It was obvious they were consumed by envy and their own mediocrity and were reacting like children. They even called me 'Steve' rather than 'Seve' just to upset me and show their contempt. Some players – never people like Nicklaus, Palmer or Watson – couldn't stomach the fact that a youngster from a village in a small country like Spain could come to the United States and beat them – or that European golfers could defeat them as they did from the 1985 Ryder Cup onwards; it was even worse when Europe beat them on their home ground in 1987. I felt Beman's policies were skewed towards the attitudes of such players. Perhaps if he'd been better disposed to dialogue, like his successor, Tim Finchem, things might have developed differently. I was shocked by the selfish views of those American golfers because when they came to Europe and earned fat appearance fees no member of the European Tour ever protested. But their behaviour towards me was nothing new. The same happened to the South African golfer Bobby Locke in 1950. When the regular US golfers protested he was winning too much prize money, he was suspended from the Tour. He was readmitted only when the best US golfers of the time campaigned in his favour.

Tony Jacklin once told me that some American professionals in his day tried to close the American Tour to foreigners. This changed eventually because it became futile. How could they refuse access to the winner of the Masters, the Open and many other big tournaments, to golfers of the calibre of Bernhard Langer, Sandy Lyle, Nick Faldo, Ian Woosnam and José María Olazábal? In 1983, the year I won my second Masters, my relationship with Beman improved when it was announced that the American Tour would change its relationships with European players and the European Tour. It was what I had been waiting for in order to join the American Tour as a fully-fledged member.

To begin with I thought I could play the fifteen statutory tournaments, despite the effort that would represent. But I couldn't. I felt very lonely, because I had no Spanish friends there, and no one I had anything in common with. I was stuck in the middle of the American night. If I'd been married or if someone else from the European Tour had been there, perhaps everything would have been different. But I was on my own.

It's hard for people who have not had this kind of experience to understand the difficulties I experienced when playing on the American Tour. At home in Spain, I get up, read the newspapers and find out what's happening in my country and the world and my immediate environment; I watch the telly, put on a video or go to the cinema and lead a relatively quiet life. Now I have a fairly good grasp of English, but at the time I struggled. I often couldn't even make out what was being said in a film where the actors were speaking American English. If you don't understand a country's language, it's very hard to communicate with the people and you end up feeling isolated and stressed out.

In spite of these drawbacks I finished 52nd in the Money List of the US Tour in 1984, even though I didn't win a single tournament. The following year I won only the USF&G Classic in New Orleans, but I earned more money per tournament played than anyone else on the Tour. This put me up to 26th in their Money List having played only nine tournaments. But as I didn't play the necessary fifteen tournaments the following year I was expelled from the Tour. I could not even take advantage of an invitation from a sponsor to play in a tournament, which I felt was a very unfair decision. I think Beman acted very strangely in this instance because the Tour had no right to set itself against invitations from sponsors. In the end, in 1986 I could only play the Grand Slam tournaments in the United States, none of which is organised by the Tour, and defend my title in New Orleans. This was one of the reasons why I was forced to practice for the Masters on the mini-circuit in Florida.

'Seve is a very difficult case. He's constantly in conflict with us and, as he's not complied with the new rules, we'll apply the old ones again,' Deane Beman said.

Beman, in his desire to punish me, also punished all other non-American players. According to the rules, any player who was among the first 125 on the USPGA's Money List had to ask permission to play in Europe, except in the Open. At the time, such a ruling affected players like Nick Faldo and Bernhard Langer. After my 'exile', in 1987 I was allowed to play on the PGA Tour again even though I wasn't a member; again I was the player with the highest earnings per tournament on the Tour. At the time the rules said that a non-member, like myself, could only play in five tournaments other than the three majors.

The following year the week before the Masters I used one of my invitations to enter the Players Championships, the flagship of the PGA Tour. The week before the US Open I used another to play the Westchester Classic in New York, which I won for the second time. This victory, plus the two Masters, meant that I'd won six PGA Tour titles.

If there was a lot of suspense when I won my first Westchester Classic in 1983, it was even more dramatic in 1988. On this occasion after 72 holes I finished level with Greg Norman, David Frost and Ken Green, having holed a five-metre putt for an eagle at the 18th. The first playoff hole was the 10th – a 270-metre par four on which a good drive would leave you on the green. Unfortunately, I put my drive in a bunker near the green. I left the ball in such a bad position I had to make my stroke with my left foot in the sand and my right outside the bunker. The shot was tricky – the aim was tight and what's more, it was downhill. Fortunately, I under-hit the ball to leave it a metre from the cup and sank the putt for a birdie. As none of the others managed less than a four, I won.

Despite this and the support I received from the best American players, I never thought for a moment that Beman intended to include me on the Tour. A section of the American press suggested the fifteen-tournament rule should only be applied to those who aspired to become full-time members of the PGA Tour. This part of the press believed that non-members who had won one of the major tournaments should be allowed to receive an unlimited number of invitations from sponsors to play on the Tour. This suggested rule change would only have impacted on Faldo and myself, because Lyle, Norman, Langer and the Japanese Tommy Nakajima were what were called non-associate foreigners, and so would have posed no organisational problems. Beman refused.

Even so, I was surprised he didn't contact me to try to find a solution to my desire to play on the PGA Tour without abandoning the European Tour. Beman was inflexible. In 1988 he refused to allow the number of compulsory tournaments to be reduced to twelve, which meant Sandy Lyle was the only European player associated with the PGA Tour.

Many people think that if I hadn't deliberately thrown away my chances of a Tour card in 1975 I would have had the opportunity to fine-tune my play on high-grade courses and also managed my back better, because although I would have played more tournaments in the United States, I would have played fewer overall. Nonetheless, I don't regret my decision and feel proud I helped to develop the European Tour.

With time, the situation was finally corrected. Tim Finchem, Beman's successor, has created a policy which ensures that the international presence on the PGA Tour is strengthened. By creating the World Championships he has made it easier for star players from other continents to play fifteen tournaments in the United States without abandoning their national circuits. The present PGA Tour set-up would have been much more favourable to my own career development in the 1980s. The problem is that I was ahead of my time. I had to go deep into the American night.

Chapter 45

Business

My priority has always been playing and winning tournaments. The business side came of its own accord. You can't be a good golfer and a good businessman without one area losing out and I've always put winning first. I'm sure if I'd tried to handle sport and business in parallel it would have been very negative for my career. I know players who have great potential talent but have put a lot of effort into the business side; they have earned a lot of money but their careers as sportsmen have turned out to be quite mediocre. For my part, I can say I feel proud of my career successes; the fact that the business has gone well is due to the efforts and efficiency of my brothers and a very professional, very caring team behind them.

The story of my business commitments begins with my professional career, my first steps in which were helped by the maestro Roberto de Vicenzo. He introduced me to a man called Ed Barner, who ran the American company UMI (Uni-Managers International), at Turnberry, during the Double Diamond Championship in September 1975.

Ed Barner, who had been a radio and television commentator and worked for a Hollywood agency, was a man who was not an expert on the game, but had an excellent portfolio of golfers, including Billy Casper, Johnny Miller, Sam Snead, Orville Moody and Lou Graham. He was a Mormon like Casper and Miller, and my brothers and I thought that he could be the man we were looking for. A month after meeting him, we put him in charge of the management of my financial interests. It took me several years to realise that I had made a mistake – a mistake that would give me headaches and cost me money.

Barner, my first manager, behaved like a sergeant major towards me. He didn't take on board that I was an adolescent who'd just left a country village. I felt that, as far as he was concerned, I was a racehorse he'd run in the usual tournaments, and a string of exhibition matches and parties – too many for a young lad who hardly spoke any English. This was one of the reasons why I took fright during the PGA Tour School and went to spend Christmas and New Year in Spain with my family, earning me a telling-off from my brother Manuel. I know what I did wasn't right, but there was no way I was going to stay by myself in the United States.

I think it was Barner who suggested that my name was too long. He suggested I should be called Seve Sota, my mother's surname. Manuel and I agreed that I should be Seve, but not Sota. I thought it was quite amusing that my name was shortened from Severiano to Seve while Miller, who was called John, had his name lengthened to Johnny.

When I started with UMI, Barner got me one contract after another. The first was signed in 1976 – $50,000 a year to play with Mizuno clubs in Japan. But this strategy soon proved difficult: I found I was playing with three makes of club, depending on whether I was in Japan, Europe or the United States. Whenever I arrived at a tournament, the first thing I had to do was ask myself, 'Where am I playing?' to know what clubs and balls I should use. I played with Mizuno in Japan, Slazenger in the UK and Sounder in the United States, Dunlop in Japan and Titleist in the rest of the world. I was changing clubs, balls and clothes all the time. It was all I did. Three days with these, two with those, playing one make, then an interview with another . . . etc., etc. It was quite mad. Subsequently I adopted only Callaway clubs and balls.

It was just as bad with the clothes I wore – Slazenger in the United Kingdom, Lacoste in mainland Europe, Izod in the United States and Munsingwear in South Africa. The Scottish brand Sunderland provided my swimming gear. I finally signed a world contract with Hugo Boss, the German company. Aside from my sporting clothes and equipment we also signed contracts with American Express, Rolex, Range Rover and Sanyo as well as agreements to represent La Manga Club in Spain and the Doral Country Club in Miami, Florida.

Now that I look back on my career I believe that if I had my time again I would do things differently. I began to disagree more and more with the advice I was getting and my relationship with UMI began to go downhill. Although it's obvious that when you end a business relationship it is because both sides are to blame, I think it would be fair to say that Ed Barner and I never really understood each other. Perhaps we both could have made more of an effort.

In 1981 I renewed my contract with UMI to allow them to represent me for another two years, but that was the last time. The ensuing negotiations to separate my business from Barner's company were long and difficult. In 1985, the day after the final round of the Masters – I was still obsessed by the fact my chip hadn't gone in for a birdie at the 16th when I was chasing Langer – I had to appear before a Los Angeles court which, at the request of UMI, was to arbitrate our contractual differences. I thought this arduous affair was finally going to be resolved, but the case was deferred. I had to wait almost two more years for a judgement. Even that wasn't the end of the matter: Barner appealed against the verdict. I was fed up with the whole affair. In the end we settled out of court. I could then breathe peacefully. Nevertheless, my relations with Ed Barner still smouldered on for a while.

In parallel, my brothers and I had founded the Fairway company to look after my business interests in my home country. The company had its headquarters in Madrid, and was headed up by Jorge Ceballos. Jorge was an old friend who'd been a manager of the Spanish PGA and a director of Iberia. The aim of Fairway was to develop and handle my business affairs in Spain, such as the Seve Tours organised with Iberia.

It was a relief to work with my family after my difficult relationship with UMI and Ed Barner. Working with them, I felt I had greater control over my own interests and that brought many benefits. I could choose what I was going to do and what I wanted to turn down. When a foreign company represents your interests it takes control and it is very difficult to reject what it proposes. For example, I've always thought it is better to play twenty tournaments and rest, because you may win a decent proportion of the tournaments you enter, rather than play thirty and be so exhausted you can't hope to win a single one. It's not worth travelling 15,000 kilometres to earn a large cheque if the journey deprives you of the opportunity to win a major.

I knew that I mustn't fill my diary with tournaments that might be financially lucrative but were much less valuable in sporting terms. Ceballos realised that my heart and soul were in playing golf and winning – not making money, going to parties and receptions.

In 1986, we reached an agreement with Roddy Carr to promote and organise events on the European Tour, and so the Amen Corner company was born. I chose the name for the famous turn holes – the 11th, 12th and 13th – at Augusta. At the present time Amen Corner also organises events in Asia, like the Royal Trophy. In addition I created Trajectory, which focuses on golf course projects. I have excellent staff there, like Gonzalo and Antonio Lavín, an engineer and an economist respectively, as well as Santiago Verastegui, an engineer, with excellent support from José Antonio and Purificación who are also engineers. Our core values are our seriousness of purpose, professionalism, honesty and efficiency. Proof of that is the fact that almost all my people have been with the company since it was set up twenty years ago. If that's important, the loyalty they show me day after day is even more so. I feel really supported.

In 1986 we offered a position of responsibility outside Spain to Joe Collett, whose aim would be to renegotiate, under Baldomero's supervision, all my contracts abroad, so I could make better use of my time. Joe Collett soon showed us we hadn't chosen the wrong man. His firm but flexible way of doing business made us think that we would have got bigger and better contracts if I'd played on the PGA Tour at the start of my career. For example, when I withdrew from the Tour in 1985 – which meant I'd be playing fewer than fifteen tournaments a year in the United States – it cost me a $500,000 contract I'd almost agreed with Nike.

In 1987 I moved to Monaco for strategic rather than tax reasons; my companies were still registered in Spain and still paid taxes there. The temperate, sunny climate of Monaco was good for my back and for training. Nice airport was nearby, and Monaco had other advantages too. I felt secure and untroubled during this period because the business, under Baldomero's guidance, was growing as we had intended.

In 1995 Joe Collett decided to devote his energies to a project entailing the creation of a world circuit. On 8 May 1995 we told the press that we had split up. Joe Collett was a colleague whom I remember with pleasure. He was courteous, correct and very professional. We immediately signed a three-year contract with Roddy Carr, the managing director of Amen Corner, about whom I have a similar opinion.

My brothers have absolute control over my professional assets and obligations. Manuel is in charge of my finances and Baldomero – who doesn't like the word 'manager' because he thinks nobody can ever run another person's life – is overall head. Baldomero, who never wants to be in a photo, always stays behind the scenes and is the touchstone of the whole family.

My brothers constitute a wonderfully caring team, along with our other colleagues. They include Rosario Sordo, the person most familiar with the idiosyncrasies of the Ballesteros family. She stands for confidentiality and professionalism in every sense. She has worked with us for many years, acting as if the company's daily work was her own and that is the example she sets her colleagues, such as Elena.

At the present time, my nephew Iván heads up Amen Corner. After working in every department of the company he is now the chief executive; he is also my representative. Iván is a very intelligent, creative and committed person and he knows how to work with me in a way that prioritises Seve the individual, which is a great help to me at this stage of my career. In our Madrid offices he is surrounded by a good team, notable for the caring and professional qualities of each member.

If I have written at length here about the development of my business interests it is not because I wanted to boast of the volume these have assumed, but because of their essential character. I've always thought that my companies must be organisations where you can feel the human touch and which reflect my image as I really am.

Chapter 46

IMG and the Japanese

After saying goodbye to my duties as Ryder Cup captain, I analysed the situation with my brothers and we concluded that it would be best if Baldomero took charge of all my business affairs. We made the change the winter before the start of the 1998 European Tour, the first tournament of which was the Dubai Desert Classic at the end of February. One night while I was in Dubai I received a call at my hotel.

'Hello, Seve, it's Mark McCormack. I understand that Roddy Carr is no longer with you. I wonder if I could resume the conversation we had twenty-five years ago about whether IMG could manage your affairs.'

IMG, the biggest, most powerful and influential management firm in the golfing world, was founded by Mark McCormack, a lawyer from Cleveland, at the beginning of the 1960s. His first three clients were Arnold Palmer, Gary Player and Jack Nicklaus, the three golfing greats. Almost twenty years later, when I'd just signed with Barner, IMG suggested I should join them and guaranteed me good money for each of the eleven tournaments I would have to play. The money seemed astronomical at the time, but the offer was conditional on exclusive participation in tournaments organised by IMG.

IMG attempted to sign me up several times afterwards, and always with the same result. Subsequently McCormack even stated that he considered his inability to recruit me as a client the biggest failure of his professional career. I have the impression that McCormack's interest may have been down to the fact that the tournaments his company organised paid appearance fees. If I had become one of his players he would have been able to reduce the total amount thanks to the commission he would have earned from me.

Lots of things had happened between the seventies and the end of the nineties, so I reckoned it would be silly to refuse to talk to McCormack. Baldomero and Mark met up during the Open, which was at Royal Birkdale that summer.

'Would Seve agree to play exhibition games on a Monday?' was the first thing Mark McCormack asked when they sat down.

'Is this what IMG is offering Seve? Games on a Monday?' Baldomero asked.

'We'll try to help as much as we can,' came the reply.

'Look, Seve can't play exhibition games on a Monday; he doesn't have to do this kind of thing – he doesn't need the money. Seve has always preferred to safeguard his sporting career. I'm sorry we can't reach an agreement,' replied Baldomero.

And that was the sum total of the offer from IMG. We didn't think it was the proposition of a man who was really interested in reaching an agreement with me, especially after he'd been the one to take the initiative.

The Lancôme Trophy was a select tournament organised by IMG. The French had always wanted me back at the tournament after I'd defeated Arnold Palmer in 1976 in an exciting game. However, as time passed, IMG's attitude became stranger and stranger. I didn't think they were really interested in whether I played or not. In 1994 IMG's Peter German said I could play in the Lancôme but they didn't anticipate paying me any match fee. That wouldn't have bothered me if I hadn't known that they were paying Greg Norman, among others. I couldn't understand this attitude because I was playing well and had won the Benson & Hedges International in May, had come eighth in the European Open in September and, the week before the Lancôme, had come second to Ian Woosnam. I wouldn't agree to play for nothing, but then Norman withdrew and they phoned me urgently. Miraculously, the money was available to pay me a match fee. I came third.

Two months after the 'tempting' offer from McCormack at Birkdale, I once again came up against Peter German at the Lancôme. The tournament organisers usually see to flights and hotels, but sometimes leading golfers will arrange these and settle up later. I did that on this occasion. Just after I'd reached the hotel where I'd made my reservation, German rang me: 'Seve, if you want you can come to the Trianon Palace,' he said. (That was the official hotel.) 'We've reserved a room for you there.'

'Peter,' I replied, realising he had spare rooms he'd contracted and paid for, 'why don't you leave me in peace? I don't think I deserve this kind of treatment after supporting this tournament for so many years. Thank you, but I'm going to stay put.'

If IMG had been representing me from the start I think I'd finally have left, as Greg Norman did. This company's main problem is its varied portfolio of clients, which allows it to negotiate sponsorship or a commercial portfolio with a broad selection of players; however, you never know whether they're negotiating on your behalf or on behalf of others. If I'd been with IMG it wouldn't have surprised me if they'd said to a sponsor, 'If you want Seve Ballesteros in this tournament you'll also have to accept so-and-so' – that is, a second- or third-ranking golfer they were interested in promoting.

IMG has undoubtedly made a big contribution to the development of the European Tour, but it has used its position to make big profits along the way. When McCormack heard this sort of criticism he would reply, 'People have to understand we were here first and we created all this.' This is certainly true, and it's also true that IMG was the first to promote marketing strategies and develop the television rights to the European Tour (through TWI and European Tour Production, the enterprise in which it and the Tour were joint partners). IMG was the first to enter the sector and, without any competition, it developed massively by monopolising the organisation and sponsorship of tournaments, controlling the representation of major golfers and implementing a policy that has prevented other agencies from challenging it in any way.

Given the way I am, I don't need a company like IMG to represent me but an honest, professional, well-qualified person that I can trust. In my view, IMG has too many conflicts of interest for it to be able to defend properly the interests of the people it represents. The flag IMG waves in support of its policy says its players earn a lot of money; but their figures are often far from the truth, at least in relation to Europe. The cry often goes up that IMG has got a particular player a fat contract of two million pounds a year. In such cases, the likelihood is that the figure of two million is correct, but often they're dollars and not pounds, and not for one year but five. Sometimes they're conditional on the golfer agreeing to a commitment of effort and time that is simply inhumane. Clearly this kind of information is part of the publicity machine aimed at promoters, sponsors and the business community, but anyone who knows this commercial world will not be fooled. IMG's rope is always round someone's neck.

Commercial contracts tie a player to a large number of commitments that take away from the time he could devote to training. I made many mistakes like this at the beginning of my career, even without IMG's help. For example, between 1980 and 1985 each year I had to spend four days over Christmas at the Doral Country Club in Miami, as stipulated in my contract. In general, everything is put to you as an attractive and easy commitment, but when the time comes you realise that things are much more restrictive and arduous than they'd seemed. But you are at fault because you or your representative hasn't done the necessary homework on the player, because you treat him like a money-making machine.

Not every company behaves in this way and some treat players very well. I remember, for example, my first visit to Japan in 1975. I was eighteen and arrived there without clubs, balls or shoes. When I entered my hotel room I found a bag from my sponsor Mizuno engraved with my name, with nine new clubs, several dozen balls, six gloves and two pairs of spikes. I felt like the happiest person in the world. I almost burst into tears, because I was alone in this distant, different country. It felt like Christmas.

Over the years, I have got on very well with the Japanese. When I was involved in an advertisement that was to be filmed in Spain for Sapporo beer, the agency brought a sixteen-person film crew over to Spain for a job you might imagine would take three days. In fact it took ten. That December, when it poured down in Sotogrande, the company spent a fortune trying to ensure we had the best possible time. I have many happy memories of these exchanges, like the one about what happened to me when I travelled to Japan to play an exhibition match with Isao Aoki. When we reached the place where we were going to play, at about 11 p.m., they told us to settle down in the clubhouse, a small building with just one bathroom. I woke up in the early hours with a desperate need to have a pee and went into the corridor. I couldn't find the bathroom so I went back to my bedroom and peered out of the window; I saw it was too high up to jump. I couldn't think what to do, until I spotted a bottle of Suntory whisky. I opened the window, emptied the bottle, and you can imagine the rest. The next morning, Aoki came into my room and the first thing he saw was the empty bottle.

'You must have been very happy last night, given you drank the whole bottle.'

I looked at him and said nothing. I didn't feel able to tell him the truth.

Another year, during the Dunlop Phoenix tournament, I was shaving in my hotel room at 7.30 a.m. – for some reason over the twenty years I travelled there I was always in room 731 – when the mirror began to vibrate. My first thought was 'We're going to have a fine day of golf, with this lousy weather!' Then the windows began to shake and the floor moved. I ran down to reception and met up with other guests who were rushing out of the hotel – we were in the middle of an earthquake.

Something similar had happened to me years before in Great Britain. On that occasion Dr Campuzano had come to see me play. He knocked on my door at 3 a.m.: 'Seve, Seve, get up, the hotel's on fire!' he shouted. But as I thought it was a joke, I slept on until the phone rang. They'd had to evacuate the hotel because it really *was* on fire.

What I like about the Japanese is that they are organised, dress elegantly, respect nature and the environment and keep their cities clean. Over the years I have noticed that the Japanese have gradually become more European, which isn't necessarily a good thing for them, because their culture could teach us a thing or two. I recall one occasion when I went to Japan to promote a golf course which I had designed that belonged to the Tezuka family. Vicente, Pedro Morán and an interpreter by the name of Yunko accompanied me. When the Tezuka children, Shun and Noriko, came out to welcome us, a helper gave me a bouquet of flowers. Pedro suggested we should take the flowers to the father of the family, whose ashes were in the attic, and offer him our prayers. His children were delighted by the idea and we went upstairs. In the room were a portrait of Mr Tezuka, rice, sake, and incense sticks to burn during prayers. Shun lit one, I lit another, and we began to pray. Minutes passed. The prayer seemed to be unending. When I could stand it no longer because of my back pain, I got up and said to Shun, 'I'm sorry but my back is hurting . . .'

Shun and Noriko got up at once and overwhelmed me with their thanks. They were very moved. That was when I discovered it is the visitor who decides on the length of time allotted to the prayer by getting up first. Nobody had ever devoted more than a minute to their father before. According to Vicente, we prayed for forty minutes.

When you leave Japan, you immediately notice the different way visitors or passengers are treated. Once, when flying from Tokyo to London, I stopped over in Moscow and, as I had a two-hour wait, I stayed in the airport, reading. When boarding was announced, I remained seated so as not to have to queue. Spotting this, a policeman came over and very rudely told me to join the queue. I told him I preferred to wait and then get on, as I was in no hurry. He reacted by shouting for my passport and I told him I wouldn't hand it over. He then spoke into his walkie-talkie and I saw a patrol coming after me. Concluding that the Russians aren't as pleasant as the Japanese, I quietly joined the queue before things got out of hand.

Chapter 47

Family Matters

I am a man who believes in family. I feel protected when surrounded by my family and I try to ensure my children feel that as well. I have felt that reassurance since childhood and, despite the pranks and excessive fondness for golf that made me neglect my school studies, my parents and brothers always understood and cared for me.

Throughout my childhood, my playing career and my business activities I have always had my family around me. We work together and I can always count on their loyalty. That's why I can live as I live, and I have spent my career in the knowledge that they will always cover my back and I can depend on their emotional support to overcome difficulties.

Nowadays Vicente lives the furthest away. I've already mentioned how close we were when we were young, but I should also add what an excellent teacher he is. (Before he settled in the south of Spain he worked as a teaching pro at Zaragoza and La Manga.) Vicente probably knows my swing best of all. On more than one occasion he has helped me correct things I'd started to change without realising.

Manuel is a financial wizard. He's been a good golfer: he has excellent technical skills, although perhaps his temperament wasn't quite right to allow him to compete at the very top. Even so, he won the Spanish Championship in 1976, the Biarritz Open in 1968, the Timex Open in 1982, and several other tournaments. When I caddied for him I learned a lot by watching how he executed his shots or confronted difficult situations.

Baldomero – Merín – is the oldest and without doubt the one we all defer to. He's also been a golfer and a great teacher. He created all our companies and he runs the show in a very down-to-earth manner. Baldomero, Manuel and Vicente accompanied me to my tournaments, protected and sheltered me so I could train and play, although they made sure I was never isolated, and on more than one occasion they caddied for me. With Baldomero and Vicente, Manuel and I became world champions.

As I've said, my brothers always played and joked with me. I've just remembered a little episode Manolo and I had at home. My mother had a small cabinet where she kept, among other things, a beautiful china service her parents gave her as a wedding present. One day she left a Manchego cheese in the cabinet. Unfortunately, both Manolo and I wanted it, and we began to fight. What a disaster! We knocked over the cabinet and broke some of the china along with five bowls we used for our breakfast milk and corn bread. Only one bowl escaped the carnage, so our mother punished us by making us take turns to eat breakfast and supper.

Marriage affected me a lot. When I married Carmen she was a very young woman. I think, because of her background, that she didn't feel as integrated into her family as I did in mine. Past conflicts determined her behaviour. I genuinely thought she could change and mature at my side and finally become the wife I needed. Unfortunately, we never gelled as a couple.

We got married in 1988, in the house Carmen's grandparents owned in Santander. Strangely enough, I won my last major just months before our wedding. The ceremony took place in the strictest privacy, because we wanted it to be an entirely family affair. Today, I wouldn't have 'hidden away' like that. Those officiating were Don Pedro Cea, the former parish priest of Rubayo, a friend of our family, and Monseñor Federico Sopeña, a friend of Carmen's family. Carmen's close family were there – grandparents, parents and brothers and sisters. My mother, brothers, sisters-in-law and nephews and niece represented my side.

My former in-laws were the only ones who took any photos, and – as I mentioned earlier – some of the photos were made public in Spain, via the shop where we'd taken the film to be developed. Funnily, in some of these photos employees of Carmen's family were described as relatives of mine. But the affair was irritating: some of the press hadn't played fairly with us.

The meal after the ceremony was really enjoyable and entertaining. Of all the guests, my family got on best with Carmen's grandparents. I retain very fond memories of them. After the short, private party, we spent a few days far from Spain before returning home. This was the house where I'd lived with my parents. Once my new house was built, we established ourselves there, but not before Carmen had made all the changes she wanted. And that's where we lived until we separated and later divorced.

From the start, Carmen didn't understand that an elite sportsman is 'different', that, to an extent, he's a very vulnerable person and he needs a great deal of peace and quiet at home. It is true that we had three wonderful children and that she cared for them as a mother should. But Carmen's real family continued to be her parents, brothers and sisters; so much so that when I had a difference of opinion with her family, she sided with me on very few occasions. Carmen's universe was her family, particularly her father.

I first got to know my former in-laws when I was an adolescent, when I replaced Vicente as their children's teacher at the age of fourteen. Two of Carmen's sisters, Ana Patricia and Paloma, won the Spanish Children's Championship (in 1974 and 1975, and 1976 and 1977 respectively). I even accompanied Carmen's father to Biarritz to play with him in a Pro-Am when I was still a caddie.

I have always had a respectful, cordial relationship with my former in-laws. I think Emilio accepted me because he thought I was a hard worker like himself and one who was, moreover, successful. I think I was his favourite son-in-law. My former father-in-law admires people who do well. I came from a very different world to theirs, but at the same time I was aware I was the best golfer in the world and one of the most famous people in the country at that time. Yet I never felt I was one of his acquisitions, as some people have remarked to me since my divorce.

Emilio Botín is a very intelligent man: he deserves everything he has achieved, for he has given his life and soul to his bank. His holidays and all that he does with his children revolve around his work and money. To keep Carmen happy I would agree to go to Switzerland or to a dinner organised by her family. I would be the only one there who would joke or tell a funny story. I did so to break the ice and provoke laughter. In the cage that was their house in

Santander, I was the one bird who could escape, because I was the only one with any independence.

As time went by I saw that Carmen's character reflected an upbringing and education distinguished by discipline and rigid attitudes, both at home and in the institutions where she'd studied abroad. As a result she found it difficult to enjoy the small things in life. I think she lacked confidence when it came to her father. She didn't dare speak to him about anything important. When she said, 'Seve, it's just how my father is,' I'd reply, 'Yes, he may be like that, but you are his daughter . . .'

When my mother died, Emilio came to my house to offer his condolences. He did so because Carmen told him, 'Papa, you must come here because Seve is very upset and depressed on account of his mother's death.' Emilio stayed in my house only for as long as he thought appropriate. Maybe he felt uncomfortable there, because there were times when we hadn't always seen eye to eye, for example when the Bank of Santander–City of Santander project in Boadilla was aired. I discovered through third parties that an American called Rees Jones was going to design the golf course. Apart from being a good designer, Rees is known as a course 'doctor', because his forte is redesigning courses that have become obsolete because of advances in club and ball technology. I wasn't amused by the fact that they'd chosen Jones without giving me an opportunity to present my ideas, and I told Emilio so. He suggested I could be a consultant, but I retorted that I wasn't a consultant or a caddie.

'If you've already contracted Jones, I've been left out of the frame.'

'Seve, you're a unique golfer, but Jones is more experienced as a designer.'

'I don't know how you can say that. You don't know what I've done. I've designed lots of courses and I think your comments are unfair and way off the mark.'

'All right,' he said because his daughter was around, 'it's agreed, you're in as co-designer, and you'll appear in all the publicity as such.'

That's how I came to work with Rees Jones on the project, with magnificent results because it is an excellent course. During the building process we made several joint visits, as a result of which changes were made to the original plans that perceptibly improved the course. My father-in-law was very positive about my contribution and

I'm sure he came round to the idea that he should have had more confidence in me from the start. In our country, where envy is the national sport, Emilio Botín has been unfairly called 'the man with a soul made of banknotes'. But I respect my former father-in-law and retain a special affection for him. He is a gentleman, and, as I've said, he is a tirelessly hard worker. I admire the success with which he oversees the Bank for 24 hours a day 365 days of the year.

With the passage of time, my relationship with Carmen deteriorated. I felt she could do whatever she wanted, such as inviting home any friend she wanted to; whenever I tried to do likewise, I was met only with reproaches. Until the day I realised that you can be tolerant – but only up to a certain point. I realised she could not give me the affection or support I needed, at a time when my career was going off the rails. Faced with no alternative, I finally said, 'That's it, Carmen, no one else will enter this house.'

So the house now became as secure as a fort. I was even more isolated. Despite this strange situation, my brothers, who were ill at ease in these circumstances, were always loyal and continued to protect and defend me against all-comers. My family usually acted like this in difficult times. Without them close at hand I felt abandoned. The situation at home and my loneliness began to have an influence both on my game and on my personality. We may have built a fantastic house but we had failed to create the home I so longed for.

When I found myself in this impasse, Carmen realised what had happened and tried to make things better, but her efforts were in vain. It was too late; I had shut myself off from her. I am sure she hadn't intended to harm me in any way. She acted as she did because she or we couldn't find a way to do things properly. Carmen is a very good mother, but her outlook on life led her to make mistakes, the worst of which was to wall me off from my world, from my brothers, my friends and the things I was used to doing. She didn't see that when I came home I needed to return to a paradise, to regain my energies; rather than that space being a tranquil haven, it had become quite the opposite, so much so that when I eventually emerged I would be more exhausted than the day I'd arrived back.

We didn't separate earlier than we did because I still thought I could save our marriage. For that reason – and for our children's sake – I spoke to Carmen's father, to see if he could talk to his daughter. I even spoke to her mother, but I did not hear back. Carmen had never got on well with her mother; if she began to in later life, that was down to me. The most natural thing in the world would have been for her mother to come and help her daughter when she was in the middle of a crisis in her marriage. Today, with hindsight, I realise that they never communicated very well.

I preferred not to see that the effort I was making to save my marriage was not bearing fruit until the time came when no solution was possible and the relationship had ended. My marriage had reached the point where it was destroying me both as a sportsman and as a person.

'Carmen,' I told her, 'we can't go on together any longer.'

'God, this is a disaster!' she replied.

'Yes, I know; but there's no way out. We can only hope time will eventually heal our wounds. I felt a similar grief when I lost my parents.'

After I'd said that, Carmen suggested a pact, because her family believed that marriage vows should never be broken: we would continue to live together but lead separate lives.

'An arrangement like that may be acceptable for others, but I can't pretend in front of people. I may believe in traditional values, but I won't accept suggestions that inhibit my future happiness,' I replied.

When everything was agreed between Carmen and myself, I suggested we issue a joint press statement, but, following advice from her family, she refused. I wanted to put a brake on all the gossip and speculation and couldn't understand why she wouldn't cooperate. Shortly afterwards, my worst fears were realised. The press picked up on a vicious rumour that our separation had been prompted by an affair I was supposed to have been having with the daughter of the restaurant manager at the Royal Golf Club of Pedreña. This was totally untrue. Fortunately, Baldomero successfully intervened and quashed the terrible story. In the UK press it was reported that I'd been forced to leave home because of my continual infidelities, something that was also not true: neither Carmen nor myself had any affairs while our marriage lasted.

When these rumours started up, I insisted we issue a press release in Britain, where the slanders being thrown at me could really damage my image, but Carmen's family opposed that as well. I even spoke to her older sister, but she wouldn't take my side. I could never issue a denial of my own because I didn't want to create problems for Carmen or her family.

After our separation, we reached an amicable financial settlement overall because, as I mentioned earlier, we married having first agreed on the legal separation of our assets.

While we were married, there could perhaps have been better communication and understanding between us. However, now that we have divorced on friendly terms, we maintain a cordial relationship. I spend weekends and holidays with my children. Naturally, I maintain an excellent, close relationship with them, although I miss not spending more time by their side. Apparently, our divorce has had no more impact on them than you would expect. The three of them study hard, and play golf and other sports a lot. I'm very proud of them, and each has a very individual personality. The two boys are very good sportsmen. Miguel was an outstanding footballer, but one day he incomprehensibly decided to give it up. It was then he began to make golf his favourite sport, and he's made a very promising start: so much so that he's already managed to beat his big brother several times, although he's two years younger and Javier plays off scratch. My daughter Carmen is a tremendous live wire. Physically, she is the strongest of the three, I think. She is as active as my mother was. All three are beginning to understand what I've always told them: 'If you want to be outstanding at something, you have to work harder than anyone else, and, above all, you have to be a good person.'

Chapter 48

Swings, Honours and Friends

As I was so young when I started to play, I let myself be led by my natural feelings when I swung a club. These came from the rhythm I found with all my clubs, from driver to putter. The driver was always one of my best clubs. I was a very powerful golfer; good proof of this are the driving competitions I won in the 1970s and 1980s. At a time when players didn't pay the attention they do now to building themselves up physically, my natural physique gave me a considerable advantage.

My swing was all hands and brain. Everything natural, my hands followed orders dictated by my brain. This allowed me to create shots, and artfulness and intuition stood out as my great virtues. This enabled me to connect with spectators, and my charisma drew a following wherever I went. This, backed by my sporting record, is what has allowed me to occupy a position in the world of golf that fills me with pride. With imagination and ideas, you develop knowledge. If you use your knowledge you can create art. If you can demonstrate you are an artist, you may become a genius.

I was a precocious golfer – I made my début as a professional aged sixteen, came second in the Open at nineteen, won on the European Tour at the same age and at the time was the youngest winner of the Masters (at twenty-three) – and my victories extended across three decades. In the 1980s, an era when world rankings didn't really exist (the first Sony Rankings date from April 1986) the fact that I was considered by the specialist media as the best player in the world was a true endorsement. In such a highly individual sport, subject to injuries, crises of confidence and fierce competition, to remain a winner for so long, and in all kinds of conditions, must count for something.

My victories included another element beyond the strictly sporting: they allowed me to build up an enormous store of encounters and experiences with leading personalities from every area of Spanish and international life. I've had the great opportunity to come in contact with every class of people all over the globe, and meet the best representatives of each.

With the passage of time we all acquire certain experiences but if you are exposed to as much of the world as I was from an early age, you grow up and mature astonishingly quickly. I wasn't a good student, but golf has enriched me as a person in a way that has helped me to get to know and judge people better.

In the course of my travels I have attended receptions, prize-giving galas, launches of golf courses I have designed, tournaments organised by my firm, or simply participated in Pro-Ams and friendly matches alongside all manner of celebrities. One of golf's great virtues is that players at different levels can compete simultaneously: professionals with amateurs and men with women. Playing in this way for more than five hours, practising one's sport and acknowledging each other's talents, enables a form of communication that is difficult to match in any other sphere of human relations. While engaged in my profession, the time I've devoted to this kind of social interaction has been considerable, and it has proved a priceless training in humanity I couldn't have acquired in any other way.

I'd like to mention some names. Lack of space means I will have to leave many out, but I have just as much affection for those I have missed out as for those that follow.

I want to begin by recording my appreciation for the King of Spain, Don Juan Carlos, and the royal family. He has shown countless kindnesses to me. I often think of the time he called me at home just after I'd won the 1980 Masters and how my father, in a great state of excitement, passed me the phone when he realised who was at the other end of the line. His Majesty has come to see me play on several occasions and I well remember his presence at the ceremony to launch the 1997 Ryder Cup in Valderrama.

My respect and admiration for the whole royal family is underlined by the fact that it was the King's father, Don Juan de Borbón, who presided over the opening of the first course I designed in Spain. That was in December 1990 at Novo Sancti Petri, Cádiz. It was one of his last public acts. We racked our brains to come up with a way in which we could both participate actively in the ceremony. We decided that I would play an approach shot onto the 9th green, next to the clubhouse, and Don Juan would finish the job off with a putt.

In his youth Don Juan was a great golfer, a member of the national amateur team, and it just so happens that he, with Doña Beatriz de Borbón and Doña María Cristina, opened the course in Pedreña in 1929.

I've also often met HRH Prince Felipe, of whom I have an especially pleasant memory from the time he awarded me the Prince of Asturias Prize for Sport in 1989.

Other notable encounters were with Nelson Mandela, on the occasion of a tournament at Sun City in South Africa; Jimmy Carter, who congratulated me after my victory in the 1980 Masters; Ronald Reagan; George Bush Senior, on several occasions, including the 1997 Ryder Cup. I have also met members of the British royal family, including the Queen, Prince Charles, Prince Edward and Princess Anne; Princess Irene of Holland, who presented me with my first trophy on the European Tour, the 1976 Dutch Open; and Emperor Akihito; as well as the royal family of Monaco whom I saw frequently when I lived in the principality.

Among the well-known individuals I have met are Muhammad Ali, Sean Connery, Christopher Lee, James Hunt, Ed Moses, George Best, Kevin Keegan, Sebastian Coe, Linford Christie, Nigel Mansell, Evander Holyfield, Bobby Charlton, Johan Cruyff, Eddy Merckx, Bernard Hainault, Ilie Nastase, Nadia Comaneci and Michael Schumacher. In South Africa I met with Alan Shepard – the only person to have played golf on the moon! Actors, actresses, models, entrepreneurs, sheikhs, chairmen of big companies, writers, painters and singers have also helped multiply my wealth of experiences.

In Spain, I particularly remember my meetings with Adolfo Suárez, a great politician and person, and the first head of government during the Spanish transition to democracy. On one occasion I played with him and Emilio Botín in Pedreña, and around the 5th hole I had to say jokingly to Emilio, 'Emilio, slow down, we can't all go at your pace', for Emilio was walking the course at top speed and Suárez found it difficult to keep up with him. I've been in the Palace of the Moncloa, the head of government's official residence, with Felipe González,

Manuel Fraga, Mariano Rajoy (because of the game I played to celebrate Xacobeo 99) and after that with President Aznar. I've often met with Juan Antonio Samaranch. He is an excellent person, recognised and admired throughout the world for his courage. I'm proud that I have intervened actively to change the image of golf in Spain: it has gone from being a sport that was considered elitist – the province of old politicians and public figures who tried to prevent it becoming popular – to a sport that has an important role in generating wealth via tourism. I am glad to see that so many people talk about golf these days. Another honour and satisfaction I have enjoyed is the distinction of being the Honorary Ambassador of Trademark Spain since 2004.

And, obviously, I have lived and shared experiences with great Spanish sportsmen like Ángel Nieto, Manolo Santana, the sadly deceased Francisco Fernández Ochoa and Miguel Induraín, whom I used to follow on the odd stage of the Tour de France. I've even played games of golf against some of them.

Finally, I'd like to acknowledge close friends, although I'm bound to have left out so many: Dr Campuzano and Lola, Dr Coloma and his wife Mercedes (personal friends and friends of my family), Jaime Zuloaga, J. Ramón Altónaga, Pedro Morán, Dr Bernardo Martín, Valentín Valle, Ángel Martín, the Miralles family, Pepe de la Cavada, Pepe Jover (President of the Golfing Federation of Murcia), Alfonso Carrascosa, Miguel Sousa (with whom I've spent many pleasant moments in Madeira, Porto Santo and the Masters), Bernard Pascassio, Gaston and Christian Barras, the Tezuka family, Gorostegui, F. Pernía, Robbie Van Erven Dorens, Renton Laidlaw, Marco Kaussler, Mitchell Platts, Tony Menai, Mario Pinzi, Tom Keane, Lincoln Venancio, Khun Arsa, Joe Ozaki, Andy Yamanaka, Andrew Yau, Kipple Chan, Enrique Ponce, Michael Robinson, Olga Viza, S. Gil, Luis del Olmo, Matías Prats, G. Riquelme, the Milá brothers. The list could go on for pages.

Chapter 49

Course Design: the Future

It was in the 1990s that I began to realise that I didn't have the same level of concentration during tournaments. I was frequently distracted on the course and rather than just thinking about my game, my mind would wander. In the middle of a round I'd start to think about the last film I'd seen or where I'd go for dinner when I'd finished, stuff like that. Of course, when this happened, a bogey was almost guaranteed. I began to lose confidence in my game.

As things didn't improve despite all my efforts, in September 1995 I announced I'd take a break for five months, to prepare for the challenge of the forthcoming Ryder Cup in Spain, although at the time I wasn't sure I would accept the captaincy. The decision was the consequence not only of the way my game was going and the dearth of victories, but also of my growing awareness of how much had changed in my life.

Until that moment I'd given my whole life over to golf from childhood, but I could no longer dedicate myself totally to my sport: there were my children to think about; they needed my attention. Without totally renouncing my passion, I had to change my ways and take a different approach to life.

When I looked back I could see that golf had been the only thing in my life. I didn't have another passion, like the fishing that entertains Jack Nicklaus so much, or hunting, José María Olazábal's enthusiasm. Although it is a privilege to be able to do what you like doing, golf and the business of golf can take up all your energy. Even so, I could have continued at the top for years, perhaps, had it not been for my back problems. I simply didn't have the physical capacity any longer.

When I went out on a course I realised the image I presented did not correspond to that of the golfer I'd always been. This made me wonder whether my previous image had been a distortion of the truth – for example, the idea that I was someone who liked conflict, which I suppose sprang from my disputes with the managers of the European and American Tours, and the supposedly bad relations I had with my caddies. I've already spoken enough about the first subject; all I can say about the second is that it was entirely others' misperceptions.

When I've changed a caddie it's basically been because I thought he failed to understand the way I am. I'm a person with a strong character, and I'm sensitive to the point of superstition. I mean that when I'm playing, my state of concentration is such that I won't allow anything to interrupt it. The first thing I tell a new caddie is that whatever happens, while I'm playing, he must never contradict me. At the end of the round he can say whatever he thinks he needs to about my game or behaviour – but not on the course, because it will adversely affect my game. In top-level competition golf, a caddie must realise he is the only companion the golfer has on the course. His job is not only to carry clubs and calculate the correct yardage; he has to be a continual source of psychological support. A caddie must try to understand his player, to put himself inside the player's skin, to know when to speak and when to keep quiet.

I almost never consult a caddie about the line of a putt, because although it's true four eyes see better than two, it's also true that two opinions can foster doubt, and doubt is the last thing a player wants at such a time. I only ask my caddie for advice on club selection if I'm not sure, and then he must answer confidently. He must never put doubt in my mind. A good caddie must understand the course; he must know the state of the greens and in which direction the grass is growing. He must also assess the wind speed, never forget to concentrate hard, and be able to withstand the pressure *he* is under. A caddie who works for me must know, moreover, that I never use a number 3 ball, because I think superstitiously that, if I do, I will end up taking three putts. He must also know to change my ball without telling me at every hole. If this doesn't happen, I will think I won't make par.

I have other superstitions too. When I go to check the line of a putt, I have a thing about always walking there and back on the right. And ever since the Dutch Open in 1976 I have made sure to wear navy blue for a final round. Sporting this colour I won three Opens and two

Masters. In the 1995 Ryder Cup, as I've already noted, I persuaded Bernard Gallacher to let us play in navy blue and not the green we'd been supposed to. Of course, we won. As people say, the only reason I'm not more superstitious is because it would bring bad luck!

To return to my caddies, I have to say that I'm hurt by claims that I only speak to them to tell them off. They're not true. A caddie is a colleague; I like to chat to them about football, films and, indeed, about golf and the round we're playing. Generally I am the one to instigate the conversation, because I think the better a caddie knows me, the better he will do his job. Aside from my brothers, the best caddie I've had is Billy Foster. But I also have very good memories of Dave Musgrove, Peter Coleman, Nick de Paul and Ian Wright.

Through a series of sporting and entrepreneurial activities, golf still occupies a central place in my life. One of these is the Seve Trophy, a biennial team tournament between mainland Europe and Great Britain and Ireland, first staged at Sunningdale in April 2000. Right from its first outing – unusually it matches the captains of the rival teams against each other in the first game of singles – it became evident that the tournament would have considerable support from the fans. My aim is to take it across the continent and stage it in Spain, France, Sweden, Germany – even in Poland.

The Seve Trophy is becoming increasingly prestigious; spectators enjoy a high level of golf. This makes me very proud, not only because the tournament bears my name, but also because my firm Amen Corner is responsible for the organisation and finding the sponsorship that makes its development possible.

With the same aim – of popularising golf in Europe – that inspired the creation of the Seve Trophy, Amen Corner has also created the Royal Trophy, the first tournament to match teams from Europe and Asia against each other. It had its first outing in January 2006. I am determined to continue working to develop interest in golf by organising tournaments and designing courses across the world. I dream of open, public courses, even one of my own, and of golf being recognised as an Olympic sport.

I am also very happy to be involved in other interesting initiatives. Take the great idea of a world golf tour that Joe Collett, my former collaborator, developed in 1994. If this project has yet to prosper, I think it's down to the advent of the World Championships. Although basically they are part of the American Tour, they constitute a good arrangement for top players. Amen Corner is focussing its activities on this new world of tournaments and championships, whether as the creator and organiser of events or representing young, talented figures.

Another area where I've particularly concentrated my efforts is in course design and construction. In 1986, I founded Trajectory with my brothers. I immersed myself in the study of course architecture with the help of Dave Thomas, one of the co-designers of the Belfry, often the setting for the Ryder Cup. Before I set up Trajectory, we worked together on the Westerwood Golf and Country Club in Scotland and on two Seve Ballesteros golf clubs in Japan.

Trajectory's success has allowed me to find a new way to express my deep love of the game. It is an exciting experience to visit a plot of land and within twelve months transform it into a fine golf course. Designing courses that respect the topography of the terrain and the environment is something that gives me great pleasure; while I'm working I always enjoy visualising shots and the challenges that will ensue.

There are traditions of course design that appear to be sacrosanct. But I wonder why, for example, courses have to follow a template of ten par 4s, four par 5s and four par 3s? I like courses to have six par 3s, six par 4s and six par 5s. I think it's very good for the game if golf courses don't all follow the same pattern. At Cypress Point, California, for example, there are consecutive par 3s; at the Old Course at St Andrews, the oldest and best of all, there are only two par 5s and two par 3s. I'm not recommending that all courses follow this model. For many reasons the Old Course only makes sense in St Andrews, the cradle of golf. What I mean is that when it comes to designing new courses we should not be afraid to break with tradition and come up with something original.

A layout with six par 3s, six par 4s and six par 5s has many advantages. Whenever I can, that's how I design my courses. And if I may say so, I've designed a good number now, and they have always been successful.

I see the virtues of this six, six, six format to be the following:

- An area of 20 per cent is saved compared with a conventional layout. Given how difficult it is to find land, this is a key factor in a project's viability.

- The creation of a sequence of holes with different pars makes for variety.
- Traditional layouts have ten par 4s. With advances in technology many can now be played with a driver and a wedge. Thus many courses have been reduced to putting competitions.
- My layout guarantees the use of all the clubs in the bag, since within each sequence (par 3, par 4 and par 5) you can incorporate short-, medium- and long-distance holes.
- You can achieve a good balance between the front and back nines. This makes it easier to start from both the 1st and 10th tees.
- You create excellent finishes: for example a great par 4 followed by a spectacular par 3, and a par 5 where anything from an eagle to a double bogey is possible, as at the 17th at Valderrama.
- It encourages spectacular play from the professionals, as there are six par 5s, but the six par 3s make the course ideal for amateurs, because there are so many good opportunities for par. And the par 5s present them with opportunities too. None of them is excessively long, in order to tempt the pros to reach them in two.
- You can set an overall par that is right for amateurs and professionals alike. The latter, even with the large number of par 5s, won't have it easy. I like all the holes I design to have greens with well-defined flag positions. This ensures that approach shots and putts won't be straightforward. Take Crans-sur-Sierre in Switzerland, a course I redesigned in 2000 and which now bears my name. Apart from converting one par 4 into a par 3, in effect I only really changed the greens and relocated the bunkers, but it's gone from being the most straightforward course on the Tour, to one of the most demanding. The second-round cut is often set at one of the highest scores of the year.

As I have said, designing courses gives me a huge amount of pride and satisfaction, and my work now takes me all over the world.

In December 2006, I announced that I would try to play some tournaments on the Seniors Tour in the United States. I just wanted to have an entertaining, enjoyable time. As it turned out, it wasn't to be, but I think that tournaments for seniors are very interesting and have enormous potential when it comes to golf as a spectacle. It's true that with age one loses some physical ability but lots of people still like to see great champions display their skills and shot-making capabilities. And as I'm a great believer in the potential of the seniors, I'm sure it won't be long before we have a Seniors Ryder Cup. It would be very positive for golf in general, particularly if the Ryder Cup restricted its own age limit to forty-five to strengthen the level of competition.

As you can see, my head and my heart are still full of dreams and passion for golf. Without any false modesty, I know I have a privileged place among the golfing greats and that confers on me a great responsibility both to my children and to the public. If I feel proud of the success I have achieved as a golfer, I also feel proud of the love and respect I receive from my children as a father and from society as a citizen.

Chapter 50

Thirty-three Years Later

Thirty-three years passed between my first outing as a professional – thirty-two from my first Open – and the announcement of my retirement as a professional golfer.

I made the decision to retire as a player at Carnoustie, the site of that first Open. Among other reasons, it was because I've always received such a warm welcome in the British Isles. Things had come full circle: I was born in the week the Masters was played and I finished my career in the week of the most important tournament in the world and the one that has given me so much satisfaction: the Open.

The reasons for my retirement as a player are very simple to sum up. Since the beginning of 2007, I'd been thinking about whether to continue or give up competitive golf. My heart urged me to continue to fight just as I always had in the pursuit of victory. However, my head was a little more realistic. It insisted I should give up playing and spend more time with my children, my family, my friends and my business activities. With my feelings divided in this way, I decided to participate in the Masters and then begin a new adventure on the Seniors Tour, so I travelled to the USA. But after playing my first tournament on the tour, my head finally won out. I decided to give up tournament golf.

I've just turned fifty and am conscious that my game will never again touch its previous heights. None of the work I put in helped me achieve great, or even good, results. Moreover, I no longer had the same driving ambition I had as a youngster to go wherever I had to, to win tournament after tournament. Fortunately, I have many good years ahead of me and I want to enjoy them, to spend my life with my children and see them grow, and even to have some time for myself – something that was impossible for me as a young man because I surrendered myself body and soul to this sport that has given me so much. Golf gave me wisdom, took me all over the world, and made me many friends. Golf gave me a sense of well-being, and made me feel at ease in life.

Today, I can spend more time working with my companies, Amen Corner and Trajectory. And this year I will create Motivation and Training, a company through which I hope to be able to help other companies and people by showing them the techniques that I used to achieve success, which I believe will enable others to achieve the objectives they set themselves.

The date of 16 July 2007 will be remembered by me as the day when I took the most difficult, complicated decision I have ever had to take. The sweet taste of many successes belong to the past, along with some of the troubles, but they are all part of the huge cake I've savoured with the greatest pleasure over the past thirty years.

Since I made my farewell I have received a huge number of really gratifying letters, the majority from anonymous fans. They have been my strength during my professional career and I shall never cease to give them my most heartfelt thanks. I hope they have all enjoyed this book.

Epilogue by Baldomero Ballesteros Sota

When Seve was born in April 1957, I was just coming up to my tenth birthday. I remember him being born. In those days, at least in small Spanish villages, mothers gave birth at home, with the aid only of a midwife and, perhaps, their neighbours. The difference in our ages allowed me to follow his development in the first years of life very closely.

Because Seve was the youngest and was protected by everyone, especially by our parents, he soon showed himself astonishingly able to take advantage of the path that his brothers had opened up before him. One of his most striking qualities as a child was his quiet powers of observation. He wasn't timid, but he was very reserved. He wasn't a bad student either but he preferred to be in the street and on the golf course, where he could lead his life his own way. There Seve found the sport to which he surrendered his childhood and youth.

Passion, faith and constant hard work were his virtues from the beginning. With them came success. His successes might have been even greater if he had decided to play on the American Tour at the beginning of the 1980s. He decided not to and, from my point of view, I think he was right in the long run: his way of playing, his style, was better suited to Europe than the United States. Seve was in his element on muddy European courses, in rain, cold and wind. In these conditions you have to play a high level of golf. Many players are good in good weather but are merely mediocre in bad conditions.

In Europe Seve forged a legend that will be difficult to emulate. His rootedness in his land and family played a decisive role in his life and career. In the British Isles he succeeded in reaching the general public; he surrendered himself to them, and they appreciated him. In this way, he helped a Tour that was finding growth difficult to develop. He brought wit, charisma, professionalism and determination to the game, and, best of all, he offered his enthusiastic supporters a passion which would satisfy both himself and them.

Seve opened up new territory and players grew at his side, as did golf itself. Fortunately, a talented generation arrived to accompany him – Faldo, Woosnam, Lyle, Langer, Olazábal, Montgomerie . . . – and now even younger players are appearing, such as Sergio Garcia and Luke Donald. If Seve had stayed in America, we might not have the level of golf in Europe that we now enjoy.

Different players have different horizons. Some see themselves as products and they are centred on achieving commercial success; and others see themselves always as golfers and are focused on achieving sporting and social goals. For this reason Seve is a symbol, not a product. Each person is a world unto himself, but if you know what you want, you'll never fail. But knowing how you want to live must go hand in hand with an intelligent approach to life.

Seve touched the hearts of all those who appreciated how special he was. If we believe that the behaviour of human beings is directly related to each individual's personality, we can similarly assume that successes are conditioned not by the times in which we live but by certain natural gifts. From this perspective, Seve's charisma and brilliance are unique. They are the product of a character that is based on profound convictions.

Clearly, the privileged place Seve occupies in world golfing history has been strengthened by the unanimous approval he has received from the people who admire and respect him. For this and many other reasons, I hope this declaration will serve to acknowledge how much those of us who enjoy the sport that he has enhanced through his amazing effort, work and dedication owe to him.

Thanks, brother. Thanks, genius.

Baldomero Ballesteros Sota